THE FIRST PRINCIPLES

A Course in Discipleship For Every Christian

Heb 5:12   For when for the time ye ought to be teachers, ye have need that one teach you again which be *the first principles* of the oracles of God; and are become such as have need of milk, and not of strong meat.

13   For every one that useth milk is unskilful in the word of righteousness: for he is a babe.

14   But strong meat belongeth to them that are of full age, even those who by reason of use have their senses exercised to discern both good and evil.

THE FIRST PRINCIPLES

A Course in Discipleship For Every Christian

A STUDY OF HEBREWS 6:1-2 FOR THE CHRISTIAN DISCIPLE

Lance Rowe

Cross Country Publishing

Dutton, Al 35744

This is a research work.
Information is drawn from many sources. I have been careful to make every effort to attribute credit where credit is due.
Unless otherwise noted all Scripture is taken from the King James Version of the Holy Bible.

Definitions for the Greek and Hebrew words contained herein are from Strong's Exhaustive Concordance of the Bible, Thayer's Greek Definitions, and Brown - Driver - Briggs' Hebrew definitions.
Commentaries used and quoted from in this work are credited where used.

Library of Congress Control Number: 2015919458

ISBN 978-0692584569

© 11/18/2015

A BRIEF

INTRODUCTION

TO

THIS STUDY

BASIC DOCTRINES OF THE CHRISTIAN FAITH

(A basic discipleship course for the new Christian written and compiled by Lance Rowe)

INTRODUCTION

Heb 5:12 For when for the time ye ought to be teachers, ye have need that one teach you again which be the first principles of the oracles of God; and are become such as have need of milk, and not of strong meat.
13 For every one that useth milk is unskilful in the word of righteousness: for he is a babe.
14 But strong meat belongeth to them that are of full age, even those who by reason of use have their senses exercised to discern both good and evil.

The writer of the book of Hebrews had just censured those whom he had addressed, telling them that though they were at an age when they should be eating meat, they were such that still needed milk. He tells them that they need to get with the program and start eating meat. He says that they ought to be teachers, but they still behave as babes.

This seems to be a perpetual problem in the Church through the ages.

The commission Jesus gave to the disciples was to go and make disciples (teach all nations), teaching them to go and teach others the things which He had commanded them ("TEACHING THEM TO OBSERVE ALL THINGS WHATSOEVER I HAVE COMMANDED YOU"- He had just commanded them to go and teach those who were entrusted to them to make disciples).

We derive our English word "discipline" from the word "Disciple." The Christian walk is a walk of discipline.

Notes-

It was to be an ongoing thing. We make disciples, and then *we teach them* to make disciples. But in order to make disciples, we ourselves should understand the basic principles that Jesus taught.

In Acts 2:42, we learn that the early Church continued in the apostle's doctrine.

Act 2:42 And they continued stedfastly in the apostles' doctrine and fellowship, and in breaking of bread, and in prayers.

What was the apostle's doctrine?

Their doctrine was the doctrine of Christ, those things that Christ taught them! See how He commissioned them after His resurrection:

Mat 28:18 And Jesus came and spake unto them, saying, All power is given unto me in heaven and in earth.
19 Go ye therefore, and teach all nations, baptizing them in the name of the Father, and of the Son, and of the Holy Ghost:
20 Teaching them to observe all things whatsoever I have commanded you: and, lo, I am with you alway, *even* unto the end of the world. Amen.

Jesus expressly charged them to make disciples, and *to teach them to observe those things that He had taught them.* So the early Church continued in those things that the apostles taught them regarding the teachings of Christ.

In verse 12 of Hebrews 5, we see the "*first principles of the oracles of God"* are mentioned.

Heb 5:12 For when for the time ye ought to be teachers, ye have need that one teach you again which be the first principles of the oracles of God; and are become such as have need of milk, and not of strong meat.

In Hebrews chapter 6, we see the "principles of the doctrine of Christ" mentioned:

Heb 6:1 Therefore leaving the principles of the doctrine of Christ, let us go on unto perfection; not laying again the foundation of repentance from dead works, and of faith toward God,

The words translated as "oracles" in Hebrews 5:12 and "doctrine" in Hebrews 6:1 both have their roots in the Greek word "logos", which means "Word".

Jesus is the Word made flesh. In John 1:1 we see that the Word was in the beginning, and the Word was with God, and the Word was God!

So many people strive to discredit the Bible. But the Bible is the Word of God. The first principles of the Word of God is what we are saved in, and according to Hebrews 6:1, those first principles are the very things that Christ set forth in His teaching.

But once we are saved, we need to go beyond those first principles, and to go on to learn how to walk in the Light of the Word and in its' Truth, so that we can teach others of the Truth that is in Christ and fulfill our purpose as ambassadors for Christ, furthering the Kingdom of God in our spheres of influence.

This is the Way of all CREATION. The baby is born, and is in the world, yet knows how to do nothing other than survive by sucking on its' mothers' breast. But eventually the baby must learn to crawl, and then to walk, and somewhere along the line, to eat solid food. Soon the baby is no longer a baby, but matures into a child, then an adolescent, and then a young adult. Even as a child, that young one passes on knowledge to others who do not yet know what he or she has learned.

Too many Christians rarely get beyond the milk stage in their walk with Christ.

If asked whether or not they know what their calling is, most Christians will say they didn't even know they had a calling. This probably is more the fault of the "parent" or the shepherd who never encourages them to grow beyond the pew in life. According to the scripture, as long as we are on the milk of the Word, we are unskilled in the Word of righteousness.

Heb 5:13 For every one that useth milk is unskilful in the word of righteousness: for he is a babe

It's time to grow up!

**Heb 6:1 Therefore leaving the principles of the doctrine of Christ, let us go on unto perfection; not laying again the foundation of repentance from dead works, and of faith toward God,
2 Of the doctrine of baptisms, and of laying on of hands, and of resurrection of the dead, and of eternal judgment.**

The writer of Hebrews says that the reader must go on to "perfection"...this is a form of the same word that is used in Heb. 5:14, which is translated as "full age". It is time to "Grow up", to walk in Christian discipline, and take some responsibility for your life as a Christian.

The maturity spoken of here is fulfilling your calling. The modern "Church" today consists for the most part of an audience and an orator. The audience listens to the orator, pays their admission (or tithe), and then returns the following week to hear what the orator comes up with next. That is a far cry from what New Testament Christianity is meant to be. Paul gives a picture of how the early Church conducted itself:

**1Co 14:26 How is it then, brethren? when ye come together, every one of you hath a psalm, hath a doctrine, hath a tongue, hath a revelation, hath an interpretation. Let all things be done unto edifying.
27 If any man speak in an *unknown* tongue, *let it be* by two, or at the most *by* three, and *that* by course; and let one interpret.
28 But if there be no interpreter, let him keep silence in the church; and let him speak to himself, and to God.
29 Let the prophets speak two or three, and let the other judge.
30 If *any thing* be revealed to another that sitteth by, let the first hold his peace.
31 For ye may all prophesy one by one, that all may learn, and all may be comforted.
32 And the spirits of the prophets are subject to the prophets.**

In every fellowship, There should be an equipping of the Body of Christ to actively further the Kingdom of God on earth.

Eph 4:11 And he gave some, apostles; and some, prophets; and some, evangelists; and some, pastors and teachers;
12 For the perfecting of the saints, for the work of the ministry, for the edifying of the body of Christ:
13 Till we all come in the unity of the faith, and of the knowledge of the Son of God, unto a perfect man, unto the measure of the stature of the fulness of Christ:
14 That we *henceforth* **be no more children, tossed to and fro, and carried about with every wind of doctrine, by the sleight of men,** *and* **cunning craftiness, whereby they lie in wait to deceive;**
15 But speaking the truth in love, may grow up into him in all things, which is the head, *even* **Christ:**
16 From whom the whole body fitly joined together and compacted by that which every joint supplieth, according to the effectual working in the measure of every part, maketh increase of the body unto the edifying of itself in love.

The purpose of the five fold ministry is that the Body of Christ is to *increase* in this world, and for the Kingdom of God to advance, and that happens as those who are in leadership equip the saints to do the work of the ministry. In Hebrews we are told to go on to perfection (maturity), and here in Ephesians the fivefold ministry (Apostles, Prophets, Evangelists, Pastors and Teachers) are the ones who are supposed to help facilitate this.

In verse one of Hebrews 6, we see the words "Not laying again", which would probably be better translated as "Not casting down again", or not laying aside the foundation on which we have been grounded, which are the following things: repentance from dead works, faith toward God, the doctrine of baptisms, and of laying on of hands, and of the resurrection of the dead, and of eternal judgment.

The Greek word translated as "laying" in verse 1 is "kataballo", which means to throw down, or to cast down. There are two other places where this word is used in the New Testament:

Rev 12:10 And I heard a loud voice saying in heaven, Now is come salvation, and strength, and the kingdom of our God, and the power of his Christ: for the accuser of our brethren is *cast down*, **which accused them before our God day and night.**

2Co 4:9 Persecuted, but not forsaken; *cast down*, **but not destroyed;**

_____
_____
_____
_____
_____
_____
_____
_____
_____
_____
_____
_____
_____
_____
_____
_____
_____
_____
_____
_____
_____
_____
_____
_____
_____
_____
_____
_____
_____
_____
_____
_____
_____

2Ti 2:1 Thou therefore, my son, be strong in the grace that is in Christ Jesus.
2 And the things that thou hast heard of me among many witnesses, the same commit thou to faithful men, who shall be able to teach others also.

Unfortunately, too many Christians don't even understand the basic doctrines outlined here in the first two verses of Hebrews chapter 6. Why is that?_____
_____
_____
_____

Many Christians in America have laid aside or *cast down* the basic doctrines in order to pursue after their own agendas in life, rather than the Will of God. Had they been taught in these basic doctrines of the Christian faith, they would probably not be so inclined to walk away from the faith, or to be complacent in the pew.

Most young Christians are generally just assimilated into the congregation, without any proper discipleship. It is left up to them to try to figure out what the preacher is talking about.

The purpose of this study is to examine these principle doctrines so that we may equip others to go on to maturity. This is what discipleship is about; teaching others those things we have been taught concerning the Kingdom of God. Although this Book is 243 pages long, the truth is that during this study, we will just scratch the surface of the depths of the understanding of God.

I would encourage the disciple to press in, take notes, make your own observations, and become that mature Christian you are supposed to be.

I would encourage the teacher to use this book to facilitate your discipling process, not as a "do this, this and this, and you've got it" type study. Head knowledge is just that; head knowledge. There is a lot of information in the Church world, and knowledge just has a tendency to puff a person up. It is the *application* of that knowledge through yielding to the Holy Spirit which will effect change in a

Heb 5:12 *For when for the time ye ought to be teachers, ye have need that one teach you again which be the first principles of the oracles of God; and are become such as have need of milk, and not of strong meat.*
13 For every one that useth milk is unskilful in the word of righteousness: for he is a babe.
14 But strong meat belongeth to them that are of full age, even those who by reason of use have their senses exercised to discern both good and evil.

Notes-

___

believer's life. There may be some teaching in this book that the teacher won't agree with, because it goes against his or her denominational or traditional background. I would recommend that you the teacher thoroughly study this book before he or she uses it in a discipleship setting, to avoid conflict.

Jesus demonstrated what it meant to make disciples; He took twelve men and lived with them, walked with them, and included them in His ministry, empowering and encouraging them to do the things that He did, so they themselves could become able ministers of the Gospel. It's every Christian's responsibility to make disciples just like Jesus did.

We are told that these basic principles are the Foundation of our faith. Remember that the word "doctrine" used here in Heb 6:1, is the Greek Logos, which means "Word". Not only are they just doctrines, but they are specifically the *doctrine of Christ.*

There are some teachers who would try to teach that the things Christ taught have no relevance to us, because Christ was under the Law, and He was teaching the Jewish people who were also under the law.

These teachers would say that only the epistles have relevance to the New Testament Christian, but the Book of Acts tells us that the Church continued in the *Apostle's doctrine*, which we have seen earlier was Christ's doctrine, since he told them to teach those things that He had taught them. And here in Hebrews 6:1, we are told that these fundamental doctrines that are listed here and in verse two are the *principles* of the doctrine of Christ.

Regardless of what some teachers may say, Jesus Christ is the Author and the Finisher of our faith, and the New Testament Christian is to walk according to the teachings of Christ.

Heb 6:1 Therefore leaving the principles of the doctrine of Christ, let us go on unto perfection; not laying again the foundation of repentance from dead works, and of faith toward God,
2 Of the doctrine of baptisms, and of laying on of hands, and of resurrection of the dead, and of eternal judgment.

Jesus mentions His Word in relation to a foundation in Luke 6:

Luke 6:47 Whosoever cometh to me, and heareth my sayings *(Greek "logos")***, and doeth them, I will shew you to whom he is like:**
48 He is like a man which built an house, and digged deep, and laid the foundation on a rock: and when the flood arose, the stream beat vehemently upon that house, and could not shake it: for it was founded upon a rock.
49 But he that heareth, and doeth not, is like a man that without a foundation built an house upon the earth; against which the stream did beat vehemently, and immediately it fell; and the ruin of that house was great.

There are many books and videos and various curriculum in the Christian market that deal with cults, religions, and heresies that threaten to creep into the Church.

I personally believe that if an individual Christian thoroughly understands the basic doctrines of his or her Christian Faith, they will not be easily persuaded to go astray, or to be "carried about with every wind of doctrine". As we proceed in this study, it is my belief that the disciple will become better prepared to deal with aberrant doctrines as we encounter them.

Throughout each lesson, you will find various numerical notations in a superscript ([1]) referring to a section entitled "cult watch" which can be found in the sidebar on that page, where false doctrines that deviate from the principle doctrines of Christ will be briefly addressed.

Let us examine carefully these elements of the foundation of our faith in the light of Jesus' words concerning them so we can give a confident answer to those who ask or challenge us regarding our Faith.

If you are blessed with the content of these studies, you may feel free to reproduce and use these studies in your own discipleship classes.

Eph 4:11 And he gave some, apostles; and some, prophets; and some, evangelists; and some, pastors and teachers;

12 For the perfecting of the saints, for the work of the ministry, for the edifying of the body of Christ:

13 Till we all come in the unity of the faith, and of the knowledge of the Son of God, unto a perfect man, unto the measure of the stature of the fulness of Christ:

14 That we henceforth be no more children, tossed to and fro, and carried about with every wind of doctrine, by the sleight of men, and cunning craftiness, whereby they lie in wait to deceive;

15 But speaking the truth in love, may grow up into him in all things, which is the head, even Christ:

16 From whom the whole body fitly joined together and compacted by that which every joint supplieth, according to the effectual working in the measure of every part, maketh increase of the body unto the edifying of itself in love.

Table of Contents

Act 4:12 Neither is there salvation in any other: for there is none other name under heaven given among men, whereby we must be saved.

WHAT WE BELIEVE:

We believe that the Bible is the infallible, inerrant Word of God, which was recorded by Holy men of God as they were inspired by the Holy Spirit to write down that which was delivered to them. We believe that the Bible is our only source for doctrine, and if one lives by the instruction of the Bible, he or she may fulfill the Will of God for their life.

We believe in one God. That God is the God of Abraham, Isaac and Jacob. In the Old Testament He was known to the people of Israel as their Deliverer. He is declared by us to be the Father, Maker of all things, whether they are visible or invisible.

We believe in one Lord, Jesus Christ, the Only Begotten Son of God; begotten, not made of the Father, of the same substance of the Father. We declare Him to be God manifest in the flesh, by whom all things were made, both things in heaven and things in earth according to Colossians 1:16.

We believe He willingly came down from His Most High estate, and was begotten by the Holy Spirit as a man through the virgin birth, dwelled among us as the Only Begotten Son of God, and was tempted in all ways like we are, yet was without sin.

He suffered, and was crucified under the authority of Pontius Pilate, died upon the cross, buried in a rich man's tomb, descended into Hades, and preached the gospel to the dead, and rose again on the third day. He was seen by over 500 eyewitnesses after His resurrection, and ascended into Heaven, where he sits at the Right Hand of the Father, and shall return one day for His Church, and to judge all men.

We believe that those who have rejected Him as their Lord and Savior will be cast into the Lake of fire where the devil and his angels shall be, to be tormented forever and ever.

We believe that those who have called upon His Name and who have received Him to be their Lord and Savior will live and be with Him forever throughout eternity, and His Kingdom shall have no end.

We believe in the Holy Spirit, Who proceeds from the Father and from the Son, of the same Substance of the Father and the Son, and Who is to be worshipped and glorified together with the Father and the Son as God. We believe Him to be our Teacher and our Comforter, and we are His Temple, sanctified by His Work that He does within us, to conform us to the Image of Jesus Christ.

We believe that His Presence in our lives is manifested by the fruit of the Spirit which will be evident to all men.

We believe in the Baptism of the Holy Spirit, whereby the Gifts of the Holy Spirit are bestowed upon the believer for the purpose of Glorifying the Name of Jesus Christ to a lost and dying world, and for equipping the believers for the Work of the Ministry. We believe that the various Gifts of the Holy Spirit are distributed by Him severally as He wills, and that these Gifts are to be earnestly desired by each member of the Church.

We believe that the Church of Jesus Christ is one, consisting of many members with various giftings and callings, and that as its members walk in the Love of Jesus Christ one toward another as brethren and not as strangers, the unsaved world will know that we are Christ's disciples.

We believe that the primary purpose of the Church is to evangelize the world and to make disciples, furthering the advancement of the Kingdom of God one soul at a time, and in the process, transforming the kingdoms of this world for the Glory of God. We are not simply waiting for the Kingdom to come sometime in the future; we are actively pursuing its establishment in the world today/

We believe in baptism by immersion in water if at all possible in obedience to the Words of our Lord Jesus Christ Who commanded to baptize in the Name of the Father, the Son, and the Holy Spirit.

We believe in the forgiveness of sins through Jesus Christ's atoning death on the cross.

We look with expectancy for the resurrection of the body, and eternal life in the Kingdom to come.

THE PRINCIPLES OF THE DOCTRINE OF CHRIST

Luk 24:46 And said unto them, Thus it is written, and thus it behoved Christ to suffer, and to rise from the dead the third day:
47 And that repentance and remission of sins should be preached in his name among all nations, beginning at Jerusalem.
48 And ye are witnesses of these things.
49 And, behold, I send the promise of my Father upon you: but tarry ye in the city of Jerusalem, until ye be endued with power from on high.

The Greek Word for repentance is:

3341 metanoia-
a change of mind (heart), as it appears to one who repents of a purpose he has formed or of something he has done

Notes-

_____
_____
_____
_____
_____
_____
_____
_____
_____
_____
_____
_____
_____
_____
_____
_____
_____
_____
_____
_____

BASIC DOCTRINES

LESSON 1

REPENTANCE FROM DEAD WORKS

Heb 6:1 Therefore leaving the principles of the doctrine of Christ, let us go on unto perfection; not laying again the foundation of repentance from dead works, and of faith toward God,
2 Of the doctrine of baptisms, and of laying on of hands, and of resurrection of the dead, and of eternal judgment.

The first doctrine mentioned in Hebrews 6:1-2 is the doctrine of REPENTANCE. It is only fitting that it is the first mentioned, because REPENTANCE is the primary condition to the New Birth, and the first requirement of the Christian Faith, and of entering into a covenant relationship with the true and living God.

It is the first message that Jesus preached:

Mat 4:17 From that time Jesus began to preach, and to say, Repent: for the kingdom of heaven is at hand.

For a person to enter into the Kingdom of God, He or she must first have a change of mind about the way they are living their life, and to have a change of mind as to whom it is they choose to serve. In Hebrews 6, we see that the operative phrase we must deal with is repentance from "dead works".

Context is always important when studying the Word of God. If a specific phrase is used in one area of a doctrinal book, and it is used again in the same book, we should pay heed to what that phrase is referring to.

Definition of the Greek Word translated as "works"

G2041
ergon
Thayer Definition:
1) business, employment, that which any one is occupied
1a) that which one undertakes to do, enterprise, undertaking
2) any product whatever, anything accomplished by hand, art, industry, or mind
3) an act, deed, thing done: the idea of working is emphasised in opp. to that which is less than work
Part of Speech: noun neuter

"Serve" is the word "latreuo".

G3000

latreuo lat-ryoo'-o

From latris (a hired menial); to minister (to God), that is, render religious homage: - serve, do the service, worship (-per).

The phrase "dead works" from which we must repent is used one other time in the New Testament, and that is also in the Book of Hebrews.

So let's look at Heb 9:14 where the phrase "dead works" is used:

Speaking of Jesus Christ, and His sacrifice for us, we read:

**Heb 9:13 For if the blood of bulls and of goats, and the ashes of an heifer sprinkling the unclean, sanctifieth to the purifying of the flesh:
14 How much more shall the blood of Christ, who through the eternal Spirit offered himself without spot to God, purge your conscience *from dead works* to serve the living God?**

Here we see that the Blood of Christ serves to PURGE our conscience from dead works, to *SERVE* the living God, and, as we have seen, the first foundational doctrine of the Christian walk mentioned in Hebrews 6:1 is repentance from *dead works*.

The word translated here in vs 14 as "serve" has a religious connotation.

The Christian's purpose is service to God. But one can serve God through a sense of religious obligation, or through a heart of gratitude and love for God.

According to Hebrews 9:14, our consciences are purged through the Blood of Jesus Christ, so that we can *SERVE* the living God in truth.

But there is a difference between Service to God, and vain religion, which is primarily what these "dead works" are referring to. To illustrate this, I bring the reader's attention to John the Baptist's words which he spoke in rebuke to the religious leaders of his day:

Mat 3:7 But when he saw many of the Pharisees and Sadducees come to his baptism, he said unto them, O generation of vipers, who hath warned you to flee from the wrath to come?
8 Bring forth therefore fruits meet for repentance:

The same message was preached years later by Paul; namely that those who he preached to were to bring forth work fit for repentance, and when he preached that message, the religious leaders sought to kill him:

Act 26:20 But shewed first unto them of Damascus, and at Jerusalem, and throughout all the coasts of Judaea, and *then* to the Gentiles, that they should repent and turn to God, and do works meet for repentance.
21 For these causes the Jews caught me in the temple, and went about to kill *me*.

John continued his message with a warning:

Mat 3:10 And now also the axe is laid unto the root of the trees: therefore every tree which bringeth not forth good fruit is hewn down, and cast into the fire.

In His conversation with His disciples, Jesus told them that just because men profess to serve God, doesn't mean they are His servants. There are those who profess to be prophets and ministers of the gospel who are unrepentant workers of iniquity, professionals who are out to make a living out of what they do in the Name of the Lord, taking advantage of many for their own personal gain instead of being servants of God.

Mat 7:15 Beware of false prophets, which come to you in sheep's clothing, but inwardly they are ravening wolves.
16 Ye shall know them by their fruits. Do men gather grapes of thorns, or figs of thistles?
17 Even so every good tree bringeth forth good fruit; but a corrupt tree bringeth forth evil fruit.
18 A good tree cannot bring forth evil fruit, neither *can* a corrupt tree bring forth good fruit.
19 Every tree that bringeth not forth good fruit is hewn down, and cast into the fire.
20 Wherefore by their fruits ye shall know them.

At this point of the study I would encourage you to open your Bible (if you haven't already done so) to Hebrews 8, and follow along.

If we back up to chapter 8, verse one, we can see that the author of Hebrews writes:

inward parts, and write it in their hearts; and will be their God, and they shall be my people.

Cult Watch:

1) Mormons, Seventh Day Adventists, Some Messianic Jewish congregations teach the necessity of observance to the Law (Mormon temple ordinances, and tithe; SDA dietary laws and Sabbath observance; Messianic Jewish festivals, dietary and Sabbath observance) as a prerequisite to Salvation.

"By the works of the Law shall no flesh be justified" (Gal 2:16).

The feasts, the Sabbaths, circumcision and the ceremonial laws as taught in the Old Testament were covenant observances between God and His Chosen people, Israel. Those who are under the New Covenant of Jesus are not bound by those laws which dictated, "touch not, taste not, handle not":

Col 2:20 Wherefore if ye be dead with Christ from the rudiments of the world, why, as though living in the world, are ye subject to ordinances,
21 (Touch not; taste not; handle not;
22 Which all are to perish with the using;) after the commandments and doctrines of men?
23 Which things have indeed a shew of wisdom in will worship, and humility, and neglecting of the body; not in any honour to the satisfying of the flesh.

The Gentile converts to Christianity were instructed in this manner concerning their conduct in Christ:

Act 15:23 And they wrote letters by them after this manner; The apostles and elders and brethren send greeting unto the brethren which are of the Gentiles in Antioch and Syria and Cilicia:

Heb 8:1 Now of the things which we have spoken this is the sum:...

And then he proceeds to define Jesus' Role in our life. We are taught that Jesus is a mediator of a better covenant than the first covenant (vs 6) which was established when God led Israel out of Egypt (vs 9).

Heb 8:6 But now hath he obtained a more excellent ministry, by how much also he is the mediator of a better covenant, which was established upon better promises.
7 For if that first *covenant* had been faultless, then should no place have been sought for the second.
8 For finding fault with them, he saith, Behold, the days come, saith the Lord, when I will make a new covenant with the house of Israel and with the house of Judah:
9 Not according to the covenant that I made with their fathers in the day when I took them by the hand to lead them out of the land of Egypt; because they continued not in my covenant, and I regarded them not, saith the Lord.

The previous covenant was a covenant of intermediaries (the priesthood in general [Hebrews 7:5], and specifically the High Priest, who would enter into the Holy of Holies once a year to offer a sacrifice on behalf of the people) between the *common people* and God. These intermediaries would serve God and offer sacrifices on behalf of the common people (laity) according to set rules and regulations (Heb 7:27). All of these rules and regulations (the Law) were simply types and shadows of heavenly things (Heb 8:4,5) but they could never make those who observed them perfect (Heb 7:11,18,19; 8:7; 10:1-4).

God instituted a better covenant through Jesus:

Heb 8:10 For this *is* the covenant that I will make with the house of Israel after those days, saith the

24 Forasmuch as we have heard, that certain which went out from us have troubled you with words, subverting your souls, saying, Ye must be circumcised, and keep the law: to whom we gave no such commandment:
25 It seemed good unto us, being assembled with one accord, to send chosen men unto you with our beloved Barnabas and Paul,
26 Men that have hazarded their lives for the name of our Lord Jesus Christ.
27 We have sent therefore Judas and Silas, who shall also tell you the same things by mouth.
28 For it seemed good to the Holy Ghost, and to us, to lay upon you no greater burden than these necessary things;
29 That ye abstain from meats offered to idols, and from blood, and from things strangled, and from fornication: from which if ye keep yourselves, ye shall do well. Fare ye well.

Cult Watch

2) Unitarians: Oneness or Jesus Only doctrine, Jehovah's Witnesses, Muslims, UPC, Universalists:

Gal 4:6 And because ye are sons, God hath sent forth the Spirit of his Son into your hearts, crying, Abba, Father.

This verse refers to the fact that because we are sons, the spirit within us cries out Abba, Father. Muslims say that Allah has no son. UPC and others declare that "Father" is a title, not a name, and that the only one that we have anything to do with is Jesus. Yet we see here that those who are sons of God and who have received the Spirit of God cry out "ABBA, Father!" There is a Father and a Son. And it is through the Son, that we have received the adoption of sons.

Lord; I will put my laws into their mind, and write them in their hearts: and I will be to them a God, and they shall be to me a people:
11 And they shall not teach every man his neighbour, and every man his brother, saying, Know the Lord: for all shall know me, from the least to the greatest.

Paul referred to this very thing in Galatians:

Gal 2:16 Knowing that a man is not justified by the works of the law, but by the faith of Jesus Christ, even we have believed in Jesus Christ, that we might be justified by the faith of Christ, and not by the works of the law: for by the works of the law shall no flesh be justified. [1]

Gal 4:1 Now I say, That the heir, as long as he is a child, differeth nothing from a servant, though he be lord of all;
2 But is under tutors and governors until the time appointed of the father.
3 Even so we, when we were children, were in bondage under the elements of the world:
4 But when the fulness of the time was come, God sent forth his Son, made of a woman, made under the law,
5 To redeem them that were under the law, that we might receive the adoption of sons.
6 And because ye are sons, God hath sent forth the Spirit of his Son into your hearts, crying, Abba, Father. [2]
7 Wherefore thou art no more a servant, but a son; and if a son, then an heir of God through Christ.
8 Howbeit then, when ye knew not God, ye did service unto them which by nature are no gods.
9 But now, after that ye have known God, or rather are known of God, how turn ye again to the weak and beggarly elements, whereunto ye desire again to be in bondage?
10 Ye observe days, and months, and times, and years. [1]
11 I am afraid of you, lest I have bestowed upon you labour in vain.

Jehovah's Witnesses say that they are witnesses of Jehovah. But the Word of God says that God has given Him (Jesus) a Name above every name (Phil 2:9, and Eph 1:17-23).

The Name of Jesus Christ is even above the Name of Jehovah! God Himself has declared this. The Jehovah's Witness Bible reads that God has given Jesus a Name above every other name (other than the Name of Jehovah), but the Greek text doesn't support that. We who are under the New Covenant are to be witnesses of Christ:

Act 1:8 But ye shall receive power, after that the Holy Ghost is come upon you: and ye shall be witnesses unto me both in Jerusalem, and in all Judaea, and in Samaria, and unto the uttermost part of the earth.

Cult Watch

3) Col 2:18 Let no man beguile you of your reward in a voluntary humility and worshipping of angels, intruding into those things which he hath not seen, vainly puffed up by his fleshly mind

Muslims, Mormons, New Age doctrine, and current trends among some believers include involvement in a fascination with angels. Mohammad claimed to have received his revelations for the Koran from Gabriel.

The angel Moroni supposedly guided Joseph Smith to the gold plates from which he claimed the Book of Mormon was translated, and many books have been written by various authors who say that they were given revelation by angelic beings that contradicts or supersedes the Bible.

There are certain modern day "prophets" who are accepted by

The word "elements" in verses 3 and 9 is the same word translated as "principles" in Hebrews 5:12:

Heb 5:12 For when for the time ye ought to be teachers, ye have need that one teach you again which be the first principles of the oracles of God; and are become such as have need of milk, and not of strong meat.

There are worldly principles and there are heavenly principles. The worldly principles are those things that our flesh understands and demands that we obey. As I pointed out a little earlier, all of the rules and regulations set forth in the Law were just types and shadows of heavenly things.

Heb 8:5 Who serve unto the example and shadow of heavenly things, as Moses was admonished of God when he was about to make the tabernacle: for, See, saith he, that thou make all things according to the pattern shewed to thee in the mount.

Col 2:16 Let no man therefore judge you in meat, or in drink, or in respect of an holyday, or of the new moon, or of the sabbath days:[1]
17 Which are a shadow of things to come; but the body is of Christ.
18 Let no man beguile you of your reward in a voluntary humility and worshipping of angels, intruding into those things which he hath not seen, vainly puffed up by his fleshly mind, [3]
19 And not holding the Head, from which all the body by joints and bands having nourishment ministered, and knit together, increaseth with the increase of God.
20 Wherefore if ye be dead with Christ from the rudiments of the world, why, as though living in the world, are ye subject to ordinances,
21 (Touch not; taste not; handle not;
22 Which all are to perish with the using;) after the commandments and doctrines of men?

certain Christian circles who speak of new revelations of mysteries that were given them by angels. The discerning Christian will ask him or herself: What does this information do for my walk with Jesus?

Cult Watch

4) A brief synopsis of The Feasts and their fulfillments:

Passover memorialized the Lord's Protection over His People as He delivered them from the Egyptian bondage (Lev 23:5), but it also signifies redemption and deliverance through the Blood of Christ, Who is our Passover (1 Cor 5:7; Heb 9:12-15).

The feast of Unleavened Bread commemorated the hasty departure of the People of Israel from Egypt in their deliverance from Pharoah's bondage, but it also symbolizes the removal of the leavening influence of the world from our lives, and the necessity to break all ties with the world. (1 Cor 5:1-12). It is a picture of repentance. We are called to be separate or "Holy". (Heb 12:14).

First Fruits was a time of thanksgiving to the Lord for His bountiful Provision to His people when they reaped the harvest of barley in the Land which He brought them (Lev 23:10-14). It was a foreshadowing of the harvest of souls that would come as a result of the establishment of the Church. In Romans 8:23, Paul refers to the early Christians as having the firstfruits of the Spirit (see also James 1:18). Christ's resurrection is referred to as the firstfruits of the dead (1 Cor 15:20-23), signifying the Promise of eternal life to those who believe in Him.

Another significance of these first three feasts is that they occurred as

26

23 Which things have indeed a shew of wisdom in will worship, and humility, and neglecting of the body; not in any honour to the satisfying of the flesh.

A child of God isn't meant to live his life according to the flesh (2 Cor 10:3; Rom 8:1,4; Gal 5:16; 2 Pet 2:10), but according to the Spirit. The natural man cannot comprehend the things of the spiritual realm, because they are spiritually discerned.

The religious man will seek to worship God according to his carnal understanding, using things in the natural world to relate to the spiritual. But Jesus said that there would come a time when the true worshippers would worship God in spirit and in truth.

**Joh 4:23 But the hour cometh, and now is, when the true worshippers shall worship the Father in spirit and in truth: for the Father seeketh such to worship him.
24 God is a Spirit: and they that worship him must worship him in spirit and in truth.**

The feasts of the Bible were simply types and shadows of heavenly realities,[4] and there are many cults and false doctrines of men that would seek to entangle the believer in the dead works of vain religion instead of allowing them to experience the Liberty that is in Christ.

Gal 2:16 Knowing that a man is not justified by the works of the law, but by the faith of Jesus Christ, even we have believed in Jesus Christ, that we might be justified by the faith of Christ, and not by the works of the law: for by the works of the law shall no flesh be justified.

Religion is fallen man trying to work his way to God on his own terms. The religious man reasons "If I do this and this and this, while not doing this, this, and an extension of each other. The feast of the **Unleavened Bread** was to happen the day after the **Passover** feast. The **Feast of the First Fruits** was to happen the day after the sabbath of the Passover.

Jesus died on the Passover, was in the tomb on the day of the feast of unleavened bread (one day after the Passover feast) and rose on the feast of the first fruits (on the morrow after the sabbath - the first day of the week [Lev 23:11]!

Pentecost or Shavuot. The feast of weeks. This feast was to occur 7 weeks after the feast of the firstfruits (Lev 23:15-) This was a time in which the Israelites were to celebrate the Summer harvest. From that harvest, the Israelites were to produce two "wave loaves' of bread to the Lord, and present them to the Lord (23:17). This was a shadow of both Jew and Gentile being accepted before the Lord. There was a drink offering of wine that was to be given, and a burnt offering (23:18). In the Book of Acts, we read that flames of fire appeared over the heads of those who were baptized with the Holy Spirit, and those who witnessed it supposed that they were drunken with new wine!

Shavuot was also a time to commemorate the giving of the Ten Commandments. In the Book of Acts, we see it's fulfillment as the Holy Spirit descends upon men, and the Law of God is written in their hearts (Acts 2:1, Ezek 36:26-27, Jer 31:33; Joel 2:28-29; Heb 8:10)

The Feast of Trumpets, or Rosh-hoshanna was to commemorate the Jewish civil New Year (Lev 23:24).

this, then I will be deserving of God's Grace". These are all dead works which need to be repented of.

Tit 3:4 But after that the kindness and love of God our Saviour toward man appeared,
5 Not by works of righteousness which we have done, but according to his mercy he saved us, by the washing of regeneration, and renewing of the Holy Ghost;
6 Which he shed on us abundantly through Jesus Christ our Saviour;
7 That being justified by his grace, we should be made heirs according to the hope of eternal life.

There is absolutely nothing we can do to merit salvation. Only through God's Mercy and God's Grace can we be saved. He showed us through the Old Covenant that we cannot keep the Law.

Gal 2:16 Knowing that a man is not justified by the works of the law, but by the faith of Jesus Christ, even we have believed in Jesus Christ, that we might be justified by the faith of Christ, and not by the works of the law: for by the works of the law shall no flesh be justified.

Religion says it is impossible to know God. Christianity is God's Work through Jesus Christ to restore fallen man's fellowship with Him. That restoration can only be done on God's terms.

2Co 5:19 To wit, that God was in Christ, reconciling the world unto himself, not imputing their trespasses unto them; and hath committed unto us the word of reconciliation.
20 Now then we are ambassadors for Christ, as though God did beseech you by us: we pray you in Christ's stead, be ye reconciled to God.
21 For he hath made him to be sin for us, who knew no sin; that we might be made the righteousness of God in him.

There are many people who choose to worship God in their own way. Catholics bow before statues of saints, and justify it by saying they are simply *venerating* the saints. But God doesn't only condemn worshipping idols; He condemns making any image and simply bowing down to it.

Exo 20:4 Thou shalt not make unto thee any graven image, or any likeness *of any thing* that *is* in heaven above, or that *is* in the earth beneath, or that *is* in the water under the earth:
5 Thou shalt not bow down thyself to them, nor serve them: for I the LORD thy God *am* a jealous God, visiting the iniquity of the fathers upon the children unto the third and fourth *generation* of them that hate me;
6 And shewing mercy unto thousands of them that love me, and keep my commandments.

Many protest and say they pray to Mary because they believe they can relate to a mother figure more than the Father. Yet the Bible expressly prohibits idolatry, both in the Old Testament, as well as the New (Acts 15:20, 2 Cor 6:16, 1 Jn 5:21). Jesus plainly said "no one can come to the Father by by me" Jn 14:6.

These are dead works that need to be repented of. They avail nothing except to keep an individual from a personal relationship with Jesus Christ. The book of Revelation speaks of the last days, and tells us that there will be those who will not repent of their dead religious works:

Rev 9:20 And the rest of the men which were not killed by these plagues yet repented not of the works of their hands, that they should not worship devils, and idols of gold, and silver, and brass, and stone, and of wood: which neither can see, nor hear, nor walk:

There are whole denominations that have dress codes, and requirements concerning the length of a man or woman's hair. Some fellowships maintain that a person should attend church in their absolute best attire, in order to honor God. Yet Jesus denounced those religious ones who loved to dress in fancy attire, and to be seen by others as being spiritual, while inwardly they are mere hypocrites (Matt 23:5-7).

Others profess to be Christians, yet live their lives like the rest of the world.

Tradition holds that this was the time of God's Creation, when all the angels shouted for joy (Job 38:7). And so we see the fulfillment of this feast in God's New Creation (2 Cor 5:17) - those who have been reconciled to God through Christ's Blood.

For 10 days following this feast, the Jew was to examine himself, and to make amends for any wrong he had done to others, and to fulfill his pledges.

Then 10 days after Rosh Hoshanna, came **Yom Kippur**, or the **Day of Atonement** (Lev 23:27). It was to be a day of afflicting one's soul, or browbeating or to humble oneself in self examination (verse 32) and repenting for one's sins. This was the day when the High Priest would enter into the Holy of holies and offer a sacrifice on behalf of the people of God. Hebrews 9:7-14 speaks of Christ being the fulfillment of this feast. Now we can come boldly before the Throne of Grace (Heb 4:14-16).

The Feast of Tabernacles was to remind the Israelites of the time when they lived in tents (tabernacles) and God dwelt among them in His own Tabernacle. It also foreshadowed a time when God's Spirit would dwell in the hearts of men, and He would tabernacle with His people again. Heb chapter 3 tells us that we are Christ's house. 2 Cor 5:1 & 4 refers to our bodies as being tabernacles. A form of the word Tabernacle is used in John 1:14. Speaking of Jesus (the Word), we read:*Joh 1:14 And the Word was made flesh, and dwelt (tabernacled) among us, (and we beheld his glory, the glory as of the only begotten of the Father,) full of grace and truth.*

There are others who are so far on the opposite spectrum of the Law, that they have no restraints in their conduct. "I am just a sinner saved by Grace", they say; "God made me this way, so He won't condemn me for what I am!" Regardless of what the outlook is, repentance is necessary for all.

**Mat 15:7 Ye hypocrites, well did Esaias prophesy of you, saying,
8 This people draweth nigh unto me with their mouth, and honoureth me with their lips; but their heart is far from me.
9 But in vain they do worship me, teaching for doctrines the commandments of men.**

Jesus Christ said He is the Way, the Truth and the Life, and no one can come to the Father except through Him (Jn 14:6). There is no other name in Heaven or earth by which anyone can be saved.

There is a difference between the Law of the Old Covenant and the Law of the New. The Old Covenant has a rule book by which to live. The Old Covenant was between God and Israel, and consisted of Statutes and Ordinances which they were unable to keep in their own ability. The statutes of feasts and Sabbaths and ceremony were between God and Israel. They were simply shadows and types of the New Covenant, and revealed Christ. There was a veil over the minds of those who were under the Law, but for those of us who have entered in through the Blood of Jesus, the veil is taken away.

Under the New Covenant, God has put His Law in our hearts and has enabled us through the indwelling of the Holy Spirit to obey that Law. By their fruit you will know the New Covenant Christian. They work, not to earn salvation, but because it is their nature to do that which is right in the sight of God.

Heb 8:10 For this *is* the covenant that I will make with the house of Israel after those days, saith the Lord; I will put my laws into their mind, and write

We are the temple of the living God. We are His Tabernacle.

This brief study of the feasts should allow the reader to see that they have all been fulfilled, and as such, we have no need to observe them anymore, since they were only given to Israel, as part of the Covenant between the Jew and God, and the Gentile who wished to embrace that Old Covenant. The truth is that the feasts were a foreshadow of those things that were to come through Jesus Christ. We who are in Christ can see how the feasts were pointing to Christ, and while we may find joy in celebrating them and their fulfillment, neither the Jew nor the Greek who has embraced the New Covenant with Christ are obligated to observe them.

The only ordinances that the believer is encouraged to keep is the communion, and the baptisms. We will deal with these in another section of this doctrinal study.

them in their hearts: and I will be to them a God, and they shall be to me a people:
11   And they shall not teach every man his neighbour, and every man his brother, saying, Know the Lord: for all shall know me, from the least to the greatest.

It is the love of a child for his or her Father that God seeks from His children. If you love Him, you will keep His Commandments, not out of obligation, but out of gratitude for what He has done for you.

HOW WOULD YOU ANSWER A PERSON WHO SAYS JESUS' WORDS ONLY APPLIED TO THOSE WHO WERE UNDER THE LAW, AND NOT TO US WHO ARE UNDER THE NEW COVENANT OF GRACE?

_____
_____
_____
_____
_____
_____
_____

WHAT WAS THE APOSTLE'S DOCTRINE?

_____
_____
_____
_____

WHAT DOES REPENTANCE MEAN?

_____
_____
_____

HOW DO YOU ANSWER THOSE WHO INSIST WE MUST KEEP THE LAW?

_____
_____
_____
_____
_____

BASIC DOCTRINES

LESSON 2

REPENTANCE FROM DEAD WORKS part 2

Heb 6:1 Therefore leaving the principles of the doctrine of Christ, let us go on unto perfection; not laying again the foundation of repentance from dead works, and of faith toward God,
2 Of the doctrine of baptisms, and of laying on of hands, and of resurrection of the dead, and of eternal judgment.

In our previous lesson, we learned that "repentance from dead works" is primarily referring to vain religious works that give credence to the fallacy that we are able to earn our way to heaven. The Pharisee who stood next to the publican justified himself in the presence of God, declaring his righteous works as a qualification for being recognized by God to be of some great value:

Luk 18:10 Two men went up into the temple to pray; the one a Pharisee, and the other a publican.
11 The Pharisee stood and prayed thus with himself, God, I thank thee, that I am not as other men are, extortioners, unjust, adulterers, or even as this publican.
12 I fast twice in the week, I give tithes of all that I possess.

By the same token, there will be those who stand before Jesus and declare all the wonderful things they did in their religious pursuits as a ticket to enter into His Presence.

Mat 7:21 Not everyone that saith unto me, Lord, Lord, shall enter into the kingdom of heaven; but he that doeth the will of my Father which is in heaven.
22 Many will say to me in that day, Lord, Lord, have we not prophesied in thy name? and in thy name have cast out devils? and in thy name done many wonderful works?

Fasting, tithes, prophesying, casting out devils and doing wonderful works are all things that God does approve of throughout the Bible, but obviously in the two cases mentioned above, there is something missing in the employment of these things. And that is the fact that we need to understand that NOTHING we can do in our own ability can ever merit our salvation.

Cult Watch

1) Jehovah's Witnesses are to be faithful to the Watchtower, in their door to door campaigns, and Mormons are under obligation to serve two years as missionaries, Seventh Day Adventists are under dietary laws and the obligation to keep the Sabbath. Some Christian denominations insist that one must be baptized under a particular formula, others insist that the only way to salvation is through baptism.

Various meditation techniques as taught by Buddhism and Hinduism, yoga, and other religions are designed to bring the practitioner to "inner peace". These various methods rely on "self discipline" on the part of the practitioner, which is learned through following a variety of step by step exercises, such as focusing your attention on certain sounds (such as the "OM" heard in Yoga), visualizations, which even many modern day "Christian" teachers encourage their disciples to do, such as "Close your eyes and visualize yourself in a field of long grass and flowers, and the cross at the center of the field. As you walk toward the cross, the grass becomes shorter, and the flowers are more obvious. Allow your sins, your bitterness and your disappointments in life to stay behind with that long grass as you step into the presence of the cross;" This is all self hypnosis and meditation that comes from the dead works of eastern religions.

The meditation that is spoken of in the Bible is pondering on the Word of God and how we can apply it in our lives'

.

Religion teaches us that if we do this, this and this, we can feel good about ourselves, and maybe the good will outweigh the bad[1]. But God plainly declares that all our Righteousness is as filthy rags.

Isa 64:6 But we are all as an unclean thing, and all our righteousnesses are as filthy rags; and we all do fade as a leaf; and our iniquities, like the wind, have taken us away.

Tit 3:3 For we ourselves also were sometimes foolish, disobedient, deceived, serving divers lusts and pleasures, living in malice and envy, hateful, and hating one another.
4 But after that the kindness and love of God our Saviour toward man appeared,
5 Not by works of righteousness which we have done, but according to his mercy he saved us, by the washing of regeneration, and renewing of the Holy Ghost;
6 Which he shed on us abundantly through Jesus Christ our Saviour;
7 That being justified by his grace, we should be made heirs according to the hope of eternal life.

Whatever good we are capable of that would be acceptable in the eyes of God is because of the work that Christ has done in us and through us.

THE WORK OF REPENTANCE ON A PERSONAL LEVEL

The way of man is to earn his way in everything. We get mad because someone who we have treated good treats us bad...we say they are ungrateful. We say "after all the things I did for him, and he treats me this way!"

But the Way of Jesus is different than the way of man. Jesus said:

Luk 6:31 And as ye would that men should do to you, do ye also to them likewise.
32 For if ye love them which love you, what thank have ye? for sinners also love those that love them.
33 And if ye do good to them which do good to you, what thank have ye? for sinners also do even the same.
34 And if ye lend to them of whom ye hope to receive, what thank have ye? for sinners also lend to sinners, to receive as much again.

As we saw in our last study, the word "repent" as used in the New Testament means to change one's mind:

G3340 metanoeo Thayer Definition: 1) to change one's mind, i.e. to repent 2) to change one's mind for better, heartily to amend with abhorrence of one's past sins

As followers of Christ, our whole thought process with regard to how we conduct our lives compared to how we used to conduct our lives as heathens must change. The Bible tells us that before we come to a saving knowledge of Christ, we are dead in our sins.

Eph 2:1 And you hath he quickened, who were dead in trespasses and sins;
2 Wherein in time past ye walked according to the course of this world, according to the prince of the power of the air, the spirit that now worketh in the children of disobedience:
3 Among whom also we all had our conversation in times past in the lusts of our flesh, fulfilling the desires of the flesh and of the mind; and were by nature the children of wrath, even as others.

Before Christ, we are wholly given over to the desires of our flesh and of our mind.

Before Christ, the flesh and the mind work together to accomplish "Self Fulfillment". The whole philosophy of the human sin nature is "If it feels good, do it". The Satanist's creed is "Do as thou wilt is the whole of the Law".

The thought process combined with the desires of the flesh is what brought Adam and Eve out of fellowship with God.

The serpent planted doubt in Eve's mind by first questioning God's credibility. Does God mean what He says? Would a loving God really condemn a person to hell? Will God really condemn you for pursuing what comes natural? He made me this way, didn't He?

Notes-

Gen 3:1 Now the serpent was more subtil than any beast of the field which the LORD God had made. And he said unto the woman, Yea, hath God said, Ye shall not eat of every tree of the garden?
2 And the woman said unto the serpent, We may eat of the fruit of the trees of the garden:
3 But of the fruit of the tree which is in the midst of the garden, God hath said, Ye shall not eat of it, neither shall ye touch it, lest ye die.
4 And the serpent said unto the woman, Ye shall not surely die:
5 For God doth know that in the day ye eat thereof, then your eyes shall be opened, and ye shall be as gods, knowing good and evil.

The same thought processes are at work in every person's life when it comes to sin and the temptation to sin. The mind and the flesh walk in cooperation with one another when it comes to sin.

Jas 1:13 Let no man say when he is tempted, I am tempted of God: for God cannot be tempted with evil, neither tempteth he any man:
14 But every man is tempted, when he is drawn away of his own lust, and enticed.

The suggestion "...Ye shall not surely die" is quickly followed by that which is enticing to the flesh (lust): "For God doth know that in the day ye eat thereof, then your eyes shall be opened, and ye shall be as gods, knowing good and evil."

Jas 1:15 Then when lust hath conceived, it bringeth forth sin: and sin, when it is finished, bringeth forth death.

Gen 3:6 And when the woman saw that the tree was good for food, and that it was pleasant to the eyes, and a tree to be desired to make one wise, she took of the fruit thereof, and did eat, and

_____
_____
_____
_____
_____
_____
_____
_____
_____

Jas 1:13 Let no man say when he is tempted, I am tempted of God: for God cannot be tempted with evil, neither tempteth he any man: 14 But every man is tempted, when he is drawn away of his own lust, and enticed.
15 Then when lust hath conceived, it bringeth forth sin: and sin, when it is finished, bringeth forth death.

Notes-

_____
_____
_____
_____
_____
_____
_____
_____
_____
_____
_____
_____
_____
_____
_____

gave also unto her husband with her; and he did eat.

It is important to understand this: The thought or the temptation wasn't the sin. ***It was when they acted on the thought that they sinned.*** While they were in the Garden, and having their encounter with the serpent, they could have changed their minds concerning the temptation and cut off communication with the serpent at any time and stayed in fellowship with God.

After the fall, man became entangled in bondage to the desires of his flesh, and has been concerned with himself and his well being more than with God's Will for his life. Man's tendency is to be his own god, determining what is right in his own eyes.

Rom 3:23 For all have sinned, and come short of the glory of God;

We fit God in to our lives in areas where it's convenient to do so, and according to our terms, instead of His. The way of man is to feel good about himself and his sin.

Eve blamed the serpent for her sin. Adam blamed the woman, and even God for his sin. After all, if God wouldn't have given the woman to him, he wouldn't have been enticed. Sure, the serpent was the author of the temptation, but each party involved was guilty of their own sin.

Joh 8:34 Jesus answered them, Verily, verily, I say unto you, Whosoever committeth sin is the servant of sin.
35 And the servant abideth not in the house for ever: but the Son abideth ever.

Prior to becoming Born Again, all we know is a life that is guided by the five senses. Whatever looks, feels, tastes, sounds, or smells good, is that which we pursue. The Bible refers to such a person as the "natural man", or "carnal".

1Co 2:14 But the natural man receiveth not the things of the Spirit of God: for they are foolishness unto him: neither can he know them, because they are spiritually discerned.

The Bible says that the flesh is at war with the spirit.

The carnal senses will mislead us concerning Spiritual truth.

Rom 8:5 For they that are after the flesh do mind the things of the flesh; but they that are after the Spirit the things of the Spirit.
6 For to be carnally minded is death; but to be spiritually minded is life and peace.
7 Because the carnal mind is enmity against God: for it is not subject to the law of God, neither indeed can be.
8 So then they that are in the flesh cannot please God.
9 But ye are not in the flesh, but in the Spirit, if so be that the Spirit of God dwell in you. Now if any man have not the Spirit of Christ, he is none of his.
10 And if Christ be in you, the body is dead because of sin; but the Spirit is life because of righteousness.
11 But if the Spirit of him that raised up Jesus from the dead dwell in you, he that raised up Christ from the dead shall also quicken your mortal bodies by his Spirit that dwelleth in you.
12 Therefore, brethren, we are debtors, not to the flesh, to live after the flesh.
13 For if ye live after the flesh, ye shall die: but if ye through the Spirit do mortify the deeds of the body, ye shall live.

How do we mortify the deeds of the body? The Bible teaches us that those of us who are in Christ no longer have a carnal mind, but in actuality, we have the "mind of Christ".

1Co 2:12 Now we have received, not the spirit of the world, but the spirit which is of God; that we might know the things that are freely given to us of God.
13 Which things also we speak, not in the words which man's wisdom teacheth, but which the Holy Ghost teacheth; comparing spiritual things with spiritual.
14 But the natural man receiveth not the things of the Spirit of God: for they are foolishness unto him: neither can he know them, because they are spiritually discerned.
15 But he that is spiritual judgeth all things, yet he himself is judged of no man.

16 For who hath known the mind of the Lord, that he may instruct him? But we have the mind of Christ.

We who have been born of the spirit are truly new creations.

2Co 5:16 Wherefore henceforth know we no man after the flesh: yea, though we have known Christ after the flesh, yet now henceforth know we him no more.
17 Therefore if any man be in Christ, he is a new creature: old things are passed away; behold, all things are become new.

Now that I have the mind of Christ, I no longer need be subject to a carnal mindset. There is a continual battle going on; the enemy of my soul tries to reason with me on my carnal level..."That sure looks good, doesn't it?" "Go ahead, taste it..." "that sure will make you feel good, if only you give in..."

But I don't have to listen to that! I am a child of God. There is a battle going on for my affections, and it is the same battle that the serpent waged in the garden with Adam and Eve. But the difference is that I don't need to buy into Satan's lies.

Now that I am a child of God, and have the Mind of Christ, I can react the way Jesus Christ would to temptation.

2Co 10:3 For though we walk in the flesh, we do not war after the flesh:
4 (For the weapons of our warfare are not carnal, but mighty through God to the pulling down of strong holds;)
5 Casting down imaginations, and every high thing that exalteth itself against the knowledge of God, and bringing into captivity every thought to the obedience of Christ;
6 And having in a readiness to revenge all disobedience, when your obedience is fulfilled.

Imaginations, knowledge and thoughts have their seat in the mind. Remember the definition of "repentance"?

In our previous lesson, we learned that the Greek word for repent is the word "Metanoia", and it literally means to change the mind. According to 2 Cor 10:5, we mortify the deeds of the body by bringing every thought into captivity to the obedience of Christ.

James 4:7 tells us that we are to resist the devil

Jas 4:7 Submit yourselves therefore to God. Resist the devil, and he will flee from you.

8 Draw nigh to God, and he will draw nigh to you. Cleanse your hands, ye sinners; and purify your hearts, ye double minded.

How do you cast down imaginations? How are you able to resist the devil?

Php 4:8 Finally, brethren, whatsoever things are true, whatsoever things are honest, whatsoever things are just, whatsoever things are pure, whatsoever things are lovely, whatsoever things are of good report; if there be any virtue, and if there be any praise, think on these things.

If your mind is filled with the Word, with worship, and with a desire and a willingness to please God, there won't be any room for vain imaginations, or entertaining thoughts that are opposed to the Will of God. There are a lot of things you may watch as entertainment that don't fit in the above categories. You need to change your mind about how you entertain yourself.

The more we practice Philippians 4:8, the more we are able to successfully resist the devil. There are strongholds that have been built up in our lives from the sin we have indulged, and those strongholds must be brought down if we are to walk a successful (read "victorious") Christian life. What is a stronghold, but a fortification whereby a person or persons gather for refuge and shelter?

Luk 11:17 But he, knowing their thoughts, said unto them, Every kingdom divided against itself is brought to desolation; and a house divided against a house falleth.
18 If Satan also be divided against himself, how shall his kingdom stand? because ye say that I cast out devils through Beelzebub.
19 And if I by Beelzebub cast out devils, by whom do your sons cast them out? therefore shall they be your judges.
20 But if I with the finger of God cast out devils, no doubt the kingdom of God is come upon you.
21 When a strong man armed keepeth his palace, his goods are in peace:
22 But when a stronger than he shall come upon him, and overcome him, he taketh from him all his armour wherein he trusted, and divideth his spoils.
23 He that is not with me is against me: and he that gathereth not with me scattereth.
24 When the unclean spirit is gone out of a man, he walketh through dry places, seeking rest; and finding none, he saith, I will return unto my house whence I came out.
25 And when he cometh, he findeth it swept and garnished.
26 Then goeth he, and taketh to him seven other spirits more wicked than himself; and they enter in, and dwell there: and the last state of that man is worse than the first

2 Co 6:16 And what agreement hath the temple of God with idols? for ye are the temple of the living God; as God hath said, I will dwell in them, and walk in them; and I will be their God, and they shall be my people.

Heb 3:4 For every house is builded by some man; but he that built all things is God.
Heb 3:5 And Moses verily was faithful in all his house, as a servant, for a testimony of those things which were to be spoken after;
6 But Christ as a son over his own house; whose house are we, if we hold fast the confidence and the rejoicing of the hope firm unto the end.
7 Wherefore (as the Holy Ghost saith, Today if ye will hear his voice,
8 Harden not your hearts, as in the provocation, in the day of temptation in the wilderness:
9 When your fathers tempted me, proved me, and saw my works forty years.
10 Wherefore I was grieved with that generation, and said, They do alway err in their heart; and they have not known my ways.
11 So I sware in my wrath, They shall not enter into my rest.)
12 Take heed, brethren, lest there be in any of you an evil heart of unbelief, in departing from the living God.
13 But exhort one another daily, while it is called To day; lest any of you be hardened through the deceitfulness of sin.
14 For we are made partakers of Christ, if we hold the beginning of our confidence stedfast unto the end;
15 While it is said, To day if ye will hear his voice, harden not your hearts, as in the provocation.

We often read Matthew 12:25-29, Mark 3:23-29, and Luke 11:17-26 in regards to casting out devils from people that we minister to.

Mat 12:25 And Jesus knew their thoughts, and said unto them, Every kingdom divided against itself is brought to desolation; and every city or house divided against itself shall not stand:
26 And if Satan cast out Satan, he is divided against himself; how shall then his kingdom stand?
27 And if I by Beelzebub cast out devils, by whom do your children cast *them* out? therefore they shall be your judges.
28 But if I cast out devils by the Spirit of God, then the kingdom of God is come unto you.
29 Or else how can one enter into a strong man's house, and spoil his goods, except he first bind the strong man? and then he will spoil his house.

But there is another and just as viable (if not more viable) way to interpret that passage.

Jesus spoke of the location of the Kingdom of God:

Luk 17:20 And when he was demanded of the Pharisees, when the kingdom of God should come, he answered them and said, The kingdom of God cometh not with observation:
21 Neither shall they say, Lo here! or, lo there! for, behold, the kingdom of God is within you.

When we become Born Again, we become citizens of the Kingdom of God. We become a temple of the Living God (1 Cor 3:16,17; 6:19). Hebrews 3:2-6 says that we are Christ's house. Through the Holy Spirit God now lives in us. In religion He is "somewhere out there"; in Christ, He lives inside us to direct and empower us to live a life of victory over sin. The Holy Spirit works within us to convict us of our sin. Jesus said that a house divided cannot stand. The Christian needs to bind the strong man from his own house in order to walk victoriously before God.

If I gossip about my neighbor, I am walking in agreement with the strongman, and contrary to the Holy Spirit. I need to repent of my Gossip if I hope to be a fit vessel for the Lord's use. If I harbor bitterness and unforgiveness in my heart, I need to take those thoughts captive and forgive. If I am prone to using alcohol or drugs, or given over to lust of the flesh and of the eyes, I need to change my mind about the life I am leading. I need to *resist* the allure and the attraction, and as I do, that strongman will flee. Why will he flee? Because we are able to say with Jesus that the prince of this world (Satan) has nothing in us (Jn 14:30).

Joh 14:30 Hereafter I will not talk much with you: for the prince of this world cometh, and hath nothing in me.

2Co 10:3 For though we walk in the flesh, we do not war after the flesh:
4 (For the weapons of our warfare *are* not carnal, but mighty through God to the pulling down of strong holds;)
5 Casting down imaginations, and every high thing that exalteth itself against the knowledge of God, and bringing into captivity every thought to the obedience of Christ;

Jesus said plainly that we cannot serve two masters. The Christian walk is one in which we walk in agreement with the Lord. You cannot agree with two conflicting sides at the same time. That is referred to in the Word of God as being double minded.

Jas 1:8 A double minded man is unstable in all his ways.

Repentance and the Gospel go hand in hand. Repentance is a Christian's friend. Repentance divests the enemy of his hold on us.

Mark 1:14 Now after that John was put in prison, Jesus came into Galilee, preaching the gospel of the kingdom of God,
15 And saying, The time is fulfilled, and the kingdom of God is at hand: repent ye, and believe the gospel.

Jesus was saying in essence, "change your mind concerning your life style, and believe the good news that I am declaring about the Kingdom of God ".

Jesus commissioned His disciples to go and preach the gospel. We see that an integral part of this gospel was that men should repent, or change their minds about the course their lives were taking.

Mark 6:12 And they went out, and preached that men should repent.

Jesus mentioned the repentance of Nineveh as a perfect illustration of God's Grace falling on a people after they repented. And then in the following verses, he demonstrates what true repentance is:

Luke 11:32 The men of Nineve shall rise up in the judgment with this generation, and shall condemn it: for they repented at the preaching of Jonas; and, behold, a greater than Jonas is here.
33 No man, when he hath lighted a candle, putteth it in a secret place, neither under a bushel, but on a candlestick, that they which come in may see the light.
34 The light of the body is the eye: therefore when thine eye is single, thy whole body also is full of light; but when thine eye is evil, thy body also is full of darkness.
35 Take heed therefore that the light which is in thee be not darkness.
36 If thy whole body therefore be full of light, having no part dark, the whole shall be full of light, as when the bright shining of a candle doth give thee light.

Jesus taught that when a person changes his mind as to the course of life he or she is following, and chooses to follow the True and Living God, it will be evident to all who know them.

When we come to God in true repentance, we have decided to set our affections on Him and the things of God, rather than on the things of the world.

The true Christian walk is one of turning our backs on the allure of the world, and turning our hearts and affections toward God. As Joshua told the Israelites, they needed to decide who they were going to serve. God is a jealous God, and He seeks those who will give Him their all.

Repentance is a matter of choice.

Repentance is truly changing our minds concerning our lives and our lifestyles, and living accordingly.

I Jn 2:15 Love not the world, neither the things that are in the world. If any man love the world, the love of the Father is not in him.
16 For all that is in the world, the lust of the flesh, and the lust of the eyes, and the pride of life, is not of the Father, but is of the world.
17 And the world passeth away, and the lust thereof: but he that doeth the will of God abideth for ever.

Rom 12:1 I beseech you therefore, brethren, by the mercies of God, that ye present your bodies a living sacrifice, holy, acceptable unto God, which is your reasonable service.
2 And be not conformed to this world: but be ye transformed by the renewing of your mind, that ye may prove what is that good, and acceptable, and perfect, will of God.

Col 3:1 If ye then be risen with Christ, seek those things which are above, where Christ sitteth on the right hand of God.
2 Set your affection on things above, not on things on the earth.
3 For ye are dead, and your life is hid with Christ in God.
4 When Christ, who is our life, shall appear, then shall ye also appear with him in glory.
5 Mortify therefore your members which are upon the earth; fornication, uncleanness, inordinate affection, evil concupiscence, and covetousness, which is idolatry:
6 For which things' sake the wrath of God cometh on the children of disobedience:
7 In the which ye also walked some time, when ye lived in them.

Jesus taught that repentance is absolutely essential for a person to be saved. But He also taught of God's longsuffering toward us.

Luke 13:1 There were present at that season some that told him of the Galilaeans, whose blood Pilate had mingled with their sacrifices.
2 And Jesus answering said unto them, Suppose ye that these Galilaeans were sinners above all the Galilaeans, because they suffered such things?
3 I tell you, Nay: but, except ye repent, ye shall all likewise perish.
4 Or those eighteen, upon whom the tower in Siloam fell, and slew them, think ye that they were sinners above all men that dwelt in Jerusalem?
5 I tell you, Nay: but, except ye repent, ye shall all likewise perish.
6 He spake also this parable; A certain man had a fig tree planted in his vineyard; and he came and sought fruit thereon, and found none.
7 Then said he unto the dresser of his vineyard, Behold, these three years I come seeking fruit on this fig tree, and find none: cut it down; why cumbereth it the ground?
8 And he answering said unto him, Lord, let it alone this year also, till I shall dig about it, and dung it:
9 And if it bear fruit, well: and if not, then after that thou shalt cut it down.

Though the Lord does bear long with us, and gives us Mercy, it is obvious that He expects us to bear fruit. True repentance will bear fruit. The Light of Christ will shine brightly in a Christian.

Acts 26:19 Whereupon, O king Agrippa, I was not disobedient unto the heavenly vision:
20 But shewed first unto them of Damascus, and at Jerusalem, and throughout all the coasts of Judaea, and then to the Gentiles, that they should repent and turn to God, and do works meet for repentance.

Acts 17:30 And the times of this ignorance God winked at; but now commandeth all men every where to repent:
31 Because he hath appointed a day, in the which he will judge the world in righteousness by that man whom he hath ordained; whereof he hath given assurance unto all men, in that he hath raised him from the dead.

No one is excluded from God's Plan of salvation. He is a Righteous Judge, and no respecter of persons. The desire of God is that all men should come to repentance.

2 Pet 3:9 The Lord is not slack concerning his promise, as some men count slackness; but is longsuffering to us-ward, not willing that any should perish, but that all should come to repentance.

See in the parable of the prodigal son (Luke 15:11-32) how the young man *changed his mind* about the course of life he was following. We are told in verse 17, that "he came to himself". He realized that the road he was on led to a dead end...so he changed his mind, and got on the right course.

Luk 15:17 And when he came to himself, he said, How many hired servants of my father's have bread enough and to spare, and I perish with hunger!
18 I will arise and go to my father, and will say unto him, Father, I have sinned against heaven, and before thee,

Remission:

859 aphesis- 1) release from bondage or imprisonment 2) forgiveness or pardon, of sins (letting them go as if they had never been committed), remission (forgiveness) of the penalty

Notes-

_____
_____
_____
_____
_____
_____
_____
_____
_____
_____
_____
_____
_____
_____
_____
_____
_____
_____
_____
_____
_____
_____
_____

Repentance and freedom from the bondage of sin go hand in hand. YOU CANNOT HAVE FREEDOM FROM SIN'S GRASP WITHOUT REPENTANCE.

**Luke 24:45 Then opened he their understanding, that they might understand the scriptures,
46 And said unto them, Thus it is written, and thus it behoved Christ to suffer, and to rise from the dead the third day:
47 And that repentance and remission of sins should be preached in his name among all nations, beginning at Jerusalem.**

When we truly repent and turn to God, sin has no more hold on us:

Rom 6:14 For sin shall not have dominion over you: for ye are not under the law, but under grace.

The Holy Spirit gives us the power to obey God once we repent:

Acts 2:38 Then Peter said unto them, Repent, and be baptized every one of you in the name of Jesus Christ for the remission of sins, and ye shall receive the gift of the Holy Ghost.

Acts 10:43 To him give all the prophets witness, that through his name whosoever believeth in him shall receive remission of sins.

Rom 3:25 Whom God hath set forth to be a propitiation through faith in his blood, to declare his righteousness for the remission of sins that are past, through the forbearance of God;

Remember that Jesus said a house or a kingdom divided against itself is brought to desolation (Lk 11:17). Our personal relationship with the Lord is broken when we walk in sin.

God's Standard of repentance is true in both the Old and the New Covenant:

Lev 26:14   But if ye will not hearken unto me, and will not do all these commandments;
15   And if ye shall despise my statutes, or if your soul abhor my judgments, so that ye will not do all my commandments, but that ye break my covenant:
16   I also will do this unto you; I will even appoint over you terror, consumption, and the burning ague, that shall consume the eyes, and cause sorrow of heart: and ye shall sow your seed in vain, for your enemies shall eat it.
17   And I will set my face against you, and ye shall be slain before your enemies: they that hate you shall reign over you; and ye shall flee when none pursueth you.
18   And if ye will not yet for all this hearken unto me, then I will punish you seven times more for your sins.
19   And I will break the pride of your power; and I will make your heaven as iron, and your earth as brass:

Mal 3:6   For I am the LORD, I change not; therefore ye sons of Jacob are not consumed.

Heb 13:8   Jesus Christ the same yesterday, and today, and forever.

Joh 8:10   When Jesus had lifted up himself, and saw none but the woman, he said unto her, Woman, where are those thine accusers? hath no man condemned thee?
11   She said, No man, Lord. And Jesus said unto her, Neither do I condemn thee: go, and sin no more.
12   Then spake Jesus again unto them, saying, I am the light of the world: he that followeth me shall not walk in darkness, but shall have the light of life.

1Jn 1:6 If we say that we have fellowship with him, and walk in darkness, we lie, and do not the truth:
7 But if we walk in the light, as he is in the light, we have fellowship one with another, and the blood of Jesus Christ his Son cleanseth us from all sin.

Unlike Adam and Eve, if the Christian assumes responsibility for his or her sin instead of blaming others or circumstances or God Himself for their sin, they will be restored to fellowship with God.

We need to change our minds about the way we are living if we want to have our fellowship with God restored. I am sure you have heard Christians say that their prayers don't seem to get past the ceiling. A little earnest self examination could change things.

1Jn 1:8 If we say that we have no sin, we deceive ourselves, and the truth is not in us.
9 If we confess our sins, he is faithful and just to forgive us our sins, and to cleanse us from all unrighteousness.
10 If we say that we have not sinned, we make him a liar, and his word is not in us.

Most Christians are aware of Jesus' words in John 14:12-14:

Joh 14:12 Verily, verily, I say unto you, He that believeth on me, the works that I do shall he do also; and greater works than these shall he do; because I go unto my Father.
13 And whatsoever ye shall ask in my name, that will I do, that the Father may be glorified in the Son.
14 If ye shall ask any thing in my name, I will do it.

Even though we say that we believe these words, we should ask ourselves, "Why then, are we not seeing this happen?" Again, Jesus said we cannot serve two masters.

Notes-

In 1st John we see a similar promise, but with it there is a condition:

1Jn 3:22 And whatsoever we ask, we receive of him, because we keep his commandments, and do those things that are pleasing in his sight.

Why do we receive whatsoever we ask?

_____

1 Jn 3:23 And this is his commandment, That we should believe on the name of his Son Jesus Christ, and love one another, as he gave us commandment.
24 And he that keepeth his commandments dwelleth in him, and he in him. And hereby we know that he abideth in us, by the Spirit which he hath given us.

Now read John 14:15:

Joh 14:15 If ye love me, keep my commandments.

Why don't we see the miraculous happening in the Church today?

Because the Church, for the most part consists of unrepentant Christians. Their house is divided, and as a result, they have a form of Godliness, but deny the Power thereof.

2Ti 3:1 This know also, that in the last days perilous times shall come.
2 For men shall be lovers of their own selves, covetous, boasters, proud, blasphemers, disobedient to parents, unthankful, unholy,
3 Without natural affection, trucebreakers, false accusers, incontinent, fierce, despisers of those that are good,
4 Traitors, heady, highminded, lovers of pleasures more than lovers of God;
5 Having a form of godliness, but denying the power thereof: from such turn away.

Rom 10:9 That if thou shalt confess with thy mouth the Lord Jesus, and shalt believe in thine heart that God hath raised him from the dead, thou shalt be saved. 10 For with the heart man believeth unto righteousness; and with the mouth confession is made unto salvation.

"For with the heart man believeth unto righteousness"

This is the standard of whether or not a person is saved. Not that they merely prayed a prayer, and took joined a fellowship; but that they believe to the point of living their lives in righteousness. God has promised that He would put His Laws in the hearts of those who are His, and they would walk in them. The Born again Christian strives to have victory over sin. This is bearing fruit fit for repentance.

1Jn 2:4 He that saith, I know him, and keepeth not his commandments, is a liar, and the truth is not in him.
5 But whoso keepeth his word, in him verily is the love of God perfected: hereby know we that we are in him.

1Jn 3:2 Beloved, now are we the sons of God, and it doth not yet appear what we shall be: but we know that, when he shall appear, we shall be like him; for we shall see him as he is.
3 And every man that hath this hope in him purifieth himself, even as he is pure.
4 Whosoever committeth sin transgresseth also the law: for sin is the transgression of the law.
5 And ye know that he was manifested to take away our sins; and in him is no sin.
6 Whosoever abideth in him sinneth not: whosoever sinneth hath not seen him, neither known him.
7 Little children, let no man deceive you: he that doeth righteousness is righteous, even as he is righteous.

Now is a good time to ask yourself: How is your house?

WHAT IS THE GREEK WORD FOR THE WORD REPENT?

_____

IS REPENTANCE NECESSARY FOR SALVATION?

_____

WHAT IS IT'S MEANING?

_____

WHAT HAPPENS IN REGARD TO THE PERSON WHO REPENTS?

_____

_____

_____

WHAT HAPPENS IN REGARD TO SIN WHEN A PERSON REPENTS?

_____

_____

_____

WHY IS "I AM JUST A SINNER SAVED BY GRACE NOT A GOOD EXCUSE FOR SIN IN A CHRISTIAN'S LIFE? (ROM 6:14)

_____

_____

_____

We have seen that the doctrine of repentance encompasses these things:

- Repentance is necessary for salvation.

- By its very definition, repentance is changing one's mind as to the course of life he or she has been pursuing, and making a conscious decision to follow the Ways of the Lord, and acting on that decision.
- One cannot merely decide to live for Jesus; there must also be a viable proof as to the effect that decision has had in one's life.
- Just calling oneself a Christian does not make a person a Christian.
- In yielding to Christ, one becomes occupied with the things of God more than he or she is with the things of this world. People will just naturally be able to see this difference.

This is bearing fruit fit for repentance.

Heb 12:3 For consider him that endured such contradiction of sinners against himself, lest ye be wearied and faint in your minds.
4 Ye have not yet resisted unto blood, striving against sin.

BASIC DOCTRINES

LESSON 3

FAITH TOWARD GOD:

FAITH AS THE AGENT OF OUR SALVATION.

Heb 6:1 Therefore leaving the principles of the doctrine of Christ, let us go on unto perfection; not laying again the foundation of repentance from dead works, and of FAITH TOWARD GOD
2 Of the doctrine of baptisms, and of laying on of hands, and of resurrection of the dead, and of eternal judgment.

Faith is the instrument by which the gift of salvation is received. Grace is the basis of salvation.

It is only by the Grace of God that any of us have a right to be saved. No man is good enough by his own merit to deserve Heaven, but God's Grace is such that He sent His Only Begotten Son to take our sins upon Himself so we would not have to personally pay the penalty for our sin.

Although Christians will and should do good works, no amount of good works can get us in heaven because none of us just aren't good enough to measure up to the Pure and Perfect Most Holy God Almighty.

Eph 2:6 And hath raised us up together, and made us sit together in heavenly places in Christ Jesus:
7 That in the ages to come he might shew the exceeding riches of his grace in his kindness toward us through Christ Jesus.
8 For by grace are ye saved through faith; and that not of yourselves: it is the gift of God:
9 Not of works, lest any man should boast.
10 For we are his workmanship, created in Christ Jesus unto good works, which God hath before ordained that we should walk in them.

Though they cannot save us, our good works will be the evidence that God has done a work of salvation in us. We receive salvation through Faith in God. It is that Faith that will compel us to live lives that are pleasing to Him. We can't work our way to salvation, but salvation will naturally result in a life of doing good works because of the Transforming Power that has been worked in our hearts through the indwelling of the Spirit of God.

Faith is absolute confidence in the Promises of God, Who cannot lie.

According to Strong's dictionary of the Greek language, Faith =

4102 pistis pis'-tis From G3982; persuasion, that is, credence; moral conviction (of religious truth, or the truthfulness of God or a religious teacher), especially reliance upon Christ for salvation; abstractly constancy in such profession; by extension the system of religious (Gospel) truth itself: -assurance, belief, believe, faith, fidelity

Faith is Substance

G5287

ὑπόστασις hupostasis hoop-os'-tas-is

From a compound of G5259 and G2476; a setting under (support), that is, (figuratively) concretely essence, or abstractly assurance (objectively or subjectively): -confidence, confident, person, substance.

2Co 9:4 Lest haply if they of Macedonia come with me, and find you unprepared, we (that we say not, ye) should be ashamed in this same confident boasting.

2Co 11:17 That which I speak, I speak it not after the Lord, but as it were foolishly, in this confidence of boasting.

Faith in God's Redemptive Work through Jesus Christ is what saves us. Again, it is only by Grace that God opted to do that Work.

In Lesson two, we let the context of the book of Hebrews define "repentance from dead works". We can do the same with the definition of faith. Hebrews 11:1 presents the definition that we should embrace as far as "Faith" is concerned.

Heb 11:1 Now faith is the substance of things hoped for, the evidence of things not seen.

FAITH IS THE SUBSTANCE

Substance (Gr. hupostasis) = confidence. There are five places where this word is used in the New Testament. Three of those places are in the Book of Hebrews. In Hebrews 3:14, this word is translated as "confidence":

Heb 3:14 For we are made partakers of Christ, if we hold the beginning of our *confidence* stedfast unto the end;

In two other places this word is translated as "confidence", and that is in 2 Cor 9:4, & 2 Cor 11:17 where Paul speaks of his "confident boasting". The only other time it is used is in Hebrews 1:3. When speaking of Christ, the author writes:

Heb 1:3 Who being the brightness of his glory, and the express image of his person, and upholding all things by the word of his power, when he had by himself purged our sins, sat down on the right hand of the Majesty on high;

We need to take a brief rabbit trail in the study of this passage in order to grasp the depth of this word that is in other places translated as "confidence". Can the reader guess which word in this passage is the same word (hupostasis) that we are looking at in Hebrews 11:1?

"Who (Jesus) being the brightness of his (God's) glory" = Speaking of Jesus' Glory, we read:

Joh 1:14 And the Word was made flesh, and dwelt among us, (and we beheld his glory, the glory as of the only begotten of the Father,) full of grace and truth.

"and the express image" of His (God's) Person" = The word translated as "*Express image*" is used only here in the New Testament = **5481 charakter khar-ak-tar' From the same as G5482; a graver (the tool or the person), that is, (by implication) engraving (["character"], the figure stamped, that is, an exact copy or [figuratively] representation): - express image.**

Of His Person = this word "Person" is the word that is elsewhere translated as "Substance" and "confidence". I really don't think we would lose anything in the translation by reading it "Who being the brightness of His Glory, and the exact representation of His (God's) confidence, (or) substance..."

The New Living translation reads:

Heb 1:3 The Son radiates God's own glory and expresses the very character of God, and he sustains everything by the mighty power of his command. When he had cleansed us from our sins, he sat down in the place of honor at the right hand of the majestic God in heaven.

Jesus was the *epitome* of what Faith is. He was Faith personified. He was the Living Word of God. He exuded confidence in all things concerning God. He spoke, and it was so, because the words He spoke were not His own, but the Father's (Jn 14:10).

Notes-

Joh 14:12 Verily, verily, I say unto you, He that believeth on me, the works that I do shall he do also; and greater works than these shall he do; because I go unto my Father.
13 And whatsoever ye shall ask in my name, that will I do, that the Father may be glorified in the Son.
14 If ye shall ask any thing in my name, I will do it.

Pro 3:5 Trust in the LORD with all thine heart; and lean not unto thine own understanding.

1679 elpi o el-pid'-zo From G1680; to expect or confide: - (have, thing) hope (-d) (for), trust.

Notes-

Joh 14:10 Believest thou not that I am in the Father, and the Father in me? the words that I speak unto you I speak not of myself: but the Father that dwelleth in me, he doeth the works.

As children of God, we are to have the same mindset. The Word of God says to "trust in the Lord with all your heart"...to have utmost confidence in Him (Prov. 3:5).

FAITH IS THE SUBSTANCE OF THINGS HOPED FOR

The next word we will look at in our definition of Faith according to Hebrews 11:1 is the word "Hope". "Faith is the substance of things hoped for"... The Greek word for "Hope" is stronger than the English word we use.

For us, the word "hope" carries with it a meaning of having at least a slight expectation that we may obtain something that we desire, like "I hope I get a motorcycle for Christmas". But the Greek word translated as "Hope", according to Strong's Dictionary is stronger than ours.

So we see that FAITH is the *confident expectation* we have that a thing that we are believing for will come to pass. Faith is the epitome of extreme TRUST in God.

Faith is my child *knowing* that if he asks for some bread from me, he will get bread, and not a rock. He has a *confident expectation* that his daddy will do right by him. If he asks for some fish, he will get some fish, and not some snake meat.

Faith is walking and living in agreement with Jesus, Who asked:

Mat 7:11 If ye then, being evil, know how to give good gifts unto your children, how much more

shall your Father which is in heaven give good things to them that ask him?

THE EVIDENCE OF THINGS NOT SEEN

The evidence (the proof or the conviction) of things not seen. My child can have utmost confidence in my promise to give him some bread, because he or she knows my love for them. The very character of a father is to provide for his children. They may not see the food in the cupboard this morning, but they know that as a father, I will do all in my power to make sure they don't go hungry. I can believe God, because I look at the creation around me, and like the psalmist, I can say

Psa 8:3 When I consider thy heavens, the work of thy fingers, the moon and the stars, which thou hast ordained;
4 What is man, that thou art mindful of him? and the son of man, that thou visitest him?

In fact, the writer of Hebrews seems to allude to this very thing when He says:

Heb 11:3 Through faith we understand that the worlds were framed by the word of God, so that things which are seen were not made of things which do appear.

Even though I have never seen God face to Face, I behold the universe and His creation, and I must conclude that there is a Creator.

So if my faith is in the One Who framed the worlds with just His Word, what is the limit to what God can do? _____

It is important to grasp the Biblical meaning of Faith in order to understand your position with God. During these next few lessons it will do the disciple

Eph 2:8 For by grace are ye saved through faith; and that not of yourselves: it is the gift of God:

good to refresh his or her mind on this Biblical definition of Faith.

So we see that FAITH is the confident expectation that we have that a thing that we are believing for will come to pass, because our expectation is based on the unchanging Word of God, Whose promises are "yea and amen".

In our current lesson, we are studying **Faith for Salvation**.

Now, we have already seen that we are saved by Grace through Faith (Eph 2:8-10). It is NOT works that saves us. It is Faith, or absolute confidence in the Work that Jesus Christ did for us on the Cross.

Other than BELIEVE that Jesus Christ is the only One Who has purchased my salvation, and receiving Him as my Lord and Savior, what can I do to be saved? Obviously, as we have learned in the previous studies, we need to repent. But other than repenting and believing the Gospel, what must you do to be saved? Take a few minutes to write your thoughts here:

_____
_____
_____
_____
_____
_____
_____
_____
_____
_____
_____
_____

Cult Watch:

1) Jehovah's Witnesses, Seventh Day Adventists, Unitarian Universalists and others deny the thought that a loving God would condemn a person to eternal torment. We will review these thoughts later in the last study of the doctrine of Hell.

Notes-
_____
_____
_____
_____
_____
_____
_____
_____
_____
_____
_____

*PROPITIATION= 2435 hilasterion- relating to an appeasing or expiating, having placating or expiating force, expiatory; a means of appeasing or expiating, a propitiation
a) used of the cover of the ark of the covenant in the Holy of Holies, which was sprinkled with the blood of the expiatory victim on the annual day of atonement (this rite signifying that the life of the people, the loss of which they had merited by their sins, was offered to God in the blood as the life of the victim, and that God by this ceremony was appeased and their sins expiated); hence, the lid of expiation, the propitiatory
b) an expiatory sacrifice
c) an expiatory victim*

If your answer to the above question is anything but "nothing", then you have a wrong view of salvation. It is not because you have some special quality above someone else that He saves you. He saves you from the bondage of sin and Hell because He loves you, and He doesn't want you to spend eternal torment in Hell[1].

The First Covenant of the Law which He established with Israel proved one thing:

No man could keep the righteous requirements whereby he could attain heaven. If he could, there would be no need for the daily sacrifices that were offered on behalf of the individuals and the priests and all who ministered before God.

**Rom 3:23 For all have sinned, and come short of the glory of God;
24 Being justified freely by his grace through the redemption that is in Christ Jesus:
25 Whom God hath set forth to be a propitiation through faith in his blood, to declare his righteousness for the remission of sins that are past, through the forbearance of God;
26 To declare, I say, at this time his righteousness: that he might be just, and the justifier of him which believeth in Jesus. (KJV)**

Jesus Christ is our propitiation. This is a big word that few people can really understand. The person who comes to God through Jesus Christ understands that Christ's sacrifice on the cross was sufficient to procure his or her forgiveness of sins they had committed against God.

O.K., what does "expiate" or "expiation" mean? Good Question.

Expiate = to appease, pacify, to expiate guilt or a crime is to perform some act which is supposed to purify the guilty person, or some act

which is accepted by the offended party as satisfaction for the injury; that is, some act by which his wrath is appeased, and his forgiveness procured.

Romans 3:25 Whom God hath set forth to be a propitiation through faith in his blood, to declare his righteousness for the remission of sins that are past, through the forbearance of God;

Jesus Christ came to blot out our sins that we have committed in the past. Christ died on our behalf, and took our deserved punishment for all of the sins we have committed against the One True Holy God upon Himself. It was His sacrifice on our behalf that has procured our forgiveness for our sins. What this means is that we begin our new life with Christ with a clean slate. Again, this demonstrates the Grace of God toward us.

The Blood that Jesus shed on Calvary's cross was more than sufficient to pay the penalty that we deserved, the penalty of death and eternity in Hell. Let's look at the verses preceding and following Romans 3:25, to get a good picture of what occurred on Calvary on behalf of humanity:

Rom 3:23 For all have sinned, and come short of the glory of God;
24 Being justified freely by his grace through the redemption that is in Christ Jesus:
25 Whom God hath set forth to be a propitiation through faith in his blood, to declare his righteousness for the remission of sins that are past, through the forbearance of God;
26 To declare, I say, at this time his righteousness: that he might be just, and the justifier of him which believeth in Jesus.

"Being justified freely by His Grace" - What an Awesome God He is! His Mercy endures forever! Your redemption was purchased by the Blood of Jesus Christ, even while you were lost in your sins! If you say you are unworthy of His Grace, you miss the point that He thought you were worthy enough to purchase your eternal life through His Blood.

THROUGH FAITH IN JESUS CHRIST, WE ARE JUSTIFIED

Tit 3:5 Not by works of righteousness which we have done, but according to his mercy he saved us, by the washing of regeneration, and renewing of the Holy Ghost;
6 Which he shed on us abundantly through Jesus Christ our Saviour;

7 That being justified by his grace, we should be made heirs according to the hope of eternal life.

The words "righteousness" in verse 5 and "justified" in verse 7 are from the same root. In the Greek Dictionary, you can find these words listed one right after another. The Strong's number for the root is 1342. This word is "dikaios" and it's a verb.

The word translated as "Righteousness" in verse 5 is "dikaiosune" (Strong's 1343) and it is a noun. The word translated as "justified" is "dikaioo" (Strong's 1344) and it is also a verb, meaning to "render righteous", or "to declare innocent".

There are popular catchphrases that preachers use to define "Justification", such as "just as if I never sinned", but I believe that detracts from the Truth that the Word of God would have us to know; which is this:

Outside of what Christ has already done in and through my life, it doesn't matter what I do to attempt to gain favor with God. Anything I do to try to earn my salvation would be seen by God as dead works. Many people say that they need to clean up their act before they give their heart to God, but that is impossible.

If a person thinks they need to give up smoking before they are worthy of giving their heart to God, they are mistaken. If they succeed in quitting smoking before they give their heart to Jesus, they can say that to some degree it is their own righteousness that made them worthy enough to receive salvation, and that is impossible. After they surrender to Jesus as their Lord and Savior, if their heart is right, they will want to quit their addictions, because their addictions are not of God.

The one that says "But Lord, didn't I prophesy in the streets in your Name? Didn't I cast out devils in Your

Rom 6:13 Neither yield ye your members as instruments of unrighteousness unto sin: but yield yourselves unto God, as those that are alive from the dead, and your members as instruments of righteousness unto God.

The word "instruments" used here can be translated as "weapons":

G3696

ὅπλον hoplon

Thayer Definition:

1) any tool or implement for preparing a thing

1a) arms used in warfare, weapons

2) an instrument

Part of Speech: noun neuter

A Related Word by Thayer's/Strong's Number: probably from a primary hepo (to be busy about)

Citing in TDNT: 5:292, 702

Mat 6:33 But seek ye first the kingdom of God, and his righteousness; and all these things shall be added unto you.

Name? In Your Name didn't I do many mighty works?" is relying on his own righteousness to justify himself in the eyes of the Lord. It doesn't matter what we do or don't do, if our hearts are not right before the Lord.

Rom 3:27 Where is boasting then? It is excluded. By what law? of works? Nay: but by the law of faith.
28 Therefore we conclude that a man is justified by faith without the deeds of the law.

The self righteous Pharisee boasted before the Lord:

Luk 18:9 And he spake this parable unto certain which trusted in themselves that they were righteous, and despised others:
10 Two men went up into the temple to pray; the one a Pharisee, and the other a publican.
11 The Pharisee stood and prayed thus with himself, God, I thank thee, that I am not as other men are, extortioners, unjust, adulterers, or even as this publican.
12 I fast twice in the week, I give tithes of all that I possess.

Those who trust in their own righteousness will justify their sloppy walk before God by comparing it with someone else.

"Well, I might smoke, but at least I don't play the lottery like so and so does."

"I might drink a little bit but at least I don't sit there and gossip about everyone like so and so does."

Sin has an "I" right in the middle of it, and even the most devoted follower of the Lord Jesus Christ will find himself or herself having to put that old man to death on a daily basis.

Just as there is nothing a person can do to earn their salvation, so there is nothing a person can do to attain righteousness. Christ has imputed His

Notes-

Righteousness to me through my faith in His Ability to redeem me from the law of sin and death.

My responsibility is to walk in that righteousness which He has bestowed upon me. I can do that because of the work Christ has done *in* me, and now He desires to work *through* me.

We will be accountable for those things which we willingly neglect. The parables of Matthew 25 illustrate that clearly:

Mat 25:14 For *the kingdom of heaven is* as a man travelling into a far country, *who* called his own servants, and delivered unto them his goods.
15 And unto one he gave five talents, to another two, and to another one; to every man according to his several ability; and straightway took his journey.
16 Then he that had received the five talents went and traded with the same, and made *them* other five talents.
17 And likewise he that *had received* two, he also gained other two.
18 But he that had received one went and digged in the earth, and hid his lord's money.
19 After a long time the lord of those servants cometh, and reckoneth with them.
20 And so he that had received five talents came and brought other five talents, saying, Lord, thou deliveredst unto me five talents: behold, I have gained beside them five talents more.
21 His lord said unto him, Well done, *thou* good and faithful servant: thou hast been faithful over a few things, I will make thee ruler over many things: enter thou into the joy of thy lord.
22 He also that had received two talents came and said, Lord, thou deliveredst unto me two talents: behold, I have gained two other talents beside them.
23 His lord said unto him, Well done, good and faithful servant; thou hast been faithful over a few things, I will make thee ruler over many things: enter thou into the joy of thy lord.

Rom 6:18 Being then made free from sin, ye became the servants of righteousness.
19 I speak after the manner of men because of the infirmity of your flesh: for as ye have yielded your members servants to uncleanness and to iniquity unto iniquity; even so now yield your members servants to righteousness unto holiness.
20 For when ye were the servants of sin, ye were free from righteousness.
21 What fruit had ye then in those things whereof ye are now ashamed? for the end of those things is death.
22 But now being made free from sin, and become servants to God, ye have your fruit unto holiness, and the end everlasting life.

Notes-

24 Then he which had received the one talent came and said, Lord, I knew thee that thou art an hard man, reaping where thou hast not sown, and gathering where thou hast not strawed:
25 And I was afraid, and went and hid thy talent in the earth: lo, *there* thou hast *that is* thine.
26 His lord answered and said unto him, *Thou* wicked and slothful servant, thou knewest that I reap where I sowed not, and gather where I have not strawed:
27 Thou oughtest therefore to have put my money to the exchangers, and *then* at my coming I should have received mine own with usury.
28 Take therefore the talent from him, and give *it* unto him which hath ten talents.
29 For unto every one that hath shall be given, and he shall have abundance: but from him that hath not shall be taken away even that which he hath.
30 And cast ye the unprofitable servant into outer darkness: there shall be weeping and gnashing of teeth.

Notice that each man was called a servant. Notice also that each was given a responsibly according to his ability (vs 15). The one who did nothing met with dire consequences. The same is true for each of these three parables in Matthew 25. Once you have repented and called on Jesus to be the Lord of your life, you are responsible to walk in that which He has called you to.

Concerning Abraham, we read that his confident expectation (faith) that what God promised He would also perform, was seen as righteousness by God. In like manner, God will impute His Righteousness to those who believe in Him, and His Saving Grace.

Rom 4:19 And being not weak in faith, he considered not his own body now dead, when he was about an hundred years old, neither yet the deadness of Sara's womb:
20 He staggered not at the promise of God through unbelief; but was strong in faith, giving glory to God;

21 And being fully persuaded that, what he had promised, he was able also to perform.
22 And therefore it was imputed to him for righteousness.
23 Now it was not written for his sake alone, that it was imputed to him;
24 But for us also, to whom it shall be imputed, if we believe on him that raised up Jesus our Lord from the dead;
25 Who was delivered for our offences, and was raised again for our justification.

Once I am saved by His Grace through faith, my dependence for everything I may hope to become in my Christian walk is in His Ability to accomplish it in and through me. It is only through faith in that Ability that I am made Righteous (justified).

When explaining God's Grace and the Work He has done in us through Jesus Christ, there always is the danger of a person embracing an attitude of indifference toward sin ("since I am just a sinner saved by Grace it really doesn't matter if I sin, because God knows that I am the sinner that I am"), which is what Paul addressed in Romans 6:1.

Rom 6:1 What shall we say then? Shall we continue in sin, that grace may abound?
2 God forbid. How shall we, that are dead to sin, live any longer therein?

Do you have faith in the ability of the Blood of Jesus Christ to deliver you from sin? Or do you believe that you will be forever bound by the bondage to sin? You may not yet see the results of freedom from the bondage of some sin in your life, but if you hold on to a confident expectation in the Work of God's Grace in your life, you will one day be living proof (evidence) of His Saving Grace.

Rom 6:11 Likewise reckon ye also yourselves to be dead indeed unto sin, but alive unto God through Jesus Christ our Lord.
12 Let not sin therefore reign in your mortal body, that ye should obey it in the lusts thereof.
13 Neither yield ye your members as instruments of unrighteousness unto sin: but yield yourselves unto God, as those that are alive from the dead, and your members as instruments of righteousness unto God.
14 For sin shall not have dominion over you: for ye are not under the law, but under grace.

Gal 6:7 Be not deceived; God is not mocked: for whatsoever a man soweth, that shall he also reap.

8 For he that soweth to his flesh shall of the flesh reap corruption; but he that soweth to the Spirit shall of the Spirit reap life everlasting.

2) A typical and very famous UES teacher wrote:

"But a man or woman who has been rescued once from a state of unforgiveness need not worry. For once 100% of a man's or woman's sins have been forgiven, the potential for being unforgiven has been done away with. The risk factor is zero. There are no more fires from which the believer needs to be saved." Eternal Security Can You Be Sure? (pp. 79,80).

The same author said this in a sermon:

"No matter what you do as a child of God, you are forgiven. You say, 'Murder?' Forgiven. 'Stealing?' Forgiven. 'Adultery?' Forgiven. 'Worshiping idols?' Forgiven." (Grace: God's Second Chance -- Grace and Continuing Sin, Tape #4, MC213.)

Some Unconditional Eternal Securitists say that if you do such things you were never saved in the first place, but this one says that as a Child of God, (if you called on the Name of Jesus), It doesn't matter what you say or do. But what does the Word of God say?

1Co 6:9 Know ye not that the unrighteous shall not inherit the kingdom of God? Be not deceived: neither fornicators, nor idolaters, nor adulterers, nor effeminate, nor abusers of themselves with mankind,

Another danger can be in embracing a Universalist ("There is no such thing as Hell and everybody will wind up in heaven") mindset of salvation. The doctrine of Unconditional Eternal Security is in my mind a universalist doctrine, with a Christian slant. While the UES adherent will say that is only through the Name of Jesus Christ that one may be saved, they will go to great lengths proving that once you say the prayer, IN JESUS' NAME, there is no way that you will lose your salvation[2].

Taken to its extreme, according to this philosophy, a Hindu can remain a Hindu as long as he has called on the Name of Jesus. A Hindu will hold on to his many gods and just add Jesus to the list of gods that he worships. There is a reason why "repentance from dead works" is listed first in the foundational doctrines of Christianity and why "Faith toward God" follows close behind. A person with the "I am just a sinner saved by Grace 'Once Saved Always Saved'" mindset reflects an unrepentant heart and an inclination to justify living a disobedient lifestyle.

The balance to this truth is this: On the other side of the cross, I walked in darkness and was ignorant as to the Way of eternal life. There was nothing I could do to earn my way to eternal life. On this side of the cross, I have a responsibility before God to be a good steward of that which He has entrusted to me.

Jesus Christ Was A Master Carpenter, And He Is Busy Renovating Us Through The Work Of The Holy Spirit.

Let's revisit Titus 3:5 for a moment:

Tit 3:5 Not by works of righteousness which we have done, but according to his mercy he saved us, by the washing of regeneration, and renewing of the Holy Ghost;

10 Nor thieves, nor covetous, nor drunkards, nor revilers, nor extortioners, shall inherit the Kingdom of God.

11 And such were some of you: but ye are washed, but ye are sanctified, but ye are justified in the name of the Lord Jesus, and by the Spirit of our God.

Renewing:

G342 anakainosis

Thayer Definition: 1) a renewal, renovation, complete change for the better Part of Speech: noun feminine A Related Word by Thayer's/Strong's Number: from G341 Citing in TDNT: 3:453, 388

As sinners we come to Jesus with the attitude that we need to change our mind (repent) about the life choices we are making, to stop serving the god of this world, choosing instead to live for Jesus.

Once we do that, then according to Titus 3:5, God cleanses us through the New Birth (regeneration), and renovates our house - *this is really what the word "renewing" means* (see the definition in the sidebar) - through the indwelling of the Holy Spirit.

The Work is God's Work, not our own work that we have done. We should be able to say that if there is ANY good in us (and there is, if Jesus dwells within us), it is only what the Lord has accomplished in our lives through His Abundant Mercy.

If we really understand that, we won't have Pharisaical attitudes toward the Christian who is struggling with a sin or sins. We will understand that we ourselves were once entangled in sin, but when the Kindness and Love of God appeared to us, He delivered us (read Titus 3:1-4) from who we were.

Because He has redeemed me through His Blood that He shed on the cross, on this side of the cross, I have been empowered to walk like I am redeemed. Because He has done the remodeling, He has enabled me to walk in obedience to His Word. If I say that I am unable to walk in obedience to His Will, I make His Word a lie. My flesh loves sin. But through Christ, I have the ability to resist the inclination to sin. And if I don't resist, then it's nobody's fault but my own, and I need to repent.

1Pe 1:13 Wherefore gird up the loins of your mind, be sober, and hope to the end for the grace that is to be brought unto you at the revelation of Jesus Christ;
14 As obedient children, not fashioning yourselves according to the former lusts (Author's note: Before the cross) in your ignorance:
15 But as he which hath called you is holy, so be ye holy in all manner of conversation;

16 Because it is written, Be ye holy; for I am holy.
17 And if ye call on the Father, who without respect of persons judgeth according to every man's work, pass the time of your sojourning here in fear:
18 Forasmuch as ye know that ye were not redeemed with corruptible things, as silver and gold, from your vain conversation received by tradition from your fathers;
19 But with the precious blood of Christ, as of a lamb without blemish and without spot:
20 Who verily was foreordained before the foundation of the world, but was manifest in these last times for you,
21 Who by him do believe in God, that raised him up from the dead, and gave him glory; that your faith and hope might be in God.

As we learned in our previous study on repentance, before we came to the cross, we were powerless to have victory over sin. But once we come to the cross, we are New Creatures (2 Cor 5:17).

Eph 4:17 This I say therefore, and testify in the Lord, that ye henceforth (*Author's Note: Henceforth = After the cross*) walk not as other Gentiles walk (*Before the cross*), in the vanity of their mind,
18 Having the understanding darkened, being alienated from the life of God through the ignorance that is in them, because of the blindness of their heart:
19 Who being past feeling have given themselves over unto lasciviousness, to work all uncleanness with greediness.
20 But ye have not so learned Christ (*After the cross*);
21 If so be that ye have heard him, and have been taught by him, as the truth is in Jesus:
22 That ye (*Your responsibility after the cross*) put off concerning the former conversation the old man, which is corrupt according to the deceitful lusts;
23 And be renewed in the spirit of your mind;
24 And that ye put on the new man, which after God is created in righteousness and true holiness.

The Spirit of God resides in us, and in His process of renovating us, He equips us to walk this Christian walk. On the other side of the cross, I had no ability in myself to be obedient to the Word of God. On the other side of the cross, I may have trusted in my dead religious works to get me some kind of favor with God. But on this side of the cross all my trust is (or should be) in Jesus and His Ability to accomplish His Work in me.

Phillipians 1:6 Being confident of this very thing, that he which hath begun a good work in you will perform it until the day of Jesus Christ:

Col 1:19 For it pleased the Father that in him should all fulness dwell; 20 And, having made peace through the blood of his cross, by him to reconcile all things unto himself; by him, I say, whether they be things in earth, or things in heaven.
21 And you, that were sometime alienated and enemies in your mind by wicked works *(Before the Cross)***, yet now hath he reconciled** *(After the cross)*
22 In the body of his flesh through death, to present you holy and unblameable and unreproveable in his sight:
23 *(our responsibility after the cross:)* **If ye continue in the faith grounded and settled, and be not moved away from the hope of the gospel, which ye have heard, and which was preached to every creature which is under heaven; whereof I Paul am made a minister;**

If we understand that it is not our own righteousness that enables us to live as Christians, we will encourage one another to press on to victory ("You can do it because it's the Holy Spirit inside you that is doing the work!"). Even the most devoted Christian will fall short of the Glory of God, but if your heart isn't right before God, you won't be too concerned about your sin. You will find a way to justify it. If your heart is right, you will strive to overcome the sin in your life.

Speaking of what we read earlier in Titus 3:5-7, Paul writes:

Tit 3:8 This is a faithful saying, and these things I will that thou affirm constantly, that they which have believed in God might be careful to maintain good works. These things are good and profitable unto men.
9 But avoid foolish questions, and genealogies, and contentions, and strivings about the law; for they are unprofitable and vain.

Since the Lord has done the renovating, you are now able to live righteously.

Some would say that Christians are unable to do so because of the Scripture that declares:

Rom 3:10 As it is written, There is none righteous, no, not one:

But that is before the cross. The next verses describe the person before the cross.

Rom 3:11 There is none that understandeth, there is none that seeketh after God.
12 They are all gone out of the way, they are together become unprofitable; there is none that doeth good, no, not one.
13 Their throat is an open sepulchre; with their tongues they have used deceit; the poison of asps is under their lips:
14 Whose mouth is full of cursing and bitterness:

15 Their feet are swift to shed blood:
16 Destruction and misery are in their ways:
17 And the way of peace have they not known:
18 There is no fear of God before their eyes.

If we stopped right there, we could agree with the false teaching that we are just sinners saved by grace, and that we will continue our lives in sin until the day we die.

With that outlook, we will. "According to your faith, so be it". But the next verses tell us that those of us who are in Christ are righteous.

Remember our earlier study on the words "Justified" and "Righteous".

Rom 3:21 But now the righteousness of God without the law is manifested, being witnessed by the law and the prophets;
22 Even the righteousness of God which is by faith of Jesus Christ unto all and upon all them that believe: for there is no difference:
23 For all have sinned, and come short of the glory of God;
24 Being justified freely by his grace through the redemption that is in Christ Jesus:
25 Whom God hath set forth to be a propitiation through faith in his blood, to declare his righteousness for the remission of sins that are past *(before the cross)***, through the forbearance of God;**
26 To declare, I say, at this time his righteousness: that he might be just, and the justifier of him which believeth in Jesus *(after the cross)***.**
27 Where is boasting then? It is excluded. By what law? of works? Nay: but by the law of faith.
28 Therefore we conclude that a man is justified *(made righteous)* **by faith without the deeds of the law.**

1Jn 3:7 Little children, let no man deceive you: he that doeth righteousness is righteous, even as he is righteous.

1Jn 2:26 These *things* **have I written unto you concerning them that seduce you.**
27 But the anointing which ye have received of him abideth in you, and ye need not that any man teach you: but as the same anointing teacheth you of all things, and is truth, and is no lie, and even as it hath taught you, ye shall abide in him.
28 And now, little children, abide in him; that, when he shall appear, we may have confidence, and not be ashamed before him at his coming.
29 If ye know that he is righteous, ye know that every one that doeth righteousness is born of him.

SANCTIFIED:

37   hagiazo-
1) to render or acknowledge, or to
be venerable or to hallow
2) to separate from profane things
and to dedicate to God
a) to consecrate things to God
b) to dedicate people to God
3) to purify
a) to cleanse externally
b) to purify by expiation: to free
from the guilt of sin
c) to purify internally by a
renewing of the soul

G38

ἁγιασμός   hagiasmos   *hag-ee-as-mos'*

From G37; properly *purification*,
that is, (the state) *purity*;
concretely (by Hebraism) a
purifier: - holiness, sanctification.

G39

ἅγιον hagion   *hag'-ee-on*

Neuter of G40; a *sacred* thing
(that is, spot): - holiest (of all),
holy place, sanctuary.

G40

ἅγιος hagios   *hag'-ee-os*

From ἅγος hagos (an *awful* thing)
compare G53, [H2282]; *sacred*
(physically *pure*, morally *blameless*
or *religious*, ceremonially
consecrated): - (most) holy (one,
thing), saint.

You can't earn your salvation, *but once you are saved, you are responsible to continue in the faith* (Col 1:23). You are no longer seen as a sinner in God's eyes; He calls you a *saint*, or a *sanctified one*.

Before Christ, you were powerless to walk in victory. After Christ, you have been given all you need to walk as a child of God should. The Holy Spirit has done a renovation in your life, and He will equip you to walk in His Righteousness.

Do you have a confident expectation that whatever temptation comes your way today, you will be able to resist it because of the Work that He has done in your life through the cross?

1Jn 5:4 For whatsoever is born of God overcometh the world: and this is the victory that overcometh the world, even our faith.

We have seen the word "Holy" mentioned several times in our study (Eph 4:24, 1Pet 1:13). Just as Righteousness and Justification are closely related, Holy, Holiness, and Sanctification are also closely related (Strong's numbers 37-42). See the definitions ◄━━━ in the side bar.

THROUGH FAITH IN JESUS CHRIST, WE ARE SANCTIFIED.

Acts 26:16 But rise, and stand upon thy feet: for I have appeared unto thee for this purpose, to make thee a minister and a witness both of these things which thou hast seen, and of those things in the which I will appear unto thee;
17 Delivering thee from the people, and from the Gentiles, unto whom now I send thee,
18 To open their eyes, and to turn them from darkness to light, and from the power of Satan unto God, that they may receive forgiveness of sins, and inheritance among them which are

G41

ἁγιότης hagiotēs *hag-ee-ot'-ace*

From G40; *sanctity* (that is, properly the state): - holiness.

_____
_____
_____
_____
_____
_____
_____
_____
_____
_____
_____
_____
_____
_____
_____
_____
_____
_____
_____

Sanctimonious = pretending to be very holy or pious; affecting sanctity or righteousness.

_____
_____
_____
_____
_____
_____

sanctified (Strong's Number 37) **by faith that is in me.**

Heb 9:13 For if the blood of bulls and of goats, and the ashes of an heifer sprinkling the unclean, sanctifieth (SN 37) to the purifying of the flesh: 14 How much more shall the blood of Christ, who through the eternal Spirit offered himself without spot to God, purge your conscience from dead works to serve the living God?

Jud 1:1 Jude, the servant of Jesus Christ, and brother of James, to them that are sanctified (SN 37) by God the Father, and preserved (to watch over, or to guard) in Jesus Christ, and called: 2 Mercy unto you, and peace, and love, be multiplied.

Col 1:21 And you, that were sometime alienated and enemies in your mind by wicked works, yet now hath he reconciled 22 In the body of his flesh through death, to present you holy (SN 40) and unblameable and unreproveable in his sight: 23 If ye continue in the faith grounded and settled, and be not moved away from the hope of the gospel, which ye have heard, and which was preached to every creature which is under heaven; whereof I Paul am made a minister;

If we understand that it is only by the Grace of God and the Work of Jesus Christ that we are sanctified, we won't become sanctimonious in our conduct toward others.

Mark Twain once went on a Steamship excursion with the Plymouth Church congregation in a tour of many famous sites around the Mediterranean sea. In his Journal, he described one of the congregation as "a solemn, unsmiling, sanctimonious old iceberg that looked like he was waiting for a vacancy in the Trinity."

We are saved through Faith. We are Justified through Faith. We are Sanctified through Faith.

On this side of the cross, the manner in which we live will bear witness to whether or not our Faith is in God's Ability to save us, or in our own works. On this side of the cross, we are exhorted to continue in the faith.

Since Christ is our Sanctification, our Propitiation, our Salvation, and our Justifier, we know that we can stand assured of His Wondrous Presence in our lives.

So when the Accuser points his finger at us for our shortcomings, we can be quick to agree with him...and repent. It is then that we can trust Jesus to be the propitiation for our sins. We are in these tabernacles of flesh, and the only thing that matters in our life is that if God is for us, no man can be against us.

Eph 6:16 Above all, taking the shield of faith, wherewith ye shall be able to quench all the fiery darts of the wicked.

If I sin (which should increasingly be the exception, and not the rule), I need to run to Jesus, who is my attorney, or my *advocate*.

1Jo 2:1 My little children, these things write I unto you, that ye sin not. And if any man sin, we have an advocate with the Father, Jesus Christ the righteous:
2 And he is the propitiation for our sins: and not for ours only, but also for the sins of the whole world.

Notice verse 1 says *IF* any man sin, not *WHEN*.

To say that we can't help but to sin is to deny the Power of the Almighty God in our lives and to give the devil more credit than he deserves. God intends for us to walk victoriously in every aspect of our lives. And we can, if we believe Him and His Word. Greater is He that is in us, than He that is in the world.

I Jn 5:4 For whatsoever is born of God overcometh the world: and this is the victory that overcometh the world, even our faith.

Salvation includes the following:

Salvation from the penalty of sin forever -- Romans 5:1, 8, 9; John 5:24; 6:37

Salvation from the power of sin daily -- Romans 6:11-14; Galatians 1:4

Salvation from the presence of sin for eternity -- I Thessalonians 4:13-18;

I John 3:1-3; John 14:1-3

1) HOW ARE WE SAVED? (Ephesians 2:8,9)

_____

_____

2) WHERE DO GOOD WORKS FIT INTO THE LIFE OF A BELIEVER? (Ephesians 2:10)

_____

_____

3) HOW ARE WE JUSTIFIED? (Romans 3:24)

_____

4) IN YOUR OWN WORDS, DEFINE "PROPITIATION". (Romans 3:25)

_____

_____

_____

5) WHAT DOES 2 CORINTHIANS 5:17 TEACH US CONCERNING OUR WALK AS CHRISTIANS?

_____

_____

_____

6) AS A CHRISTIAN, WHAT SHOULD MY ATTITUDE BE CONCERNING SIN? (1 John 2:1)

_____

_____

7) WHAT DOES ROMANS 6:14 ASSURE ME OF?

_____

_____

_____

8) HOW DO I OVERCOME THE WORLD? (1 JN 5:4)

_____
_____
_____

9) WHAT DOES 1 JOHN 4:4 TELL ME CONCERNING HE THAT IS IN ME?

_____
_____

10) WHO IS JESUS, ACCORDING TO HEBREWS 12:2?

_____

WRITE DOWN YOUR TESTIMONY OF WHAT GOD SAVED YOU FROM AND HOW YOU WERE SAVED:

_____
_____
_____
_____
_____
_____
_____
_____
_____
_____
_____
_____
_____
_____
_____
_____
_____
_____
_____
_____
_____
_____

BASIC DOCTRINES

LESSON 4
FAITH TOWARD GOD:

TRUE FAITH BELIEVES GOD FOR ALL THAT HE PROMISES

Heb 6:1 Therefore leaving the principles of the doctrine of Christ, let us go on unto perfection; not laying again the foundation of repentance from dead works, and of FAITH TOWARD GOD,
2 Of the doctrine of baptisms, and of laying on of hands, and of resurrection of the dead, and of eternal judgment.

TRUE FAITH BELIEVES GOD IN ALL THAT HE SAYS

As we have seen in the previous study, when we come to a saving faith in Jesus Christ, we are empowered by Christ to live a life of victory in every aspect of our life. But we still have choices before us. We can choose to walk in faith or in unbelief. Disobedience amounts to unbelief, and results in varying degrees of success and failure in our Christian walk.

IN THE AREA WHERE WE FAIL IN TRUSTING GOD, WE WILL FAIL IN OUR WALK WITH HIM.

The Word of God encourages us to stand fast in the faith.

1 Cor 16:13 Watch ye, stand fast in the faith, quit you like men, be strong.

We know the 11th chapter of Hebrews to be the "faith chapter".

Here we have living examples of men and women of God who had faith toward God. These models of faith were persuaded that the One who they believed in was able to do more than they could ever ask or think. In Hebrews 11:6, we are told that it is impossible to please God if we do not have faith:

Heb 11:6 But without faith it is impossible to please him: for he that cometh to God must believe that he is, and that he is a rewarder of them that diligently seek him. (KJV)

Doubt:

G1252

διακρίνω diakrinō

Thayer Definition:

1) to separate, make a distinction, discriminate, to prefer

2) to learn by discrimination, to try, decide

2a) to determine, give judgment, decide a dispute

3) to withdraw from one, desert

4) to separate one's self in a hostile spirit, to oppose, strive with dispute, contend

5) to be at variance with one's self, hesitate, doubt

Part of Speech: verb

A Related Word by Thayer's/Strong's Number: from G1223 and G2919

Citing in TDNT: 3:946, 469

Notes-
_____
_____
_____
_____
_____
_____
_____
_____
_____
_____
_____
_____
_____
_____
_____
_____

Faith and doubt are not partners that go hand in hand with one another.

We read that Jesus taught the following:

Matt 21:21 Jesus answered and said unto them, Verily I say unto you, If ye have faith, and doubt not, ye shall not only do this which is done to the fig tree, but also if ye shall say unto this mountain, Be thou removed, and be thou cast into the sea; it shall be done.
22 And all things, whatsoever ye shall ask in prayer, believing, ye shall receive.

Doubt is a destroyer of faith. Faith is a product of the spiritual realm. Doubt emanates from the flesh. Jesus said if we have faith, and DOUBT NOT, all things whatsoever we will ask we will receive. Just as the flesh is at war with the Spirit, so doubt battles against faith.

The word translated as "doubt" is a Greek word that is composed of two words, made into one: "diakrino".

Dia means "through", and *krino* means to judge in a manner in which one passes a sentence, usually in an unfavorable light. *The two words together mean to compare things, or to think things through, and to make distinctions between those things.*

We have a tendency to reason within ourselves:

"Yes, Jesus said 'if you say unto this mountain be thou removed, and be cast into the sea, it shall be done,' but he was just talking figuratively." or "yes, but I'm looking at mount Everest right now. Surely he wasn't talking about anything of this magnitude".

But in Matthew Jesus is saying in essence, *"I tell you the Truth, if you have a confident expectation that a thing will come to pass, and you don't allow yourself to evaluate the situation to the point that you explain this Promise away, you can say to this mountain, be thou removed and be cast into the sea, and it will be done."*

Jesus said "Whatever you shall ask in prayer, if you ask in FAITH, you SHALL receive." The question we have to ask ourselves is if we believe Jesus was a deceiver. When He declared Himself to be the TRUTH, was He lying or was He telling the Truth? Are The Words of Jesus meant to be believed, or not? Jesus said:

Joh 6:63 It is the spirit that quickeneth; the flesh profiteth nothing: the words that I speak unto you, they are spirit, and they are life.
64 But there are some of you that believe not. For Jesus knew from the beginning who they were that believed not, and who should betray him.

As we learned in our last study, Jesus was the epitome of Faith. He was Faith manifest in the flesh. Every word that Jesus spoke was life. Every word that Jesus spoke still has life. After He spoke these words in John 6:63-64, we read:

Joh 6:66 From that time many of his disciples went back, and walked no more with him.

They could not accept nor comprehend the fact that every word that Jesus spoke was spirit and life.

I don't want to make a big deal out of this, but notice that this passage is 6:66, which is the number of the name of the Beast in Revelation 13. I have written a book entitled "Three Questions, A Study of the Last Days Based On Matthew 24", which, among other things deals with the Beast, and other issues concerning the last days. You can find it for sale on line at crosscountry4jesus.com. Just follow the link.

Doubt IS the seat of the manifestation of the spirit of everything that is contrary to the Word of God. It is a result of doubt in the Truth of the Word of God that there will be a falling away in the last days.

Doubt IS anti-Christ (against Christ).

Remember that in our last lesson, we learned that FAITH is the confident expectation we have that a thing that we are believing for will come to pass.

The Bible says that doubt is being double minded concerning an issue...

James 1:5 If any of you lack wisdom, let him ask of God, that giveth to all men liberally, and upbraideth not; and it shall be given him.

CULT WATCH

1) One great doubt producer is the argument that the Bible was just written by men. But the Bible tells us otherwise. It says that All Scripture was divinely imparted (the Greek word actually means "breathed in") to us. In the creation account, we read that man became a living soul because God breathed into man the breath of life. In 2 Ti 3:16, we read that all scripture is God breathed as holy men of God were used as tools by God to write His Word, and to convey His Will to mankind:

2Ti 3:16 All scripture is given by inspiration of God (G2315 theopneustos theh-op'-nyoo-stos From G2316 and a presumed derivative of G4154; divinely breathed in: - given by inspiration of God. Strong's Hebrew and Greek dictionaries) **, and is profitable for doctrine, for reproof, for correction, for instruction in righteousness:**
17 That the man of God may be perfect, throughly furnished unto all good works.

Just prior to these verses, Paul warns Timothy that evil men will grow worse and worse, and they will live to deceive others. He says that by holding to the Word of God, he will become wise concerning salvation and faith.

2Ti 3:13 But evil men and seducers shall wax worse and worse, deceiving, and being deceived.
14 But continue thou in the things which thou hast learned and hast been assured of, knowing of whom thou hast learned them;

6 But let him ask in faith, nothing wavering. For he that wavereth is like a wave of the sea driven with the wind and tossed.
7 For let not that man think that he shall receive any thing of the Lord.
8 A double minded man is unstable in all his ways. (KJV)

Double mindedness is in effect saying, "I know God can do this, but..." The word "but" effectively dispels the faith.

The first step in walking in Faith concerning the Promises of God, is absolutely believing that the Bible is absolutely true.

You can't have faith in the Promises of God, unless you believe the Bible is the infallible, inerrant Word of God.

If you will allow Satan to convince you that there are areas of the Bible that are not true, then he will be able to convince you that there are promises in the Bible that you can't stand on[1].

It was God's Word that created everything that we see and know.

To walk in Faith is to trust in His Word as a personal promise to you from God.

Mat 4:4 But he answered and said, It is written, Man shall not live by bread alone, but by every word that proceedeth out of the mouth of God.

When we see a Promise in God's Word, it is important that we are able to read that promise with simple child-like faith. A child doesn't think away a promise. Only as they grow older and are faced with numerous disappointments and failures do they learn to think away the promises.

We must remember that Faith is the conviction or our confidence in the truth of God's Word.

15 And that from a child thou hast known the holy scriptures, which are able to make thee wise unto salvation through faith which is in Christ Jesus.

One aspect of the Mormon's creed is *"We believe the Bible is true insofar as it is correctly translated."* This very statement is designed to instill doubt in the believer's mind.

Cult Watch

2) Concerning the argument that the Gifts of God were done away with when the last apostle died:

Speaking of Israel, and their position as God's chosen people after the New Covenant through Jesus' Blood provided access for the Gentiles as children of God as well, Paul wrote:

Rom 11:29 For the gifts and calling of God are without repentance.

This is saying in essence, that God doesn't change His mind concerning His Gifts. Once He instituted His spiritual Gifts for the establishment of the Church, it was "a done deal". He is the same today as He was the day He imparted the Gifts and established the Church.

The Word "gifts" here is the same Greek word that is used when describing the spiritual gifts in 1 Corinthians 12, and Romans 12:6, which relates to spiritual gifts.

If one has a conviction as to the truth of a matter, one will not compromise in that conviction. In my walk as a Christian, I have had no doubt that the Bible is the infallible inerrant Word of God. All that it says is True. I know this. And yet, sometimes my life doesn't reflect this, because I have a tendency in some areas to say "I know God said this, but..." The "But" shows that sometimes I do doubt that the Bible is the infallible inerrant Word of God.

WE NEED TO GET OFF OUR BUTS AND STAND ON THE WORD OF GOD.

A very real instance of doubt in a Christian's mind is the ungodly doctrine that says "I know that the gifts of the Holy Spirit were written about in the Bible, but they were done away with when the last apostle died".[2]

These ungodly doctrines of unbelief would cut out 1 Corinthians 12, 13, and 14, and Romans 12.

Satan is the one who instills doubt in a person. His very name means adversary. He is opposed to everything concerning our walk with God. See how he operated in the garden, when he asked a question of Eve that was designed to instill doubt in her mind:

Gen 3:1 Now the serpent was more subtil than any beast of the field which the LORD God had made. And he said unto the woman, Yea, hath God said, Ye shall not eat of every tree of the garden?

Once the question - which was designed to bring some incredulity to the Word of God - was asked, then the enemy of her soul took her through a process of thinking which eventually dispelled her trust in the Truth of God's Word. This resulted in disobedience to God, which ended in breaking the fellowship with God.

G4100

πιστεύω pisteuō

Thayer Definition:

1) to think to be true, to be persuaded of, to credit, place confidence in

1a) of the thing believed

1a1) to credit, have confidence

1b) in a moral or religious reference

1b1) used in the NT of the conviction and trust to which a man is impelled by a certain inner and higher prerogative and law of soul

1b2) to trust in Jesus or God as able to aid either in obtaining or in doing something: saving faith

2) to entrust a thing to one, i.e. his fidelity

2a) to be intrusted with a thing

Part of Speech: verb

A Related Word by Thayer's/Strong's Number: from G4102

Citing in TDNT: 6:174, 849

G4101

πιστικός pistikos

Thayer Definition:

1) pertaining to belief

1a) having the power of persuading, skilful in producing belief

1b) trusty, faithful, that can be relied on

Part of Speech: adjective

A Related Word by Thayer's/Strong's Number: from G4102

G4102

πίστις pistis

Thayer Definition:

1) conviction of the truth of anything, belief; in the NT of a conviction or belief respecting man's relationship to God and divine things, generally with the

Throughout the Bible, we can see that it is lack of faith (the conviction that God's Word is absolutely true) that causes people to err.

Throughout the books of the Old Testament we can see that the root of Israel's many occasions of stumbling was the result of their lack of faith in God's Word. Satan tried to get even Jesus to doubt Who He was.

**Matt 4: 3 And when the tempter came to him, he said, If thou be the Son of God, command that these stones be made bread.
4 But he answered and said, It is written, Man shall not live by bread alone, but by every word that proceedeth out of the mouth of God.
5 Then the devil taketh him up into the holy city, and setteth him on a pinnacle of the temple,
6 And saith unto him, If thou be the Son of God, cast thyself down: for it is written, He shall give his angels charge concerning thee: and in their hands they shall bear thee up, lest at any time thou dash thy foot against a stone.
7 Jesus said unto him, It is written again, Thou shalt not tempt the Lord thy God.
8 Again, the devil taketh him up into an exceeding high mountain, and sheweth him all the kingdoms of the world, and the glory of them;
9 And saith unto him, All these things will I give thee, if thou wilt fall down and worship me.
10 Then saith Jesus unto him, Get thee hence, Satan: for it is written, Thou shalt worship the Lord thy God, and him only shalt thou serve. (KJV)**

Notice that in each instance, Jesus answered the temptation with the Word of God. I can't emphasize this truth enough: *The core of our faith is in the very Word of God, which the enemy is constantly trying to undermine.*

Jesus' firm conviction in the Absolute Truth of the Word of God enabled Him to resist the temptations that the enemy threw at Him.

In John 1:1, we can see that Jesus Christ IS the Word. We Trust the Word of God, because we Trust Jesus, Who was the very epitome of Faith.

A life of faith is daily living in the Truth of the Word of God.

While men attempt to undermine the Word of God in this day and age, the Christian who embraces its' Truth will not be disappointed. We need to throw down the thought process that battles against the Truth of the Word of God.

2 Cor 10:4 (For the weapons of our warfare are not carnal, but mighty through God to the pulling down of strong holds;)
5 Casting down imaginations, and every high thing that exalteth itself against the knowledge of God, and bringing into captivity every thought to the obedience of Christ (KJV)

Prov 3:5 Trust in the LORD with all thine heart; and lean not unto thine own understanding.
6 In all thy ways acknowledge him, and he shall direct thy paths. (KJV)

My eyes may tell me one thing, but if the Word of God tells me just the opposite of what I see, I need to go with the Word of God.

2 Cor 5:7 (For we walk by faith, not by sight:)

Just as Faith is the second basic principle mentioned in Hebrews Chapter 6, and Repentance from dead works was the first thing mentioned, we can see that Repentance and Faith go hand in hand.

Mark 1:14 Now after that John was put in prison, Jesus came into Galilee, preaching the gospel of the kingdom of God,
15 And saying, The time is fulfilled, and the kingdom of God is at hand: repent ye, and believe (the same word translated as "faith" elsewhere) **the gospel. (KJV)**

When we are faced with an attitude of unbelief in relation to the Word of God, we need to change our minds (*repent*) concerning that attitude.

G4102 (Continued)

included idea of trust and holy fervour born of faith and joined with it

1a) relating to God

1) the conviction that God exists and **is** the creator and ruler of all things, the provider and bestower of eternal salvation through Christ

1b) relating to Christ

1b1) a strong and welcome conviction or belief that Jesus is the Messiah, through whom we obtain eternal salvation in the kingdom of God

1c) the religious beliefs of Christians

1d) belief with the predominate idea of trust (or confidence) whether in God or in Christ, springing from faith in the same

2) fidelity, faithfulness

2a) the character of one who can be relied on

Part of Speech: noun feminine

A Related Word by Thayer's/Strong's Number: from G3982

Citing in TDNT: 6:174, 849

Notes-

_____
_____
_____
_____
_____
_____
_____
_____
_____
_____
_____
_____
_____
_____
_____
_____

In our last study, we saw that the Greek words translated as "Righteousness" and "Justified" in Titus 3:5 and 7 were closely related, having the same root word. The words "believe" and "faith" are also from the same root word.

The word translated as "believe" is a form of the word "pistis" which we have been studying, which is translated as "faith" (Strong's number 4100).

So in Mark 1:15, Jesus was saying in effect, "change your mind as to your old way of thinking, and have faith in the Good News of the Kingdom of God".

But just saying we believe in Him is not the answer. If we have a firm conviction or confidence concerning Him and the Truth of His Word, we will walk in that conviction. Our lives will reflect what we believe. We will continue in His Word.

John 8: 31 Then said Jesus to those Jews which believed on him, If ye continue in my word, then are ye my disciples indeed;
32 And ye shall know the truth, and the truth shall make you free.

Thayer's lexicon of the Greek language includes this definition for the word translated as Faith (4102):

a) relating to God: the conviction that God exists and is the creator and ruler of all things, the provider and bestower of eternal salvation through Christ

Since God exists and is the Creator and ruler of all things...nothing is too difficult for Him.

When Jesus called Lazarus from the tomb, He prayed a prayer to the Father that shows us His confidence toward the Father:

John 11:40 Jesus saith unto her, Said I not unto thee, that, if thou wouldest believe, thou shouldest see the glory of God?

41 Then they took away the stone from the place where the dead was laid. And Jesus lifted up his eyes, and said, Father, I thank thee that thou hast heard me.
42 And I knew that thou hearest me always: but because of the people which stand by I said it, that they may believe that thou hast sent me.
43 And when he thus had spoken, he cried with a loud voice, Lazarus, come forth.

Jesus knew that the Father heard him at all times. Do *you* know that the Father hears you at all times? The only reason He wouldn't is because you are compromising with sin.

Isa 59:1 Behold, the LORD'S hand is not shortened, that it cannot save; neither his ear heavy, that it cannot hear:
2 But your iniquities have separated between you and your God, and your sins have hid *his* face from you, that he will not hear.

Jesus encouraged others to believe in God, and demonstrated His Faith so others would be able to believe.

In what areas of your life are you glorifying God?

What are you doing to instill faith in others?

Let's look at another aspect of Thayer's definition of faith (4102):

d) belief with the predominate idea of trust (or confidence) whether in God or in Christ, springing from faith in the same

When we walk in faith toward God, we see His Glory evidenced in our lives. Let's look at the account of Jesus and Lazarus again:

John 11:38 Jesus therefore again groaning in himself cometh to the grave. It was a cave, and a stone lay upon it.
39 Jesus said, Take ye away the stone. Martha, the sister of him that was dead, saith unto him, Lord, by this time he stinketh: for he hath been dead four days.

Notes-

_____
_____
_____
_____
_____
_____
_____
_____
_____
_____
_____
_____
_____
_____
_____
_____
_____
_____
_____
_____
_____
_____
_____
_____
_____

2Co 1:19 For the Son of God, Jesus Christ, who was preached among you by us, even by me and Silvanus and Timotheus, was not yea and nay, but in him was yea.
20 For all the promises of God in him are yea, and in him Amen, unto the glory of God by us.

40 Jesus saith unto her, Said I not unto thee, that, if thou wouldest believe, thou shouldest see the glory of God?
41 Then they took away the stone from the place where the dead was laid. And Jesus lifted up his eyes, and said, Father, I thank thee that thou hast heard me.
42 And I knew that thou hearest me always: but because of the people which stand by I said it, that they may believe that thou hast sent me.
43 And when he thus had spoken, he cried with a loud voice, Lazarus, come forth.
44 And he that was dead came forth, bound hand and foot with graveclothes: and his face was bound about with a napkin. Jesus saith unto them, Loose him, and let him go.
45 Then many of the Jews which came to Mary, and had seen the things which Jesus did, believed on him. (KJV)

In verse 40, Jesus told Martha that if she believed, she would see the glory of God. We can see that the Glory of God was about to manifest itself in the miracle of Lazarus rising from the dead. We know that God's Glory is revealed in the wondrous miracles He works. Our lives should reflect His Glory as we walk in absolute confidence in Him.

It is important at this point to mention the final definition of the word faith as defined by Thayer's lexicon:

2) fidelity, faithfulness; the character of one who can be relied on

This is a two way street. We Trust God and His Word, because we know that He is One Who can be relied on. But we ourselves also must abide in that fidelity and faithfulness before Him, if we are truly walking in faith.

Just saying we have faith in Him and His Word doesn't mean anything if we are not being faithful to His Word. But our unfaithfulness or our lack of faith will never negate the Truth of His Word.

2Ti 2:11 It is a faithful saying: For if we be dead with him, we shall also live with him:
12 If we suffer, we shall also reign with him: if we deny him, he also will deny us:
13 If we believe not, yet he abideth faithful: he cannot deny himself.
14 Of these things put them in remembrance, charging them before the Lord that they strive not about words to no profit, but to the subverting of the hearers.
15 Study to shew thyself approved unto God, a workman that needeth not to be ashamed, rightly dividing the word of truth.
16 But shun profane and vain babblings: for they will increase unto more ungodliness.

He will honor His Word because all the Promises in Him are Yea and Amen (2 Cor 1:20), but our unfaithfulness to His Word will be the evidence of our unbelief, and we will wrestle with (doubt) whether a Promise applies to us because of our guilty conscience.

1Jn 3:20 For if our heart condemn us, God is greater than our heart, and knoweth all things.
21 Beloved, if our heart condemn us not, then have we confidence toward God.
22 And whatsoever we ask, we receive of him, because we keep his commandments, and do those things that are pleasing in his sight.
23 And this is his commandment, That we should believe on the name of his Son Jesus Christ, and love one another, as he gave us commandment.
24 And he that keepeth his commandments dwelleth in him, and he in him. And hereby we know that he abideth in us, by the Spirit which he hath given us.

Just as Faith and doubt are exact opposites with one another, faith and obedience go hand in hand. If we have a clear conscience, we can have confidence that He hears us. We won't wrestle with whether He hears us or not.

Luke 6: 46 And why call ye me, Lord, Lord, and do not the things which I say? (KJV)

According to Matthew 7:21-23, there will be those who will have exercised Faith toward God and perform miracles, yet whose lives do not reflect that of a Christian:

Mat 7:21 Not every one that saith unto me, Lord, Lord, shall enter into the kingdom of heaven; but he that doeth the will of my Father which is in heaven.
22 Many will say to me in that day, Lord, Lord, have we not prophesied in thy name? and in thy name have cast out devils? and in thy name done many wonderful works?
23 And then will I profess unto them, I never knew you: depart from me, ye that work iniquity.

Obviously sin does not negate the principles of faith which are established by the Word of God, just as the principles of gravity doesn't negate the principles of aerodynamics. God will honor His Word, because His Word is Truth. Those who misuse His Word will have to answer to Him in the Day of Judgment.

2Co 1:20 For all the promises of God in him *are* yea, and in him Amen, unto the glory of God by us.

All of the promises of God are yea and Amen. Men wrestle with His promises, and negate the Truth of His Word.

Mar 16:15 And he said unto them, Go ye into all the world, and preach the gospel to every creature.
16 He that believeth and is baptized shall be saved; but he that believeth not shall be damned.
17 And these signs shall follow them that believe; In my name shall they cast out devils; they shall speak with new tongues;
18 They shall take up serpents; and if they drink any deadly thing, it shall not hurt them; they shall lay hands on the sick, and they shall recover.

What is the promise here? _____

Jas 5:14 Is any sick among you? let him call for the elders of the church; and let them pray over him, anointing him with oil in the name of the Lord:
15 And the prayer of faith shall save the sick, and the Lord shall raise him up; and if he have committed sins, they shall be forgiven him.

What is the promise here? _____

1Jn 5:13 These things have I written unto you that believe on the name of the Son of God; that ye may know that ye have eternal life, and that ye may believe on the name of the Son of God.

What is the promise here? _____

1Jn 5:14 And this is the confidence that we have in him, that, if we ask any thing according to his will, he heareth us:
15 And if we know that he hear us, whatsoever we ask, we know that we have the petitions that we desired of him.

What is the Promise here? _____

1Jn 5:4 For whatsoever is born of God overcometh the world: and this is the victory that overcometh the world, even our faith
5 Who is he that overcometh the world, but he that believeth that Jesus is the Son of God?

What is the Promise here? _____

To sum up this lesson, it is important for the reader to understand that God's Word is True. While there are conditional promises in the Word of God (prefaced with the word "*IF*"), there are also definite promises that only become conditional as far as our Faith or lack thereof in those promises is concerned.

HOW DO WE FAIL IN OUR CHRISTIAN WALK?

_____

_____

WHAT DOES HEBREWS 11:6 TELL US?

_____

WHAT IS THE CONDITION TO ANSWERED PRAYER ACCORDING TO JESUS' WORDS IN MATTHEW 21:21?

_____

_____

HOW ARE WE TO APPROACH GOD CONCERNING HIS WILL IN OUR LIVES ACCORDING TO JAMES 1:5?

_____

_____

WHAT DOES THE BIBLE SAY ABOUT THE PERSON WHO DOUBTS WHEN HE APPROACHES GOD CONCERNING A THING? (JAMES 1:7-8)

_____

_____

2 COR 13:5 GIVES US A WONDERFUL PRESCRIPTION FOR OUR WALK WITH GOD. WHAT IS IT?

_____

_____

JUST AS FAITH AND _____ ARE EXACT OPPOSITES OF ONE ANOTHER, FAITH AND _____ GO HAND IN HAND.

LIKE JESUS, HOW ARE WE TO RESPOND TO TEMPTATION?

_____

_____

WHAT DOES PROVERBS 3:5-6 SAY?

_____

_____

1 CORINTHIANS 4:2 SAYS WHAT?

_____

_____

_____

11. WHAT DOES 2 CORINTHIANS 5:7 MEAN TO YOU?

_____

_____

_____

_____

Heb 11:6 Without faith it is impossible to please God, because he that comes to Him must believe that He is who He says He is, and that He is a rewarder of those who diligently seek Him.

JEHOVAH ROHI
OUR SHEPHERD

Psa 23:1 A Psalm of David. The LORD *is* my shepherd; I shall not want.
2 He maketh me to lie down in green pastures: he leadeth me beside the still waters.
3 He restoreth my soul: he leadeth me in the paths of righteousness for his name's sake.
4 Yea, though I walk through the valley of the shadow of death, I will fear no evil: for thou *art* with me; thy rod and thy staff they comfort me.
5 Thou preparest a table before me in the presence of mine enemies: thou anointest my head with oil; my cup runneth over.
6 Surely goodness and mercy shall follow me all the days of my life: and I will dwell in the house of the LORD for ever.

Jesus manifested the Name of God

Joh 10:11 I am the good shepherd: the good shepherd giveth his life for the sheep.

Joh 10:14 I am the good shepherd, and know my sheep, and am known of mine.

BASIC DOCTRINES

FAITH TOWARD GOD

LESSON 5

BELIEVING GOD FOR WHO HE IS

Heb 6:1 Therefore leaving the principles of the doctrine of Christ, let us go on unto perfection; not laying again the foundation of repentance from dead works, and of faith toward God,
2 Of the doctrine of baptisms, and of laying on of hands, and of resurrection of the dead, and of eternal judgment.

TRUE FAITH BELIEVES GOD FOR ALL HE SAYS HE IS

THE NAMES OF GOD REVEAL HIS PROMISES

If we know Who God is, we will be able to have confidence in Him when we make our petitions known to Him. The various Names of God throughout the Bible teach us that He is Who He says He is. In this Lesson, we will study the Names of God as revealed in the Bible.

Remember, Hebrews 11:6 tells us that *without faith it is impossible to please God, because he that comes to Him must believe that He is who He says He is, and that He is a rewarder of those who diligently seek Him.*

In that light, we need to know Who He says He is in various parts of the Bible.

JEHOVAH ROHI
OUR SHEPHERD

His Glory is manifested when we believe in His Name which declares Him to be our Shepherd (-Rohi), and we see Him lead us safely through whatever situation we may be faced with.

Because He is my Shepherd, I have no need for anything. He takes me to places of provision, and gives me food to eat (both spiritually and physically), and quenches my thirst, both spiritually and physically. Look at what Jesus, the Good Shepherd teaches us:

Matt 6:25 Therefore I say unto you, Take no thought for your life, what ye shall eat, or what ye shall drink; nor yet for your body, what ye shall put on. Is not the life more than meat, and the body than raiment?

When He says to take no thought for these things, He means it. DON'T WORRY...The Lord is a Good Shepherd, and He will Provide for you. Christians get in a dither about their situation, but the Good Shepherd won't let us down. We need to learn to rest in Him. Christians who get excited about their financial situation or their provision, don't really know Him as their Shepherd.

He restores our soul...

This Word "restore" means He brings us back to Him. If we slip away, He has a way of getting us back, even if it means with the rod of correction. If we have a loved one who has gone astray, we need to believe that the Good Shepherd will go and find him. The Word of God says that He is the Author and the Finisher of our faith, and that He Who began a good work in us will be faithful to complete it.

Phi 1:6 Being confident of this very thing, that he which hath begun a good work in you will perform it until the day of Jesus Christ:

Matt 18: 11 For the Son of man is come to save that which was lost.
12 How think ye? if a man have an hundred sheep, and one of them be gone astray, doth he not leave the ninety and nine, and goeth into the mountains, and seeketh that which is gone astray?
13 And if so be that he find it, verily I say unto you, he rejoiceth more of that sheep, than of the ninety and nine which went not astray.
14 Even so it is not the will of your Father which is in heaven, that one of these little ones should perish.

WITHOUT FAITH, IT IS IMPOSSIBLE TO PLEASE GOD, BECAUSE HE WHO COMES TO GOD MUST BELIEVE THAT HE IS (JEHOVAH ROHI-OUR SHEPHERD) AND THAT HE IS A REWARDER OF THOSE WHO DILLEGENTLY SEEK HIM.

JEHOVAH JIREH OUR PROVIDER

Gen 22:14 And Abraham called the name of that place Jehovahjireh: as it is said to this day, In the mount of the LORD it shall be seen.

Deu 28:1 And it shall come to pass, if thou shalt hearken diligently unto the voice of the LORD thy God, to observe *and* to do all his commandments which I command thee this day, that the LORD thy God will set thee on high above all nations of the earth:
2 And all these blessings shall come on thee, and overtake thee, if thou shalt hearken unto the voice of the LORD thy God.
3 Blessed *shalt* thou *be* in the city, and blessed *shalt* thou *be* in the field.
4 Blessed *shall be* the fruit of thy body, and the fruit of thy ground, and the fruit of thy cattle, the increase of thy kine, and the flocks of thy sheep.
5 Blessed *shall be* thy basket and thy store.
6 Blessed *shalt* thou *be* when thou comest in, and blessed *shalt* thou *be* when thou goest out.
7 The LORD shall cause thine enemies that rise up against thee to be smitten before thy face: they shall come out against thee one way, and flee before thee seven ways.
8 The LORD shall command the blessing upon thee in thy storehouses, and in all that thou settest thine hand unto; and he shall bless thee in the land which the LORD thy God giveth thee.
9 The LORD shall establish thee an holy people unto himself, as he hath sworn unto thee, if thou shalt keep the commandments of the LORD thy God, and walk in his ways.

JEHOVAH JIREH OUR PROVIDER

His Glory is manifested when we believe in His Name which proclaims Him to be our Provider (Jehovah [or Yahweh] Jireh) (Genesis 22:14). God saw the need, and we see that provision come to pass.

The Lord has said that He will withhold no good thing from those who seek Him,

Ps 34:10 The young lions do lack, and suffer hunger: but they that seek the LORD shall not want any good thing.

Ps 84:11 For the LORD God is a sun and shield: the LORD will give grace and glory: no good thing will he withhold from them that walk uprightly. 12 O LORD of hosts, blessed is the man that trusteth in thee.

....and that He will supply all of our NEEDS according to His Riches in Glory:

Phil 4: 19 But my God shall supply all your need according to his riches in glory by Christ Jesus.

As we have seen, the walk of the Christian is to be centered on obedience toward God. The condition to our blessings is IF we are obedient to God. If we have been obedient to Him, and have diligently purposed to walk in His Will, instead of our own, we can believe that He will provide all our needs according to His Riches in Glory.

Abraham responded in obedience to God's command, and he knew that God, Who had promised that his seed would be as the sand of the sea would be true to His Promise. As such, God provided the sacrifice that Abraham had confidence that He would provide.

10 And all people of the earth shall see that thou art called by the name of the LORD; and they shall be afraid of thee.
11 And the LORD shall make thee plenteous in goods, in the fruit of thy body, and in the fruit of thy cattle, and in the fruit of thy ground, in the land which the LORD sware unto thy fathers to give thee.
12 The LORD shall open unto thee his good treasure, the heaven to give the rain unto thy land in his season, and to bless all the work of thine hand: and thou shalt lend unto many nations, and thou shalt not borrow.
13 And the LORD shall make thee the head, and not the tail; and thou shalt be above only, and thou shalt not be beneath; if that thou hearken unto the commandments of the LORD thy God, which I command thee this day, to observe and to do *them:*
14 And thou shalt not go aside from any of the words which I command thee this day, *to* the right hand, or *to* the left, to go after other gods to serve them.

Heb 12:1 Wherefore seeing we also are compassed about with so great a cloud of witnesses, let us lay aside every weight, and the sin which doth so easily beset *us,* and let us run with patience the race that is set before us,
2 Looking unto Jesus the author and finisher of *our* faith; who for the joy that was set before him endured the cross, despising the shame, and is set down at the right hand of the throne of God.
3 For consider him that endured such contradiction of sinners against himself, lest ye be wearied and faint in your minds.
4 Ye have not yet resisted unto blood, striving against sin.

Deuteronomy 28:1-14, and Matthew 7:21-25 are passages in the Bible that complement one another. Faith and Obedience are constant companions.

**Matt 7:21 Not every one that saith unto me, Lord, Lord, shall enter into the kingdom of heaven; but he that doeth the will of my Father which is in heaven.
22 Many will say to me in that day, Lord, Lord, have we not prophesied in thy name? and in thy name have cast out devils? and in thy name done many wonderful works?
23 And then will I profess unto them, I never knew you: depart from me, ye that work iniquity.
24 Therefore whosoever heareth these sayings of mine, and doeth them, I will liken him unto a wise man, which built his house upon a rock:
25 And the rain descended, and the floods came, and the winds blew, and beat upon that house; and it fell not: for it was founded upon a rock.**

The bottom line of our walk in Covenant with the Lord is that we are to walk in obedience to Him.

He also provides the ability to walk in obedience to Him:

1Co 10:13 There hath no temptation taken you but such as is common to man: but God is faithful, who will not suffer you to be tempted above that ye are able; but will with the temptation also make a way to escape, that ye may be able to bear it.

To say that we cannot resist the sin when temptation comes our way is to walk in unbelief toward His Word, and to call God a liar.

The Truth of the matter is that a person who continually gives into the temptation to indulge in his or her sin loves the sin more than they love God. When they become confronted with that Truth, then they need to repent of their sin, confess it to God, and make up their minds that with His Help, they

Mat 6:19 Lay not up for yourselves treasures upon earth, where moth and rust doth corrupt, and where thieves break through and steal:

20 But lay up for yourselves treasures in heaven, where neither moth nor rust doth corrupt, and where thieves do not break through nor steal:

21 For where your treasure is, there will your heart be also.

22 The light of the body is the eye: if therefore thine eye be single, thy whole body shall be full of light.

23 But if thine eye be evil, thy whole body shall be full of darkness. If therefore the light that is in thee be darkness, how great is that darkness!

24 No man can serve two masters: for either he will hate the one, and love the other; or else he will hold to the one, and despise the other. Ye cannot serve God and mammon.

25 Therefore I say unto you, Take no thought for your life, what ye shall eat, or what ye shall drink; nor yet for your body, what ye shall put on. Is not the life more than meat, and the body than raiment?

26 Behold the fowls of the air: for they sow not, neither do they reap, nor gather into barns; yet your heavenly Father feedeth them. Are ye not much better than they?

27 Which of you by taking thought can add one cubit unto his stature?

28 And why take ye thought for raiment? Consider the lilies of the field, how they grow; they toil not, neither do they spin:

29 And yet I say unto you, That even Solomon in all his glory was not arrayed like one of these.

30 Wherefore, if God so clothe the grass of the field, which today is, and tomorrow is cast into the oven, shall he not much more clothe you, O ye of little faith?

31 Therefore take no thought, saying, What shall we eat? or, What shall we drink? or, Wherewithal shall we be clothed?

32 (For after all these things do the Gentiles seek:) for your heavenly Father knoweth that ye have need of all these things.

will take the escape route the next time the temptation comes. God understands that we are weak and prone to sin. But it is our faith in Him (not in ourselves) that overrides the inclination to sin, and gives us victory over sin.

1Jo 5:4 For whatsoever is born of God overcometh the world: and this is the victory that overcometh the world, even our faith.
5 Who is he that overcometh the world, but he that believeth that Jesus is the Son of God?

Deuteronomy 28:15-68 and Matthew 7:26-27 also parallel one another, and tells us that if we don't walk in willing obedience to His word, we will live under a curse.

Many Christians try to stand on the Promises of the Lord when they are walking in disobedience to His Word.

Deuteronomy 28:4,5, and 8 promises prosperity to the obedient people of God. But many Christians focus on obtaining the things of this world more than they do the furtherance of the Kingdom of God.

Col 3:1 If ye then be risen with Christ, seek those things which are above, where Christ sitteth on the right hand of God.
2 Set your affection on things above, not on things on the earth.
3 For ye are dead, and your life is hid with Christ in God.
4 When Christ, who is our life, shall appear, then shall ye also appear with him in glory.
5 Mortify therefore your members which are upon the earth; fornication, uncleanness, inordinate affection, evil concupiscence, and covetousness, which is idolatry:
6 For which things' sake the wrath of God cometh on the children of disobedience:
7 In the which ye also walked some time, when ye lived in them.

33 But seek ye first the kingdom of God, and his righteousness; and all these things shall be added unto you.

Jesus manifested the Name of God when He provided the wine at the wedding at Cana (Jn 21:1-10), when He provided the food for the multitude (Lk 9:12-17), or the abundance of fish when the fish weren't around (Lk 5:4-7), or when He summoned the fish with a coin in its mouth to pay tax (Matt 17:24-27).

JEHOVAH ROPHE
THE LORD OUR HEALER

*Exo 15:22 So Moses brought Israel from the Red sea, and they went out into the wilderness of Shur; and they went three days in the wilderness, and found no water.
23 And when they came to Marah, they could not drink of the waters of Marah, for they were bitter: therefore the name of it was called Marah.
24 And the people murmured against Moses, saying, What shall we drink?
25 And he cried unto the LORD; and the LORD shewed him a tree, which when he had cast into the waters, the waters were made sweet: there he made for them a statute and an ordinance, and there he proved them,
26 And said, If thou wilt diligently hearken to the voice of the LORD thy God, and wilt do that which is right in his sight, and wilt give ear to his commandments, and keep all his statutes, I will put none of these diseases upon thee, which I have brought upon the Egyptians: for I am the LORD that healeth thee.*

Jesus manifested the Name of God when he healed the multitudes of their diseases.

As we are obedient to the Lord, those things that we lay our hands to will prosper. It will be a natural result of our obedience. Jesus said we don't have to take any thought for those things that we need, if we are truly seeking first His Kingdom *AND* His Righteousness in our lives.

God isn't a liar. His Word is True. Many Christians behave as though they have to convince God to be true to His promises. God just simply wants us to rest in Who He is, and to walk in obedience to His Word. If I am faithful to examine myself on a daily basis, and am willing to repent of those things in my life that are contrary to the Will of God, God will be true to His Name. Disobedience is a result of unbelief.

JUST AS HIS NAME DECLARES, HE IS OUR PROVIDER. "WITHOUT FAITH, IT IS IMPOSSIBLE TO PLEASE GOD, BECAUSE HE THAT COMETH TO GOD MUST BELIEVE THAT HE IS (JEHOVAH JIREH, OUR PROVIDER), AND THAT HE IS A REWARDER OF THOSE WHO DILIGENTLY SEEK HIM."

JEHOVAH ROPHE
THE LORD OUR HEALER

His Glory is manifested when we believe in His Name, which declares Him to be our Healer (Jehovah [Yahweh] Rophe (Exodus 15:22-26), and when we see that Healing come to pass.

Exod 15:26 And said, If thou wilt diligently hearken to the voice of the LORD thy God, and wilt do that which is right in his sight, and wilt give ear to his commandments, and keep all his statutes, *I will put none of these diseases upon*

***thee,* which I have brought upon the Egyptians: for I am the LORD that healeth thee.**

Ps 103:2 Bless the LORD, O my soul, and forget not all his benefits: 3 Who forgiveth all thine iniquities; who healeth all thy diseases;

Isa 53:5 But he was wounded for our transgressions, he was bruised for our iniquities: the chastisement of our peace was upon him; and with his stripes we are healed.

Jesus Christ was God manifested in the flesh...as He walked among us, He healed the people that came to Him.

In Matthew 8:7-13, we are told of when a centurion came to Jesus and asked that He would heal his servant. The centurion told Jesus all He needed to do was speak His Word, and his servant would be healed.

It is the Word of God which is True, and we must learn to believe His Word above whatever any circumstances may seem to say.

WE WALK BY FAITH, AND NOT BY SIGHT.

Again, to be able to stand firm on the promises of God, we ourselves need to be walking in obedience to His Word.

The Word of God says that many people in the Body of Christ are weak and sickly, because they partake of the Lord's supper unworthily...When we take communion, we are proclaiming that we understand what the Lord has done for us in His death on the cross.

If we just flippantly exercise a form of religion (*dead works*), and eat and drink the bread and the wine despite the fact that we are given over to adultery, or drunkenness, or addiction, or cheating or stealing, because it's just what we do on Sunday, giving no thought to the fact that Christ came to save us *from* our sins, and that He took our sins on Himself so we would not have to pay the penalty for our sins, we are in essence, doing despite to the Spirit of Grace.

We need to examine ourselves, and determine whether we are in the Will of God or not.

1 Cor 11:26 For as often as ye eat this bread, and drink this cup, ye do shew the Lord's death till he come.
27 Wherefore whosoever shall eat this bread, and drink this cup of the Lord, unworthily, shall be guilty of the body and blood of the Lord.

Oftentimes it is Sin that opens the door to sickness:

1Jn 5:18 We know that whosoever is born of God sinneth not; but he that is begotten of God keepeth himself, and that wicked one toucheth him not.

Repentance and Confession will close the door to sickness.

Jas 5:14 Is any sick among you? let him call for the elders of the church; and let them pray over him, anointing him with oil in the name of the Lord:
15 And the prayer of faith shall save the sick, and the Lord shall raise him up; and if he have committed sins, they shall be forgiven him.
16 Confess your faults one to another, and pray one for another, that ye may be healed. The effectual fervent prayer of a righteous man availeth much.

Notes-
_____
_____
_____
_____
_____
_____
_____
_____
_____
_____
_____
_____
_____
_____
_____
_____
_____
_____

28 But let a man examine himself, and so let him eat of that bread, and drink of that cup.
29 For he that eateth and drinketh unworthily, eateth and drinketh damnation to himself, not discerning the Lord's body.
30 For this cause many are weak and sickly among you, and many sleep.
31 For if we would judge ourselves, we should not be judged.
32 But when we are judged, we are chastened of the Lord, that we should not be condemned with the world.

Sickness in Christians can often times (but not always) be a result of chastisement from the Lord. Because of our disobedience, many times the Lord removes His Protecting Hand from us, and we find ourselves walking in that sickness.

The Word of God says we are not to be conformed to the world. Let us examine ourselves and see if we have allowed the world to slip into our lives.

The Word of God says we are not to set our affections on the things of this world. Let us examine ourselves and see if that is what we have done.

The Word of God says that we are not to be liars, backbiters, gossips, thieves, covetous, jealous, bitter, adulterous, idolators, drunkards, greedy, selfish, divisive, filled with hate, unforgiving, etc. etc.. If we are sick, we need to examine ourselves, and determine if the Lord has withdrawn His Protective Hand from us.

Regarding sickness, James tells us:

James 5:14 Is any sick among you? let him call for the elders of the church; and let them pray over him, anointing him with oil in the name of the Lord:
15 And the prayer of faith shall save the sick, and the Lord shall raise him up; and if he have committed sins, they shall be forgiven him.

JEHOVAH NISSI THE LORD OUR BANNER

Exo 17:8 Then came Amalek, and fought with Israel in Rephidim.
9 And Moses said unto Joshua, Choose us out men, and go out, fight with Amalek: to morrow I will stand on the top of the hill with the rod of God in mine hand.
10 So Joshua did as Moses had said to him, and fought with Amalek: and Moses, Aaron, and Hur went up to the top of the hill.
11 And it came to pass, when Moses held up his hand, that Israel prevailed: and when he let down his hand, Amalek prevailed.
12 But Moses' hands *were* heavy; and they took a stone, and put *it* under him, and he sat thereon; and Aaron and Hur stayed up his hands, the one on the one side, and the other on the other side; and his hands were steady until the going down of the sun.
13 And Joshua discomfited Amalek and his people with the edge of the sword.
14 And the LORD said unto Moses, Write this *for* a memorial in a book, and rehearse *it* in the ears of Joshua: for I will utterly put out the remembrance of Amalek from under heaven.
15 And Moses built an altar, and called the name of it Jehovahnissi:

Christ, on the cross, had His arms suspended by the nails that held Him in place. Through His death on the cross, He purchased victory over the world for those who would come to Him. Christ is our Banner.

1Jn 5:4 For whatsoever is born of God overcometh the world: and this is the victory that overcometh the world, even our faith.

16 Confess your faults one to another, and pray one for another, that ye may be healed. The effectual fervent prayer of a righteous man availeth much.
17 Elias was a man subject to like passions as we are, and he prayed earnestly that it might not rain: and it rained not on the earth by the space of three years and six months.
18 And he prayed again, and the heaven gave rain, and the earth brought forth her fruit.
19 Brethren, if any of you do err from the truth, and one convert him;
20 Let him know, that he which converteth the sinner from the error of his way shall save a soul from death, and shall hide a multitude of sins.

Confession, healing and forgiveness appear to go hand in hand in a Christian's life. If our conscience is clear, then we can trust our Lord to heal us.

HIS NAME DECLARES HIM TO BE OUR HEALER. WITHOUT FAITH IT IS IMPOSSIBLE TO PLEASE HIM, BECAUSE HE THAT COMETH TO HIM MUST BELIEVE THAT HE IS (JEHOVAH ROPHE, THE LORD OUR HEALER), AND THAT HE IS A REWARDER OF THOSE WHO DILIGENTLY SEEK HIM.

JEHOVAH NISSI THE LORD OUR BANNER

His Glory is manifested when we believe in His Name which declares Him to be our Banner (-Nissi Exodus 17:8-15) and we see Victory over our enemy.

The Word of God says that our battle is not with flesh and blood...but that we are battling a spiritual battle as Christians.

Eph 6: 12 For we wrestle not against flesh and blood, but against principalities, against powers,

against the rulers of the darkness of this world, against spiritual wickedness in high places.

James 4: 7 Submit yourselves therefore to God. Resist the devil, and he will flee from you.

Christians believe that since they were born in the flesh, they are subject to sin. But when we became born of God, we were delivered from the power of sin in our lives (Romans 6:14).

Ephesians 6:12-18 tells us that the warfare that we are fighting is spiritual warfare. It tells us how to battle this:

Eph 6:12 For we wrestle not against flesh and blood, but against principalities, against powers, against the rulers of the darkness of this world, against spiritual wickedness in high places.
13 Wherefore take unto you the whole armour of God, that ye may be able to withstand in the evil day, and having done all, to stand.
14 Stand therefore, having your loins girt about with truth, and having on the breastplate of righteousness;
15 And your feet shod with the preparation of the gospel of peace;
16 Above all, taking the shield of faith, wherewith ye shall be able to quench all the fiery darts of the wicked.
17 And take the helmet of salvation, and the sword of the Spirit, which is the word of God:
18 Praying always with all prayer and supplication in the Spirit, and watching thereunto with all perseverance and supplication for all saints;

Many commentaries have been written, and many sermons have been preached on this passage of Scripture. But the simple fact is that we have been empowered to do the Will of God, and to overcome the enemy of our souls in every aspect of our lives when we received Jesus Christ as our Lord and Savior.

According to verse 14, we are to walk in Truth. The Word of God is True. We have seen how Jesus resisted the temptations of the devil with the Word of God. If we believe in the Word of God, we can walk in the Truth, and the Truth will make us free.

As we walk in the Truth of God, we will walk in Righteousness before God. We will make decisions that are pleasing to God, rather than merely decisions that are pleasing to our flesh.

In verse 15, we are exhorted to take the gospel wherever we go. If we carry the testimony of what the Lord has done in our lives, we will be able to share it with others, and impact their lives for the furtherance of the Kingdom of God in our community.

In verse 16, we learn that it is our faith in God which enables us to overcome all the attacks that the enemy of our souls throws at us. Our faith tells us that we are Children of the Most High God, and that if He is for us, no one can stand against us.

Verse 17 mentions taking the helmet of salvation. The knowledge that we are saved from the wrath of God allows us to walk in confidence when the enemy tries to heap condemnation on us, and he does try to heap condemnation on us every time we fail; but the Truth of the matter is this:

Rom 8: 35 Who shall separate us from the love of Christ? shall tribulation, or distress, or persecution, or famine, or nakedness, or peril, or sword?
36 As it is written, For thy sake we are killed all the day long; we are accounted as sheep for the slaughter.
37 Nay, in all these things we are more than conquerors through him that loved us.
38 For I am persuaded, that neither death, nor life, nor angels, nor principalities, nor powers, nor things present, nor things to come,
39 Nor height, nor depth, nor any other creature, shall be able to separate us from the love of God, which is in Christ Jesus our Lord.

This is where the final item in the armor of God comes in.

The Sword of the Spirit, which is the Word of God.

The flesh doesn't profit anything, but it is the Spirit of God which gives us life, and the Sword of the Spirit is the Word of God. The Word of God does not minister to the flesh, but to the Spirit of man. The Word of God is absolutely true. The enemy of our souls tempts us to yield to the lusts of the flesh so he

G3528

νικάω   nikaō   *nik-ah'-o*

From G3529; to *subdue* (literally or figuratively): - conquer, overcome, prevail, get the victory.

Total KJV occurrences: 28

Notes-

_____
_____
_____
_____
_____
_____
_____
_____
_____
_____
_____
_____
_____
_____
_____
_____
_____
_____
_____
_____
_____
_____
_____
_____
_____
_____
_____

can get us under condemnation. The Word of God, if it is rooted deeply in our hearts, will enable us to resist the temptation to yield to the lusts of the flesh.

The flesh is at war with the Spirit, and we will be overcomers if we wield the Sword of the Spirit in every aspect of our lives.

**Gal 1: 3 Grace be to you and peace from God the Father, and from our Lord Jesus Christ,
4 Who gave himself for our sins, that he might deliver us from this present evil world, according to the will of God and our Father:**

The Banner was the standard which was flown in the battle, proclaiming whose kingdom the various armies represented. Moses' arms were lifted up in intercession for Israel in their battle with the Amalekites. Under the New Covenant, Jesus is our Standard. As long as the Name of the Most High God is lifted up, He will fight our battles, and no power on earth can withstand the Power of God.

**Col 1: 9 For this cause we also, since the day we heard it, do not cease to pray for you, and to desire that ye might be filled with the knowledge of his will in all wisdom and spiritual understanding;
10 That ye might walk worthy of the Lord unto all pleasing, being fruitful in every good work, and increasing in the knowledge of God;
11 Strengthened with all might, according to his glorious power, unto all patience and longsuffering with joyfulness;
12 Giving thanks unto the Father, which hath made us meet to be partakers of the inheritance of the saints in light:
13 Who hath delivered us from the power of darkness, and hath translated us into the kingdom of his dear Son:**

WITHOUT FAITH, IT IS IMPOSSIBLE TO PLEASE GOD, BECAUSE HE WHO COMES TO GOD MUST BELIEVE THAT HE IS (JEHOVAH NISSI- THE LORD OUR BANNER), AND THAT HE IS A

REWARDER OF THOSE WHO DILIGENTLY SEEK HIM.

The Lord intends for us to be over comers, and not defeated people in all aspects of our lives. He will give us victory over the sins that so easily beset us. We are called and enabled to overcome:

Rev 2:7 He that hath an ear, let him hear what the Spirit saith unto the churches; To him that overcometh will I give to eat of the tree of life, which is in the midst of the paradise of God.

Rev 2:11 He that hath an ear, let him hear what the Spirit saith unto the churches; He that overcometh shall not be hurt of the second death.

Rev 2:17 He that hath an ear, let him hear what the Spirit saith unto the churches; To him that overcometh will I give to eat of the hidden manna, and will give him a white stone, and in the stone a new name written, which no man knoweth saving he that receiveth *it*.

Rev 2:26 And he that overcometh, and keepeth my works unto the end, to him will I give power over the nations:

Rev 3:5 He that overcometh, the same shall be clothed in white raiment; and I will not blot out his name out of the book of life, but I will confess his name before my Father, and before his angels.

Rev 3:12 Him that overcometh will I make a pillar in the temple of my God, and he shall go no more out: and I will write upon him the name of my God, and the name of the city of my God, *which is* new Jerusalem, which cometh down out of heaven from my God: and *I will write upon him* my new name.

**Rev 3:21 To him that overcometh will I grant to sit with me in my throne, even as I also overcame, and am set down with my Father in his throne.
22 He that hath an ear, let him hear what the Spirit saith unto the churches.**

1Jn 5:4 For whatsoever is born of God overcometh the world: and this is the victory that overcometh the world, *even* our faith.

JEHOVAH SHAMMAH
THE LORD IS HERE

Eze 48:30 And these *are* the goings out of the city on the north side, four thousand and five hundred measures.
31 And the gates of the city *shall be* after the names of the tribes of Israel: three gates northward; one gate of Reuben, one gate of Judah, one gate of Levi.
32 And at the east side four thousand and five hundred: and three gates; and one gate of Joseph, one gate of Benjamin, one gate of Dan.
33 And at the south side four thousand and five hundred measures: and three gates; one gate of Simeon, one gate of Issachar, one gate of Zebulun.
34 At the west side four thousand and five hundred, *with* their three gates; one gate of Gad, one gate of Asher, one gate of Naphtali.
35 *It was* round about eighteen thousand *measures:* and the name of the city from *that* day *shall be,* The LORD *is* there.

Jesus manifested the Name of the Father when He said

Mat 18:20 For where two or three are gathered together in my name, there am I in the midst of them.

Mat 28:18 And Jesus came and spake unto them, saying, All power is given unto me in heaven and in earth.
19 Go ye therefore, and teach all nations, baptizing them in the name of the Father, and of the Son, and of the Holy Ghost:
20 Teaching them to observe all things whatsoever I have commanded you: and, lo, I am with you alway, even unto the end of the world. Amen.

Rom 12:21 Be not overcome of evil, but overcome evil with good.

1Jn 4:3 And every spirit that confesseth not that Jesus Christ is come in the flesh is not of God: and this is that *spirit* of antichrist, whereof ye have heard that it should come; and even now already is it in the world.
4 Ye are of God, little children, and have overcome them: because greater is he that is in you, than he that is in the world.
5 They are of the world: therefore speak they of the world, and the world heareth them.
6 We are of God: he that knoweth God heareth us; he that is not of God heareth not us. Hereby know we the spirit of truth, and the spirit of error.

Rev 12:11 And they overcame him by the blood of the Lamb, and by the word of their testimony; and they loved not their lives unto the death.

In the Sidebar on the previous page, one of the definition of the Greek word translated as "Overcome" is "to subdue". God had given commandment to Adam and Eve to subdue the earth, and in Christ, we are also called to subdue the works of the enemy. We are able to do that as we abide in Christ, our Banner.

JEHOVAH SHAMMAH
THE LORD IS HERE

His Glory is manifested when we believe in His Name which declares Him to be "here" (-Shammah Ezekiel 48:35), and we know that the Ever Present One will never leave us or forsake us, and we are comforted in the midst of our trials with that knowledge.

Ps 46: 1 God is our refuge and strength, a very present help in trouble.
2 Therefore will not we fear, though the earth be removed, and though the mountains be carried into the midst of the sea;

3 Though the waters thereof roar and be troubled, though the mountains shake with the swelling thereof. Selah.
4 There is a river, the streams whereof shall make glad the city of God, the holy place of the tabernacles of the most High.
5 God is in the midst of her; she shall not be moved: God shall help her, and that right early.
6 The heathen raged, the kingdoms were moved: he uttered his voice, the earth melted.
7 The LORD of hosts is with us; the God of Jacob is our refuge. Selah.
8 Come, behold the works of the LORD, what desolations he hath made in the earth.
9 He maketh wars to cease unto the end of the earth; he breaketh the bow, and cutteth the spear in sunder; he burneth the chariot in the fire.
10 Be still, and know that I am God: I will be exalted among the heathen, I will be exalted in the earth.
11 The LORD of hosts is with us; the God of Jacob is our refuge. Selah.

No other so-called "god" in all the religions of the world is like the One True God that the Christian faith reveals. As the Psalm declares, He is a very present Help in times of trouble.

He has promised us that He would never leave nor forsake us.

He is ready to help all those who call on Him out of a pure heart. The Bible declares the nation whose God is the Lord to be blessed!

Deut 4: 7 For what nation is there so great, who hath God so nigh unto them, as the LORD our God is in all things that we call upon him for?

Ps 145:18 The LORD is nigh unto all them that call upon him, to all that call upon him in truth.
19 He will fulfil the desire of them that fear him: he also will hear their cry, and will save them.
20 The LORD preserveth all them that love him: but all the wicked will he destroy.
21 My mouth shall speak the praise of the LORD: and let all flesh bless his holy name for ever and ever.

Jesus assured us that He is with us Always.

Matt 28:19 Go ye therefore, and teach all nations, baptizing them in the name of the Father, and of the Son, and of the Holy Ghost:
20 Teaching them to observe all things whatsoever I have commanded you: and, lo, I am with you alway, even unto the end of the world. Amen.

JEHOVAH SHALOM
THE LORD OUR PEACE

Jdg 6:19 And Gideon went in, and made ready a kid, and unleavened cakes of an ephah of flour: the flesh he put in a basket, and he put the broth in a pot, and brought *it* out unto him under the oak, and presented *it*.
20 And the angel of God said unto him, Take the flesh and the unleavened cakes, and lay *them* upon this rock, and pour out the broth. And he did so.
21 Then the angel of the LORD put forth the end of the staff that *was* in his hand, and touched the flesh and the unleavened cakes; and there rose up fire out of the rock, and consumed the flesh and the unleavened cakes. Then the angel of the LORD departed out of his sight.
22 And when Gideon perceived that he *was* an angel of the LORD, Gideon said, Alas, O Lord GOD! for because I have seen an angel of the LORD face to face.
23 And the LORD said unto him, Peace *be* unto thee; fear not: thou shalt not die.
:24 Then Gideon built an altar there unto the LORD, and called it Jehovahshalom: unto this day it *is* yet in Ophrah of the Abiezrites.

Jesus was the Manifestation of Jehovah Shalom in the Flesh when He promised

Joh 14:27 Peace I leave with you, my peace I give unto you: not as the world giveth, give I unto you. Let not your heart be troubled, neither let it be afraid.

He is with us in the midst of our trials:

Rom 8: 28 And we know that all things work together for good to them that love God, to them who are the called according to his purpose.

We see that He is with us even in the trials of our faith. But there is one other thing that we must consider about this One Whose Name declares that He is Here.

THE GREATEST DEMONSTRATION OF UNBELIEF IS THAT WHICH WE DO WHEN WE BELIEVE THAT NO HUMAN EYES CAN SEE US.

While this may be true, God is here in our presence, and He sees what we do behind closed doors. If that revelation could sink into our hearts and minds, our walk with Him will be a walk without hypocrisy.

WITHOUT FAITH, IT IS IMPOSSIBLE TO PLEASE HIM, BECAUSE HE THAT COMES TO HIM MUST BELIEVE THAT HE IS (JEHOVAH SHAMMAH - THE LORD IS HERE) AND THAT HE IS A REWARDER OF THOSE WHO DILIGENTLY SEEK HIM.

JEHOVAH SHALOM
THE LORD OUR PEACE

We see His Glory manifested when we are caught in a situation that threatens to destroy our peace, and we see the God of Peace (-Shalom: Judges 6:24) intervene in our lives, and we experience a peace that passes all understanding.

We must remember that He is a God of Covenant, and His Name reflects the covenant He has promised us. If we OBEY Him, we will be able to rest in His Promises.

Lev 26:1 Ye shall make you no idols nor graven image, neither rear you up a standing image, neither shall ye set up any image of stone in your land, to bow down unto it: for I am the LORD your God.

2 Ye shall keep my sabbaths, and reverence my sanctuary: I am the LORD.

3 If ye walk in my statutes, and keep my commandments, and do them;

4 Then I will give you rain in due season, and the land shall yield her increase, and the trees of the field shall yield their fruit.

5 And your threshing shall reach unto the vintage, and the vintage shall reach unto the sowing time: and ye shall eat your bread to the full, and dwell in your land safely.

6 And I will give peace in the land, and ye shall lie down, and none shall make you afraid: and I will rid evil beasts out of the land, neither shall the sword go through your land.

7 And ye shall chase your enemies, and they shall fall before you by the sword.

8 And five of you shall chase an hundred, and an hundred of you shall put ten thousand to flight: and your enemies shall fall before you by the sword.

9 For I will have respect unto you, and make you fruitful, and multiply you, and establish my covenant with you.

10 And ye shall eat old store, and bring forth the old because of the new.

11 And I will set my tabernacle among you: and my soul shall not abhor you.

12 And I will walk among you, and will be your God, and ye shall be my people.

13 I am the LORD your God, which brought you forth out of the land of Egypt, that ye should not be their bondmen; and I have broken the bands of your yoke, and made you go upright.

As I mentioned earlier, God is a Covenant God, and His Promises are contingent upon our obedience. See the warning He gave His people Israel:

Deut 29:19 And it come to pass, when he heareth the words of this curse, that he bless himself in his heart, saying, I shall have peace, though I walk in the imagination of mine heart, to add drunkenness to thirst:
20 The LORD will not spare him, but then the anger of the LORD and his jealousy shall smoke against that man, and all the curses that are written in this book shall lie upon him, and the LORD shall blot out his name from under heaven.

For those who would insist that this is the Old Testament and we are under the Covenant of Grace of the New Testament, we will look at what the New Testament has to say:

Heb 10:28 He that despised Moses' law died without mercy under two or three witnesses:
29 Of how much sorer punishment, suppose ye, shall he be thought worthy, who hath trodden under foot the Son of God, and hath counted the blood of the covenant, wherewith he was sanctified, an unholy thing, and hath done despite unto the Spirit of grace?
30 For we know him that hath said, Vengeance belongeth unto me, I will recompense, saith the Lord. And again, The Lord shall judge his people.
31 It is a fearful thing to fall into the hands of the living God.

We are under a New Covenant, one of Grace, and not the works of the Law. But the God Who we serve is the same today as He was yesterday, and He calls us to Obedience. If we walk in obedience toward Him, He will give us peace.

Ps 4:1 Hear me when I call, O God of my righteousness: thou hast enlarged me when I was in distress; have mercy upon me, and hear my prayer.
2 O ye sons of men, how long will ye turn my glory into shame? how long will ye love vanity, and seek after leasing? Selah.
3 But know that the LORD hath set apart him that is godly for himself: the LORD will hear when I call unto him.
4 Stand in awe, and sin not: commune with your own heart upon your bed, and be still. Selah.
5 Offer the sacrifices of righteousness, and put your trust in the LORD.
6 There be many that say, Who will shew us any good? LORD, lift thou up the light of thy countenance upon us.
7 Thou hast put gladness in my heart, more than in the time that their corn and their wine increased.
8 I will both lay me down in peace, and sleep: for thou, LORD, only makest me dwell in safety.

JEHOVAH M'KADDESH THE LORD OUR SANCTIFICATION

Lev 20:7 Sanctify yourselves therefore, and be ye holy: for I *am* the LORD your God.
8 And ye shall keep my statutes, and do them: I *am* the LORD which sanctify you.

Sanctify

6942 qadash-
to consecrate, to sanctify, to prepare, to dedicate, to be hallowed, to be holy, to be sanctified, to be separate
a) 1) to be set apart, to be consecrated 2) to be hallowed 3) consecrated, tabooed
b) 1) to show oneself sacred or majestic 2) to be honored, to be treated as sacred 3) to be holy
c) 1) to set apart as sacred, to consecrate, to dedicate 2) to observe as holy, to keep sacred 3) to honor as sacred, to hallow 4) to consecrate
d) 1) to be consecrated 2) consecrated, dedicated e) 1) to set apart, to devote, to consecrate 2) to regard or treat as sacred or hallow 3) to consecrate
f) 1) to keep oneself apart or separate 2) to cause Himself to be hallowed (used of God) 3) to be observed as holy 4) to consecrate oneself

Holy

6918 qadowsh or qadosh-
sacred, holy, the Holy One, a saint, set apart

104

Ps 29:11 The LORD will give strength unto his people; the LORD will bless his people with peace.

When we receive Jesus as our Lord and Saviour, the Kingdom of God is established in our hearts:

Rom 14:17 For the kingdom of God is not meat and drink; but righteousness, and peace, and joy in the Holy Ghost.
18 For he that in these things serveth Christ is acceptable to God, and approved of men.
19 Let us therefore follow after the things which make for peace, and things wherewith one may edify another.

Because of our desire to walk in obedience toward God, He will give us peace in the midst of all our trials:

Rom 16:19 For your obedience is come abroad unto all men. I am glad therefore on your behalf: but yet I would have you wise unto that which is good, and simple concerning evil.
20 And the God of peace shall bruise Satan under your feet shortly. The grace of our Lord Jesus Christ be with you. Amen.

WITHOUT FAITH, IT IS IMPOSSIBLE TO PLEASE GOD, BECAUSE HE THAT COMES TO HIM MUST BELIEVE THAT HE IS (-SHALOM; OUR PEACE) AND THAT HE IS A REWARDER OF THOSE WHO DILIGENTLY SEEK HIM.

JEHOVAH M'KADDESH THE LORD OUR SANCTIFICATION

We see His Glory manifested when we believe that He is the one Who has made us Holy, Who has sanctified us (Leviticus 20:7), and Who has Purified us.

We cannot take any credit for the Work He does in us, but He *enables* us to obey His commandments. He tells us to sanctify ourselves, and then He says that He sanctifies us.

Lev 20:7 Sanctify yourselves therefore, and be ye holy: for I am the LORD your God.
8 And ye shall keep my statutes, and do them: I am the LORD which sanctify you.

He empowers the Born again Christian to walk in His Will.

In the Bible, where you see the words translated as "Holy" and "sanctify", you will see that they are closely related to one another (look at the side bar on the previous page).

Over and over again, throughout the Bible, we see God Almighty telling His people to be Holy, because His is Holy.

We will look at just a few of those places for the purpose of this study:

Lev 11:45 For I am the LORD that bringeth you up out of the land of Egypt, to be your God: ye shall therefore be holy, for I am holy.

Lev 19:2 Speak unto all the congregation of the children of Israel, and say unto them, Ye shall be holy: for I the LORD your God am holy.
3 Ye shall fear every man his mother, and his father, and keep my sabbaths: I am the LORD your God.
4 Turn ye not unto idols, nor make to yourselves molten gods: I am the LORD your God.

Lev 20:26 And ye shall be holy unto me: for I the LORD am holy, and have severed you from other people, that ye should be mine.

It is important to note this last passage, because the Lord says that He has severed His people from other people. They were to live differently than the people in the world. The standard hasn't changed under the New Covenant:

Rom 12: 1 I beseech you therefore, brethren, by the mercies of God, that ye present your bodies a living sacrifice, holy, acceptable unto God, which is your reasonable service.
2 And be not conformed to this world: but be ye transformed by the renewing of your mind, that ye may prove what is that good, and acceptable, and perfect, will of God.

Many Christians fail in this respect...they have not presented their bodies as a living sacrifice, holy and acceptable to God, because of their conformity to the ways of the world.

Like Israel of old, many Christians want the things of the world more than they desire the things of God. A renewed mind will esteem the things that the world has to offer as refuse, or a little thing. A renewed mind will want to seek the establishment of Kingdom of God and His Righteousness.

And this is a wonderful Work that the Lord Has done in their hearts, when the yielded Christian is more concerned about the furtherance of God's Kingdom than his own well being!

True sanctification or holiness is being separate. Seeking only to please the Lord, and not our own selves.

But when we reach a place where we esteem the things of this world as nothing, and our hearts are fully set on serving the Lord with all of our being; we can't compare ourselves to others, and think we have arrived when they have not. The Lord Warns us:

Rom 12:3 For I say, through the grace given unto me, to every man that is among you, not to think of himself more highly than he ought to think; but to think soberly, according as God hath dealt to every man the measure of faith.

Let me point out here in the light of this passage, that true men and women of Faith understand that the things of this world are nothing, and that being separate unto the Lord is everything to the true child of Faith:

Heb 11:32 And what shall I more say? for the time would fail me to tell of Gedeon, and of Barak, and of Samson, and of Jephthae; of David also, and Samuel, and of the prophets:
33 Who through faith subdued kingdoms, wrought righteousness, obtained promises, stopped the mouths of lions,
34 Quenched the violence of fire, escaped the edge of the sword, out of weakness were made strong, waxed valiant in fight, turned to flight the armies of the aliens.
35 Women received their dead raised to life again:

Most Christians would want to stop here, and concentrate on these mighty deeds of faith...they subdued kingdoms, wrought righteousness, obtained promises, stopped the mouths of lions, quenched the violence of fire, escaped

_____
_____
_____
_____
_____
_____
_____
_____
_____
_____
_____
_____
_____
_____
_____
_____
_____
_____
_____
_____
_____
_____
_____
_____

Php 4:11 Not that I speak in respect of want: for I have learned, in whatsoever state I am, therewith to be content.
12 I know both how to be abased, and I know how to abound: every where and in all things I am instructed both to be full and to be hungry, both to abound and to suffer need.
13 I can do all things through Christ which strengtheneth me.

the edge of the sword, waxed valiant in fight, turned to flight the armies of the aliens, women received their dead raised to life again...What promises!

But as we can see by looking just a little further in this passage of Scripture, a person who is walking in Holiness before God Almighty, separate from the world understands that the most important thing in the world is that God is glorified in our lives, no matter what comes our way:

Heb 11:35 ...and others were tortured, not accepting deliverance; that they might obtain a better resurrection:
36 And others had trial of cruel mockings and scourgings, yea, moreover of bonds and imprisonment:
37 They were stoned, they were sawn asunder, were tempted, were slain with the sword: they wandered about in sheepskins and goatskins; being destitute, afflicted, tormented;
38 (Of whom the world was not worthy:) they wandered in deserts, and in mountains, and in dens and caves of the earth.
39 And these all, having obtained a good report through faith, received not the promise:
40 God having provided some better thing for us, that they without us should not be made perfect.

The promise was that the world would be reconciled unto God. That both Jews and Gentiles would know the One True God Who created them for Himself. A sanctified Christian has learned to be content, whether he is abased, or whether he abounds (See Philippians 4:11-13).

The Blessing of God is that in all things, we are more than conquerors. At the Cross, Jesus gave us power over sin. Because of the Work God has done in his or her heart, the Christian disciple will strive to overcome the power of sin that seems to so easily beset them.

Heb 12:4 Ye have not yet resisted unto blood, striving against sin.

True sanctification results in this attitude:

Rom 8:35 Who shall separate us from the love of Christ? shall tribulation, or distress, or persecution, or famine, or nakedness, or peril, or sword?
36 As it is written, For thy sake we are killed all the day long; we are accounted as sheep for the slaughter.
37 Nay, in all these things we are more than conquerors through him that loved us.
38 For I am persuaded, that neither death, nor life, nor angels, nor principalities, nor powers, nor things present, nor things to come,
39 Nor height, nor depth, nor any other creature, shall be able to separate us from the love of God, which is in Christ Jesus our Lord.

We are called to be Holy under the New Covenant:

1 Pet 1: 13 Wherefore gird up the loins of your mind, be sober, and hope to the end for the grace that is to be brought unto you at the revelation of Jesus Christ;
14 As obedient children, not fashioning yourselves according to the former lusts in your ignorance:
15 But as he which hath called you is holy, so be ye holy in all manner of conversation;
16 Because it is written, Be ye holy; for I am holy.
17 And if ye call on the Father, who without respect of persons judgeth according to every man's work, pass the time of your sojourning here in fear:
18 Forasmuch as ye know that ye were not redeemed with corruptible things, as silver and gold, from your vain conversation received by tradition from your fathers;
19 But with the precious blood of Christ, as of a lamb without blemish and without spot:

In Deuteronomy 7, we see that the Lord warns Israel from becoming conformed to the ways of the world around them, and then He reminds them that they are chosen because He loves them, not for any redeeming qualities of their own:

Deuteronomy 7:6 ....For thou art an holy people unto the LORD thy God: the LORD thy God hath chosen thee to be a special people unto himself, above all people that are upon the face of the earth.
7 The LORD did not set his love upon you, nor choose you, because ye were more in number than any people; for ye were the fewest of all people:
8 But because the LORD loved you, and because he would keep the oath which he had sworn unto your fathers, hath the LORD brought you out

---

Just as the Father is our Sanctification, so also is the Son.

Joh 17:19 And for their sakes I sanctify myself, that they also might be sanctified through the truth.

Heb 13:12 Wherefore Jesus also, that he might sanctify the people with his own blood, suffered without the gate.

JEHOVAH TSIDKENU THE LORD OUR RIGHTEOUSNESS

Jer 23:5 Behold, the days come, saith the LORD, that I will raise unto David a righteous Branch, and a King shall reign and prosper, and shall execute judgment and justice in the earth.
6 In his days Judah shall be saved, and Israel shall dwell safely: and this is his name whereby he shall be called, THE LORD OUR RIGHTEOUSNESS.

Jesus is our Righteousness.

Rom 5:17 For if by one man's offence death reigned by one; much more they which receive abundance of grace and of the gift of righteousness shall reign in life by one, Jesus Christ.)
18 Therefore as by the offence of one judgment came upon all men to condemnation; even so by the righteousness of one the free gift came upon all men unto justification of life.

with a mighty hand, and redeemed you out of the house of bondmen, from the hand of Pharaoh king of Egypt.

As we yield ourselves to God, in sincerity and truth, He will purify us unto Himself, and will make us a people zealous of good works.

Titus 2:11 For the grace of God that bringeth salvation hath appeared to all men,
12 Teaching us that, denying ungodliness and worldly lusts, we should live soberly, righteously, and godly, in this present world;
13 Looking for that blessed hope, and the glorious appearing of the great God and our Saviour Jesus Christ;
14 Who gave himself for us, that he might redeem us from all iniquity, and purify unto himself a peculiar people, zealous of good works.
15 These things speak, and exhort, and rebuke with all authority. Let no man despise thee.

Where it seems impossible for us to walk in the Holiness of God, it IS POSSIBLE, if we just rely on Him to perfect the work He has begun in us.

WITHOUT FAITH, IT IS IMPOSSIBLE TO PLEASE GOD, BECAUSE HE THAT COMES TO HIM MUST BELIEVE THAT HE IS (JEHOVAH MAKADDESH, OUR SANCIFICATION), AND THAT HE IS A REWARDER OF THOSE WHO DILIGENTLY SEEK HIM.

JEHOVAH TSIDKENU THE LORD OUR RIGHTEOUSNESS

We see His Glory manifested when we believe that He is our righteousness (Jehovah Tsidkenu - Jeremiah 23:5,6) and we let His Righteousness shine through us.

In Romans 3:10 we are told that none of us as human beings are righteous.

**Rom 3:10 As it is written, There is none righteous, no, not one:
11 There is none that understandeth, there is none that seeketh after God.
12 They are all gone out of the way, they are together become unprofitable; there is none that doeth good, no, not one.
13 Their throat is an open sepulchre; with their tongues they have used deceit; the poison of asps is under their lips:
14 Whose mouth is full of cursing and bitterness:
15 Their feet are swift to shed blood:
16 Destruction and misery are in their ways:
17 And the way of peace have they not known:
18 There is no fear of God before their eyes.**

But that is no surprise to God, so He set forth a remedy for all of humanity:

**Rom 3: 19 Now we know that what things soever the law saith, it saith to them who are under the law: that every mouth may be stopped, and all the world may become guilty before God.
20 Therefore by the deeds of the law there shall no flesh be justified in his sight: for by the law is the knowledge of sin.
21 But now the righteousness of God without the law is manifested, being witnessed by the law and the prophets;
22 Even the righteousness of God which is by faith of Jesus Christ unto all and upon all them that believe: for there is no difference:
23 For all have sinned, and come short of the glory of God;
24 Being justified freely by his grace through the redemption that is in Christ Jesus:
25 Whom God hath set forth to be a propitiation through faith in his blood, to declare his righteousness for the remission of sins that are past, through the forbearance of God;
26 To declare, I say, at this time his righteousness: that he might be just, and the justifier of him which believeth in Jesus.**

Romans 10:10 says it is with the heart that man believes unto righteousness.

Before Christ, I was captured by sin. Now in Christ, sin has no more dominion over me. As I once practiced sin, so now I practice resisting sin, and bringing my thoughts into captivity to the obedience of Christ. His Holy Spirit now dwells in me, and I am able to walk according to His leading in my life.

Jesus taught us what our attitude should be concerning righteousness:

Matt 5: 6 Blessed are they which do hunger and thirst after righteousness: for they shall be filled.

1Jn 3:5 And ye know that he was manifested to take away our sins; and in him is no sin.

6 Whosoever abideth in him sinneth not: whosoever sinneth hath not seen him, neither known him.

7 Little children, let no man deceive you: he that doeth righteousness is righteous, even as he is righteous.

8 He that committeth sin is of the devil; for the devil sinneth from the beginning. For this purpose the Son of God was manifested, that he might destroy the works of the devil.

9 Whosoever is born of God doth not commit sin; for his seed remaineth in him: and he cannot sin, because he is born of God.

10 In this the children of God are manifest, and the children of the devil: whosoever doeth not righteousness is not of God, neither he that loveth not his brother.

11 For this is the message that ye heard from the beginning, that we should love one another.

12 Not as Cain, who was of that wicked one, and slew his brother. And wherefore slew he him? Because his own works were evil, and his brother's righteous.

13 Marvel not, my brethren, if the world hate you.

14 We know that we have passed from death unto life, because we love the brethren. He that loveth not his brother abideth in death.

15 Whosoever hateth his brother is a murderer: and ye know that no murderer hath eternal life abiding in him.

16 Hereby perceive we the love of God, because he laid down his life for us: and we ought to lay down our lives for the brethren.

17 But whoso hath this world's good, and seeth his brother have need, and shutteth up his bowels of compassion from him, how dwelleth the love of God in him?

18 My little children, let us not love in word, neither in tongue; but in deed and in truth.

The Born Again child of God will want to please the Father in all that he does. Jesus said if we HUNGER and THIRST after righteousness, we will be filled. As we grow in the knowledge of the Lord, we obtain more understanding of what the Righteousness of God is.

Rom 1:16 For I am not ashamed of the gospel of Christ: for it is the power of God unto salvation to everyone that believeth; to the Jew first, and also to the Greek.
17 For therein is the righteousness of God revealed from faith to faith: as it is written, The just shall live by faith.

As God does a work in our hearts, we may still occasionally battle with the desires of our unrighteous flesh, but as we grow in our relationship with our Father, the righteousness of God will manifest itself in our lives.

We will bear the Spiritual fruit of righteousness in our lives. As we continue (which is what the word "abide" means) in Him, our desire for the works of unrighteousness will decrease, as He increases in our lives.

Righteousness is a gift from God. As a Gift, it is intended to be put to use by the one to whom it was bestowed.

Rom 5:17 For if by one man's offence death reigned by one; much more they which receive abundance of grace and of the gift of righteousness shall reign in life by one, Jesus Christ.

We are given the ability through Jesus to reign over our natural inclination to sin. There are many teachers who corrupt the Word of God, and say that is not possible, but the truth is we can walk in the righteousness that has been given us through Jesus Christ. You are an over comer if you are in Christ.

1Jn 3:19 And hereby we know that we are of the truth, and shall assure our hearts before him.
20 For if our heart condemn us, God is greater than our heart, and knoweth all things.
21 Beloved, if our heart condemn us not, then have we confidence toward God.
22 And whatsoever we ask, we receive of him, because we keep his commandments, and do those things that are pleasing in his sight.
23 And this is his commandment, That we should believe on the name of his Son Jesus Christ, and love one another, as he gave us commandment.
24 And he that keepeth his commandments dwelleth in him, and he in him. And hereby we know that he abideth in us, by the Spirit which he hath given us.

Mat 1:21 And she shall bring forth a son, and thou shalt call his name JESUS: for he shall save his people from their sins.

Cult watch

1. "I am just a sinner saved by grace" is nowhere to be found in the Word of God.

The Christian was once a sinner, given over to the lusts of the flesh, bound by addiction and uncontrollable urges. But now through the Grace of God, the Christian is a saint of God, a holy man or woman of God who strives to live his or her life no longer under the dominion of sin. As they continue in their obedience to the Word of God, they become more and more like their Savior. Sin no longer has the hold over us like it once used to. Those who once were habitual liars no longer habitually lie because it is not in their nature any longer. This applies to all aspects of the Christian walk.

1 John is a tough book for those who want to hold on to their sin-justifying doctrine. 1 Jn 3: 7 and 8 seems especially harsh to the one who struggles against sin.

1 JN 3:7 Little children, let no man deceive you: he that doeth righteousness is righteous, even as he is righteous.
8 He that committeth sin is of the devil; for the devil sinneth from the beginning. For this purpose the Son of God was manifested, that he might destroy the works of the devil.

This passage opens with "let no man decieve you". Some say you cannot be saved from sin in this life. Yet Jesus' very name was given Him because it was declared that He would save His people from their sin.

Some deceivers say once you say the "sinner's prayer" you are adopted into the family of God, and it doesn't matter if you sin, because you are just a sinner saved by Grace. But the scripture here says let no man deceive you. He that commits sin is of the devil.

There are some who would teach that a person who is striving to walk in obedience to the Word of God is trying to earn his or her salvation. But the true disciple of Christ will want to be more and more like Christ. The word "committeth" speaks of a person who is given over to the indulgence of sin in their life. It is what you do. It is in your nature to sin[1]. But if you are a child of God, it is no longer your nature to sin. Though you may find yourself sinning, your desire will to have victory over it, not to wallow in it.

Rom 6:13 Neither yield ye your members as instruments of unrighteousness unto sin: but yield yourselves unto God, as those that are alive from the dead, and your members as instruments of righteousness unto God.
14 For sin shall not have dominion over you: for ye are not under the law, but under grace.

15 What then? shall we sin, because we are not under the law, but under grace? God forbid.
16 Know ye not, that to whom ye yield yourselves servants to obey, his servants ye are to whom ye obey; whether of sin unto death, or of obedience unto righteousness?
17 But God be thanked, that ye were the servants of sin, but ye have obeyed from the heart that form of doctrine which was delivered you.
18 Being then made free from sin, ye became the servants of righteousness.
19 I speak after the manner of men because of the infirmity of your flesh: for as ye have yielded your members servants to uncleanness and to iniquity unto iniquity; even so now yield your members servants to righteousness unto holiness.
20 For when ye were the servants of sin, ye were free from righteousness.
21 What fruit had ye then in those things whereof ye are now ashamed? for the end of those things is death.
22 But now being made free from sin, and become servants to God, ye have your fruit unto holiness, and the end everlasting life.
23 For the wages of sin is death; but the gift of God is eternal life through Jesus Christ our Lord.

Faith and obedience walk hand in hand.

If we truly believe in God, we will want to be obedient to Him. As we walk in faith toward God, we will be obedient, and His Righteousness will manifest itself in us.

Rom 1:17 For therein is the righteousness of God revealed from faith to faith: as it is written, The just shall live by faith.

Our own righteousness will get us nowhere in our walk with God. It is God Who has instilled in us the understanding of how we need to walk toward Him. It is God's Righteousness that the Born again Christian walks in, not his own.

Self Righteousness fosters pride. If we actually understand that it is God's Righteousness which works in us, we will have no room for pride in our hearts.

WITHOUT FAITH, IT IS IMPOSSIBLE TO PLEASE HIM, BECAUSE HE THAT COMES TO HIM MUST BELIEVE THAT HE IS (OUR RIGHTEOUSNESS, JEHOVAH TSIDKENU), AND THAT HE IS A REWARDER OF THOSE WHO DILIGENTLY SEEK HIM.

GOD ALMIGHTY
ELSHADDAI

GOD ALMIGHTY
EL-SHADDAI

Gen 17:1 And when Abram was ninety years old and nine, the LORD appeared to Abram, and said unto him, I *am* the Almighty God; walk before me, and be thou perfect.
2 And I will make my covenant between me and thee, and will multiply thee exceedingly.

We see His Glory when we believe that He is our Almighty God. (El Shaddai - Genesis 17:1-2). The Almighty God caused Sarai to conceive when it was impossible in a human perspective.

Genesis 35:11 shows that the Almighty God can cause a great nation to come from the seed of one man.

Gen 35:11 And God said unto him, I am God Almighty: be fruitful and multiply; a nation and a company of nations shall be of thee, and kings shall come out of thy loins;

Psalm 27 tells us that the Almighty God will protect us in time of trouble:

Jesus manifested the Name of "God Almighty" When He declared:

Ps 27: 4 One thing have I desired of the LORD, that will I seek after; that I may dwell in the house of the LORD all the days of my life, to behold the beauty of the LORD, and to inquire in his temple.
5 For in the time of trouble he shall hide me in his pavilion: in the secret of his tabernacle shall he hide me; he shall set me up upon a rock.
6 And now shall mine head be lifted up above mine enemies round about me: therefore will I offer in his tabernacle sacrifices of joy; I will sing, yea, I will sing praises unto the LORD.

Mat 28:18 And Jesus came and spake unto them, saying, All power is given unto me in heaven and in earth.

Notes

_____
_____
_____
_____
_____
_____
_____
_____
_____
_____
_____
_____
_____
_____
_____
_____
_____
_____
_____

When we have put all of our trust in Him, the Almighty God will be our refuge and our fortress.

Truly, the Word of God does not say in vain,

Ps 91:1 He that dwelleth in the secret place of the most High shall abide under the shadow of the Almighty.
2 I will say of the LORD, He is my refuge and my fortress: my God; in him will I trust.
3 Surely he shall deliver thee from the snare of the fowler, and from the noisome pestilence.
4 He shall cover thee with his feathers, and under his wings shalt thou trust: his truth shall be thy shield and buckler.

5 Thou shalt not be afraid for the terror by night; nor for the arrow that flieth by day;

6 Nor for the pestilence that walketh in darkness; nor for the destruction that wasteth at noonday.

7 A thousand shall fall at thy side, and ten thousand at thy right hand; but it shall not come nigh thee.

8 Only with thine eyes shalt thou behold and see the reward of the wicked.

9 Because thou hast made the LORD, which is my refuge, even the most High, thy habitation;

10 There shall no evil befall thee, neither shall any plague come nigh thy dwelling.

11 For he shall give his angels charge over thee, to keep thee in all thy ways.

12 They shall bear thee up in their hands, lest thou dash thy foot against a stone.

13 Thou shalt tread upon the lion and adder: the young lion and the dragon shalt thou trample under feet.

14 Because he hath set his love upon me, therefore will I deliver him: I will set him on high, because he hath known my name.

15 He shall call upon me, and I will answer him: I will be with him in trouble; I will deliver him, and honour him.

16 With long life will I satisfy him, and shew him my salvation.

Rom 8:31 What shall we then say to these things? If God be for us, who can be against us?

32 He that spared not his own Son, but delivered him up for us all, how shall he not with him also freely give us all things?

33 Who shall lay any thing to the charge of God's elect? It is God that justifieth.

34 Who is he that condemneth? It is Christ that died, yea rather, that is risen again, who is even at the right hand of God, who also maketh intercession for us.

35 Who shall separate us from the love of Christ? shall tribulation, or distress, or persecution, or famine, or nakedness, or peril, or sword?

36 As it is written, For thy sake we are killed all the day long; we are accounted as sheep for the slaughter.

37 Nay, in all these things we are more than conquerors through him that loved us.

38 For I am persuaded, that neither death, nor life, nor angels, nor principalities, nor powers, nor things present, nor things to come,

39 Nor height, nor depth, nor any other creature, shall be able to separate us from the love of God, which is in Christ Jesus our Lord.

EL-ELYON
MOST HIGH GOD

Gen 14:18 And Melchizedek king of Salem brought forth bread and wine: and he *was* the priest of the most high God.
19 And he blessed him, and said, Blessed *be* Abram of the most high God, possessor of heaven and earth:
20 And blessed be the most high God, which hath delivered thine enemies into thy hand. And he gave him tithes of all.

Jesus manifested the Glory of God when He walked in complete submission to the Father, and has recieved a Name above every Name, which would make Him El Elyon

Php 2:8 And being found in fashion as a man, he humbled himself, and became obedient unto death, even the death of the cross.
9 Wherefore God also hath highly exalted him, and given him a name which is above every name:
10 That at the name of Jesus every knee should bow, of things in heaven, and things in earth, and things under the earth;
11 And that every tongue should confess that Jesus Christ is Lord, to the glory of God the Father.

Notes

_____
_____
_____
_____
_____
_____
_____
_____
_____
_____

WITHOUT FAITH, IT IS IMPOSSIBLE TO PLEASE HIM, BECAUSE HE THAT COMES TO HIM MUST BELIEVE THAT HIS IS (GOD ALMIGHTY- EL SHADDAI) AND THAT HE IS A REWARDER OF THOSE WHO DILIGENTLY SEEK HIM.

EL-ELYON
MOST HIGH GOD

We see His Glory manifested when we believe that He is (El Elyon, Gen 14:19) the Most High. He is the Possessor of the Heavens and the earth.

Ps 9:1 I will praise thee, O LORD, with my whole heart; I will shew forth all thy marvellous works.
2 I will be glad and rejoice in thee: I will sing praise to thy name, O thou most High.
3 When mine enemies are turned back, they shall fall and perish at thy presence.

We know that the Word of God says that our battle is not with flesh and blood, but it is a spiritual battle. We have overcome by the blood of the Lamb. The enemies of our soul will be turned back by the Most High God, Who possesses the heaven and the earth.

Ps 47:1 O clap your hands, all ye people; shout unto God with the voice of triumph.
2 For the LORD most high is terrible; he is a great King over all the earth.
3 He shall subdue the people under us, and the nations under our feet.
4 He shall choose our inheritance for us, the excellency of Jacob whom he loved. Selah.

The Most High God is not to be taken lightly. We are to walk according to and be obedient to His Will in our lives.

Ps 50:14 Offer unto God thanksgiving; and pay thy vows unto the most High:
15 And call upon me in the day of trouble: I will deliver thee, and thou shalt glorify me.

JEHOVAH QANNA
THE LORD IS JEALOUS

Exo 34:14 For thou shalt worship no other god: for the LORD, whose name is Jealous, is a jealous God:
15 Lest thou make a covenant with the inhabitants of the land, and they go a whoring after their gods, and do sacrifice unto their gods, and one call thee, and thou eat of his sacrifice;
16 And thou take of their daughters unto thy sons, and their daughters go a whoring after their gods, and make thy sons go a whoring after their gods.

Jesus demonstrated the Jealousness of God when he cleansed the temple:

Mat 21:12 And Jesus went into the temple of God, and cast out all them that sold and bought in the temple, and overthrew the tables of the moneychangers, and the seats of them that sold doves,
13 And said unto them, It is written, My house shall be called the house of prayer; but ye have made it a den of thieves.

Notes

_____
_____
_____
_____
_____
_____
_____
_____
_____
_____
_____
_____
_____
_____

16 But unto the wicked God saith, What hast thou to do to declare my statutes, or that thou shouldest take my covenant in thy mouth?
17 Seeing thou hatest instruction, and castest my words behind thee.
18 When thou sawest a thief, then thou consentedst with him, and hast been partaker with adulterers.
19 Thou givest thy mouth to evil, and thy tongue frameth deceit.
20 Thou sittest and speakest against thy brother; thou slanderest thine own mother's son.
21 These things hast thou done, and I kept silence; thou thoughtest that I was altogether such an one as thyself: but I will reprove thee, and set them in order before thine eyes.
22 Now consider this, ye that forget God, lest I tear you in pieces, and there be none to deliver.
23 Whoso offereth praise glorifieth me: and to him that ordereth his conversation aright will I shew the salvation of God.

WITHOUT FAITH, IT IS IMPOSSIBLE TO PLEASE HIM, BECAUSE HE THAT COMES TO HIM MUST BELIEVE THAT HE IS (EL-ELYON, THE MOST HIGH GOD), AND THAT HE IS A REWARDER OF THOSE WHO DILIGENTLY SEEK HIM.

JEHOVAH QANNA
THE LORD IS JEALOUS

Since He is the Most High God, we are not to have any gods before Him. Worldliness, covetousness, materialism, lust, food, pride, drunkenness, family, friends...all these can be gods that we have deemed more important than the Most High God. We can see His Glory manifested when we believe that He is (Jehovah Qanna - Exodus 34:14) a Jealous God.

The New Testament parallel to this passage is found in Romans 12:1-2:

Rom 12:1 I beseech you therefore, brethren, by the mercies of God, that ye present your bodies a living sacrifice, holy, acceptable unto God, which is your reasonable service.
2 And be not conformed to this world: but be ye transformed by the renewing of your mind, that ye may prove what is that good, and acceptable, and perfect, will of God.

And...

2 Cor 6: 14 Be ye not unequally yoked together with unbelievers: for what fellowship hath righteousness with unrighteousness? and what communion hath light with darkness?
15 And what concord hath Christ with Belial? or what part hath he that believeth with an infidel?
16 And what agreement hath the temple of God with idols? for ye are the temple of the living God; as God hath said, I will dwell in them, and walk in them; and I will be their God, and they shall be my people.
17 Wherefore come out from among them, and be ye separate, saith the Lord, and touch not the unclean thing; and I will receive you,
18 And will be a Father unto you, and ye shall be my sons and daughters, saith the Lord Almighty.

There is much compromise in the church today. Worldliness and pursuit after the things of the world abounds among those who are supposed to be separate from the world, and there are many false teachers who encourage this type of lifestyle. They teach the Christians to believe that they can be recipients of the blessings of God without obedience to Him and His Word. This worldliness that has crept into many churches today is teaching Christians to be disobedient to the very Word of God.

Deut 4:23 Take heed unto yourselves, lest ye forget the covenant of the LORD your God, which he made with you, and make you a graven image, or the likeness of anything, which the LORD thy God hath forbidden thee.
24 For the LORD thy God is a consuming fire, even a jealous God.
25 When thou shalt beget children, and children's children, and ye shall have remained long in the land, and shall corrupt yourselves, and make a graven image, or the likeness of any thing, and shall do evil in the sight of the LORD thy God, to provoke him to anger:
26 I call heaven and earth to witness against you this day, that ye shall soon utterly perish from off the land whereunto ye go over Jordan to possess it; ye shall not prolong your days upon it, but shall utterly be destroyed.
27 And the LORD shall scatter you among the nations, and ye shall be left few in number among the heathen, whither the LORD shall lead you.

28 And there ye shall serve gods, the work of men's hands, wood and stone, which neither see, nor hear, nor eat, nor smell.
29 But if from thence thou shalt seek the LORD thy God, thou shalt find him, if thou seek him with all thy heart and with all thy soul.
30 When thou art in tribulation, and all these things are come upon thee, even in the latter days, if thou turn to the LORD thy God, and shalt be obedient unto his voice;
31 (For the LORD thy God is a merciful God;) he will not forsake thee, neither destroy thee, nor forget the covenant of thy fathers which he sware unto them.

See what the first commandment was to Israel:

Deut 5:6 I am the LORD thy God, which brought thee out of the land of Egypt, from the house of bondage.
7 Thou shalt have none other gods before me.
8 Thou shalt not make thee any graven image, or any likeness of any thing that is in heaven above, or that is in the earth beneath, or that is in the waters beneath the earth:
9 Thou shalt not bow down thyself unto them, nor serve them: for I the LORD thy God am a jealous God, visiting the iniquity of the fathers upon the children unto the third and fourth generation of them that hate me,
10 And shewing mercy unto thousands of them that love me and keep my commandments.

The Most important thing In a Christian's walk is his or her relationship with God. This relationship will result in obedience and walking in His Righteousness. This is fulfilling the first and greatest commandment, which is to Love the Lord with all your, heart, with all your soul and all your mind (Matt 22:37).

The second most important thing is Glorifying His Holy Name to the world, and to further the Kingdom of God on this earth, and this is done through proclaiming His Reality to those who are still in darkness. This is fulfilling the second commandment, which is to love your neighbor as yourself. You don't want to go to hell... how can you be silent while those around you are heading to Hell?

If we are faithful in these two things, we won't have to worry about the blessings of the Lord, because they will overtake us.

WITHOUT FAITH, IT IS IMPOSSIBLE TO PLEASE HIM, BECAUSE HE THAT COMES TO HIM MUST BELIEVE THAT HE IS (JEHOVAH QANNA - THE

Notes

ABBA
FATHER

Gal 4: 6 And because ye are sons,
God hath sent forth the Spirit of his
Son into your hearts, crying, Abba,
Father.
7 Wherefore thou art no more a
servant, but a son; and if a son,
then an heir of God through Christ.

LORD IS JEALOUS), AND THAT HE IS A REWARDER OF THOSE WHO DILIGENTLY SEEK HIM.

ABBA
FATHER

We can see His Glory manifested when we believe that He is our Father, our Abba; when we make Him our all in all.

Abba is a term that slaves were forbidden to use in addressing the head of the family. According to "Vine's" dictionary of the Greek language, it *"approximates to a personal name, in contrast to 'Father' with which it is always joined in the New Testament. This is probably due to the fact that, abba having practically become a proper name, Greek-speaking Jews added the Greek word pater, "father," from the language they used.*

Abba is the word framed by the lips of infants, and betokens unreasoning trust; "father" expresses an intelligent apprehension of the relationship. The two together express the love and intelligent confidence of the child."

**Gal 4: 6 And because ye are sons, God hath sent forth the Spirit of his Son into your hearts, crying, Abba, Father.
7 Wherefore thou art no more a servant, but a son; and if a son, then an heir of God through Christ.**

Believing that He is our Father, we know that we can approach Him boldly concerning any petition, and He will hear us. As a loving Father Who has our best interests at heart, He will grant our wishes according to His Wisdom, and He will chasten us when we are disobedient. But this always results in our growth in Him.

The child most generally reflects what kind of parents he has:

Matt 5:44 But I say unto you, Love your enemies, bless them that curse you, do good to them that hate you, and pray for them which despitefully use you, and persecute you;
45 That ye may be the children of your Father which is in heaven: for he maketh his sun to rise on the evil and on the good, and sendeth rain on the just and on the unjust.
46 For if ye love them which love you, what reward have ye? do not even the publicans the same?
47 And if ye salute your brethren only, what do ye more than others? do not even the publicans so?
48 Be ye therefore perfect, even as your Father which is in heaven is perfect.

Our Heavenly Father is a Good Father. He has our best interests at heart.

Matt 7:9 Or what man is there of you, whom if his son ask bread, will he give him a stone?
10 Or if he ask a fish, will he give him a serpent?
11 If ye then, being evil, know how to give good gifts unto your children, how much more shall your Father which is in heaven give good things to them that ask him?
12 Therefore all things whatsoever ye would that men should do to you, do ye even so to them: for this is the law and the prophets.

WITHOUT FAITH, IT IS IMPOSSIBLE TO PLEASE GOD, BECAUSE HE THAT COMES TO HIM MUST BELIEVE THAT HE IS (OUR FATHER, ABBA) AND THAT HE IS A REWARDER OF THOSE WHO DILIGENTLY SEEK HIM.

When we really BELIEVE that He is Who He says He is, we see His Glory manifested in our lives, and we become eyewitnesses of His Majesty, or His Glory, just as the disciples were in the beginning.

2 Pet 1:16 For we have not followed cunningly devised fables, when we made known unto you the power and coming of our Lord Jesus Christ, but were eyewitnesses of his majesty.
17 For he received from God the Father honour and glory, when there came such a voice to him from the excellent glory, This is my beloved Son, in whom I am well pleased. (KJV)

In John 11, we see an account where Jesus resurrected a dead man. There is an important point here that should be noticed by the Christian, and that is the Trust that Jesus had for His Father:

Joh 11:37 And some of them said, Could not this man, which opened the eyes of the blind, have caused that even this man should not have died?
38 Jesus therefore again groaning in himself cometh to the grave. It was a cave, and a stone lay upon it.
39 Jesus said, Take ye away the stone. Martha, the sister of him that was dead, saith unto him, Lord, by this time he stinketh: for he hath been dead four days.
40 Jesus saith unto her, Said I not unto thee, that, if thou wouldest believe, thou shouldest see the glory of God?
41 Then they took away the stone from the place where the dead was laid. And Jesus lifted up his eyes, and said, Father, I thank thee that thou hast heard me.
42 And I knew that thou hearest me always: but because of the people which stand by I said it, that they may believe that thou hast sent me.
43 And when he thus had spoken, he cried with a loud voice, Lazarus, come forth.
44 And he that was dead came forth, bound hand and foot with graveclothes: and his face was bound about with a napkin. Jesus saith unto them, Loose him, and let him go.
45 Then many of the Jews which came to Mary, and had seen the things which Jesus did, believed on him.

Notice that in verse 42, Jesus said "I knew that thou hearest me always..." Jesus is our example of faith. He knew that the Father heard Him always.

What would happen if Christians had that kind of knowledge? You can have that confidence if you resolve to walk in obedience toward Him as He did toward the Father. Jesus tells us what would happen if we had that confidence.

John 14: 12 Verily, verily, I say unto you, He that believeth on me, the works that I do shall he do also; and greater works than these shall he do; because I go unto my Father.
13 And whatsoever ye shall ask in my name, that will I do, that the Father may be glorified in the Son.
14 If ye shall ask any thing in my name, I will do it. (KJV)

Faith, as Jesus was teaching it, is not a source of power for the person who wants to do magic tricks to impress people. Jesus was expressing the fact that with God, nothing is impossible. There is no situation that a person could find themselves in, that God couldn't deliver them from.

The key is BELIEVING. Not just saying "I believe", but actually KNOWING that it is true, and living a life that expresses that faith.

There are schools of thought today that purport to teach faith principles, but which are actually Christianizing New Age teachings. WE ARE NOT TO HAVE FAITH IN OUR FAITH. WE ARE TO HAVE FAITH IN THE ONE WHO IS THE AUTHOR AND THE FINISHER OF OUR FAITH!

TRUE FAITH IS BELIEVING THAT GOD IS ALL THAT HE SAYS HE IS.

1. WRITE THE NAMES OF GOD AND WHAT THEY MEAN TO YOU IN YOUR PRESENT SITUATION:

_____
_____
_____
_____
_____
_____
_____
_____
_____
_____
_____
_____
_____
_____
_____
_____
_____
_____
_____
_____
_____
_____
_____
_____
_____
_____
_____
_____

BASIC DOCTRINES

FAITH TOWARD GOD

LESSON 6

PRAYING IN FAITH

Heb 6:1 Therefore leaving the principles of the doctrine of Christ, let us go on unto perfection; not laying again the foundation of repentance from dead works, and of faith toward God,
2 Of the doctrine of baptisms, and of laying on of hands, and of resurrection of the dead, and of eternal judgment.

FAITH TO PRAY

Nelson's Bible dictionary defines FAITH in this way:

FAITH A belief in or confident attitude toward God, involving commitment to His will for one's life.

This definition seems to fit Jesus' Words in Mark 11:

Mark 11:22 And Jesus answering saith unto them, Have faith in God.
23 For verily I say unto you, That whosoever shall say unto this mountain, Be thou removed, and be thou cast into the sea; and shall not doubt in his heart, but shall believe that those things which he saith shall come to pass; he shall have whatsoever he saith.
24 Therefore I say unto you, What things soever ye desire, when ye pray, believe that ye receive them, and ye shall have them.
25 And when ye stand praying, forgive, if ye have ought against any: that your Father also which is in heaven may forgive you your trespasses.
26 But if ye do not forgive, neither will your Father which is in heaven forgive your trespasses. (KJV)

We see a condition to answered prayer. Jesus said when you stand praying (asking the Father for that which you desire), you are to have a forgiving heart to all.

Luke 17:3 Take heed to yourselves: If thy brother trespass against thee, rebuke him; and if he repent, forgive him.
4 And if he trespass against thee seven times in a day, and seven times in a day turn again to thee, saying, I repent; thou shalt forgive him.

The Lord's disciples thought this was a hard requirement that the Lord was putting on them, and they asked Him to "increase their faith" so they could obey His Words. What Jesus told them next is a revealing statement.

We CAN walk in forgiveness...it is a choice that each one of us have to make. Jesus said that if we have faith as a grain of mustard seed, we could say to a tree or a mountain to be removed, and it would be removed.

Forgiveness doesn't require faith...it requires an obedient servant's heart.

Luke 17:5 And the apostles said unto the Lord, Increase our faith.
6 And the Lord said, If ye had faith as a grain of mustard seed, ye might say unto this sycamine tree, Be thou plucked up by the root, and be thou planted in the sea; and it should obey you.
7 But which of you, having a servant plowing or feeding cattle, will say unto him by and by, when he is come from the field, Go and sit down to meat?
8 And will not rather say unto him, Make ready wherewith I may sup, and gird thyself, and serve me, till I have eaten and drunken; and afterward thou shalt eat and drink?
9 Doth he thank that servant because he did the things that were commanded him? I trow not.
10 So likewise ye, when ye shall have done all those things which are commanded you, say, We are unprofitable servants: we have done that which was our duty to do. (KJV)

It is our duty to do what the Word of God instructs us to do. As we have seen, Repentance and Faith go hand in hand with one another. Obedience to the Word of God is the result of a repentant heart. If we ask anything in line with and in obedience to His Will, it will be given to us.

But the condition is obvious. Believing the Word, Abiding in Christ, Living in Truth. If we are walking according to these conditions, then the things we desire will not be contrary to His Will.

We will look at some Biblical examples of prayers of faith, and we will see that a prayer of Faith will not demand things for our own selfish gain, because a child of God has been instructed to deny himself.

Mar 8:34 And when he had called the people unto him with his disciples also, he said unto them, Whosoever will come after me, let him deny himself, and take up his cross, and follow me.

Through a contextual study of the Word of God, we can see that a prayer of faith will not be about material possessions for ones' own creature comforts, because we have been told to lay up treasures in the Kingdom of God, rather than treasures on earth where moth and rust corrupt and thieves break in to steal.

Matt 6: 19 Lay not up for yourselves treasures upon earth, where moth and rust doth corrupt, and where thieves break through and steal:
20 But lay up for yourselves treasures in heaven, where neither moth nor rust doth corrupt, and where thieves do not break through nor steal:
21 For where your treasure is, there will your heart be also.

A prayer of faith will be prayed more often for others than for ourselves.

Gal 6:2 Bear ye one another's burdens, and so fulfil the law of Christ.

A prayer of faith will be about souls and furthering the Kingdom of God. Jesus and the apostles were our examples. Let us see how they prayed.

1) They prayed for more laborers in the harvest field.

Matt 9:37 Then saith he unto his disciples, The harvest truly is plenteous, but the labourers are few;
38 Pray ye therefore the Lord of the harvest, that he will send forth labourers into his harvest

Why were they instructed to pray for laborers? _____
_____

2) They prayed to see people delivered from demonic strongholds.

Matt 17:21 Howbeit this kind goeth not out but by prayer and fasting.

Fasting is a practice of denying the cravings of the flesh. It enables one to be more sensitive to the leading of the Holy Spirit in various situaltions.

3) They prayed that people would be healed.

Acts 9:40 But Peter put them all forth, and kneeled down, and prayed; and turning him to the body said, Tabitha, arise. And she opened her eyes: and when she saw Peter, she sat up.
41 And he gave her his hand, and lifted her up, and when he had called the saints and widows, presented her alive.

42 And it was known throughout all Joppa; and many believed in the Lord.

What was the result of answered prayers to healing (Vs 42)? _____
_____

4) They prayed for those who are in authority, and others.

1 Tim 2:1 I exhort therefore, that, first of all, supplications, prayers, intercessions, and giving of thanks, be made for all men;
2 For kings, and for all that are in authority; that we may lead a quiet and peaceable life in all godliness and honesty.
3 For this is good and acceptable in the sight of God our Saviour;
4 Who will have all men to be saved, and to come unto the knowledge of the truth.

According to verse two, what is the end goal of praying for all who are in authority?
_____
_____

5) Jesus instructed His disciples to pray for those who treat us wrong.

Matt 6:12 And forgive us our debts, as we forgive our debtors.

Luke 6:28 Bless them that curse you, and pray for them which despitefully use you.

Why would we pray for those who do us wrong?

_____
_____

Look up Matthew 5:43 through 48, and explain Jesus reasoning behind this _____
_____
_____
_____

6) **They prayed that others would receive the Holy Spirit:**

Acts 8: 14 Now when the apostles which were at Jerusalem heard that Samaria had received the word of God, they sent unto them Peter and John:

15 Who, when they were come down, prayed for them, that they might receive the Holy Ghost:

According to Jesus, what is the primary purpose of the Baptism of the Holy Spirit? (Acts 1:8) _____

_____

_____

7) They prayed for each other, that they would become all that Christ wanted them to become

Eph 1:16 Cease not to give thanks for you, making mention of you in my prayers;
17 That the God of our Lord Jesus Christ, the Father of glory, may give unto you the spirit of wisdom and revelation in the knowledge of him:
18 The eyes of your understanding being enlightened; that ye may know what is the hope of his calling, and what the riches of the glory of his inheritance in the saints,
19 And what is the exceeding greatness of his power to us-ward who believe, according to the working of his mighty power,
20 Which he wrought in Christ, when he raised him from the dead, and set him at his own right hand in the heavenly places,
21 Far above all principality, and power, and might, and dominion, and every name that is named, not only in this world, but also in that which is to come:
22 And hath put all things under his feet, and gave him to be the head over all things to the church,
23 Which is his body, the fulness of him that filleth all in all.

Eph 6: 17 And take the helmet of salvation, and the sword of the Spirit, which is the word of God:
18 Praying always with all prayer and supplication in the Spirit, and watching thereunto with all perseverance and supplication for all saints;
19 And for me, that utterance may be given unto me, that I may open my mouth boldly, to make known the mystery of the gospel,

Phil 1:9 And this I pray, that your love may abound yet more and more in knowledge and in all judgment;
10 That ye may approve things that are excellent; that ye may be sincere and without offence till the day of Christ;
11 Being filled with the fruits of righteousness, which are by Jesus Christ, unto the glory and praise of God.

Col 1:9 For this cause we also, since the day we heard it, do not cease to pray for you, and to desire that ye might be filled with the knowledge of his will in all wisdom and spiritual understanding;
10 That ye might walk worthy of the Lord unto all pleasing, being fruitful in every good work, and increasing in the knowledge of God;
11 Strengthened with all might, according to his glorious power, unto all patience and longsuffering with joyfulness;

1Thes 5:23 And the very God of peace sanctify you wholly; and I pray God your whole spirit and soul and body be preserved blameless unto the coming of our Lord Jesus Christ.

II Th 1: 11 Wherefore also we pray always for you, that our God would count you worthy of this calling, and fulfil all the good pleasure of his goodness, and the work of faith with power:
12 That the name of our Lord Jesus Christ may be glorified in you, and ye in him, according to the grace of our God and the Lord Jesus Christ.

We can see a pattern in those instances where Christians *pray for themselves*:

1) They prayed for boldness to proclaim the Word of God.

Acts 4:29 And now, Lord, behold their threatenings: and grant unto thy servants, that with all boldness they may speak thy word,

2) They prayed that the Lord would be glorified in their ministry.

Acts 4:30 By stretching forth thine hand to heal; and that signs and wonders may be done by the name of thy holy child Jesus. 31 And when they had prayed, the place was shaken where they were assembled together; and they were all filled with the Holy Ghost, and they spake the word of God with boldness.

3) We are to pray that we won't enter into temptation.

Matt 6: 13 And lead us not into temptation, but deliver us from evil: For thine is the kingdom, and the power, and the glory, for ever. Amen.

131

Mar 11:23 For verily I say unto you, That whosoever shall say unto this mountain, Be thou removed, and be thou cast into the sea; and shall not doubt in his heart, but shall believe that those things which he saith shall come to pass; he shall have whatsoever he saith.
24 Therefore I say unto you, What things soever ye desire, when ye pray, believe that ye receive them, and ye shall have them.
25 And when ye stand praying, forgive, if ye have ought against any: that your Father also which is in heaven may forgive you your trespasses.
26 But if ye do not forgive, neither will your Father which is in heaven forgive your trespasses.

Notes

_____
_____
_____
_____
_____
_____
_____
_____
_____
_____
_____
_____
_____
_____
_____
_____

Matt 26:41 Watch and pray, that ye enter not into temptation: the spirit indeed is willing, but the flesh is weak.

Luke 21:36 Watch ye therefore, and pray always, that ye may be accounted worthy to escape all these things that shall come to pass, and to stand before the Son of man.

4) They prayed for wisdom in appointing others to ministry:

Acts 1:23 And they appointed two, Joseph called Barsabas, who was surnamed Justus, and Matthias.
24 And they prayed, and said, Thou, Lord, which knowest the hearts of all men, shew whether of these two thou hast chosen,
25 That he may take part of this ministry and apostleship, from which Judas by transgression fell, that he might go to his own place.
26 And they gave forth their lots; and the lot fell upon Matthias; and he was numbered with the eleven apostles.

5) They prayed that God's Will would be done in their lives:

Matt 6: 10 Thy kingdom come. Thy will be done in earth, as it is in heaven.

6) Even in the face of the greatest adversity, Jesus prayed that the Father's Will would be done in His Life:

Matt 26:39 And he went a little further, and fell on his face, and prayed, saying, O my Father, if it be possible, let this cup pass from me: nevertheless not as I will, but as thou wilt.

In the model of prayer that the Lord gave us, we see we are to pray for our daily bread. This means that we are not to worry about tomorrow's provision. The Lord's provision today is sufficient for our needs.

We are to pray with a clear conscience.

1 Tim 2:8 I will therefore that men pray every where, lifting up holy hands, without wrath and doubting.

Throughout the gospel accounts, we can see that Jesus' life was a life of prayer:

Mark 1:35 And in the morning, rising up a great while before day, he went out, and departed into a solitary place, and there prayed.

Mark 6:46 And when he had sent them away, he departed into a mountain to pray.

Luke 5:16 And he withdrew himself into the wilderness, and prayed.

Luke 6:12 And it came to pass in those days, that he went out into a mountain to pray, and continued all night in prayer to God.

Luke 9:28 And it came to pass about an eight days after these sayings, he took Peter and John and James, and went up into a mountain to pray.

Jesus taught us to pray with expectancy.

Luke 11:1 And it came to pass, that, as he was praying in a certain place, when he ceased, one of his disciples said unto him, Lord, teach us to pray, as John also taught his disciples.
2 And he said unto them, When ye pray, say, Our Father which art in heaven, Hallowed be thy name. Thy kingdom come. Thy will be done, as in heaven, so in earth.
3 Give us day by day our daily bread.
4 And forgive us our sins; for we also forgive every one that is indebted to us. And lead us not into temptation; but deliver us from evil.
5 And he said unto them, Which of you shall have a friend, and shall go unto him at midnight, and say unto him, Friend, lend me three loaves;
6 For a friend of mine in his journey is come to me, and I have nothing to set before him?
7 And he from within shall answer and say, Trouble me not: the door is now shut, and my children are with me in bed; I cannot rise and give thee.
8 I say unto you, Though he will not rise and give him, because he is his friend, yet because of his importunity he will rise and give him as many as he needeth.
9 And I say unto you, Ask, and it shall be given you; seek, and ye shall find; knock, and it shall be opened unto you.
10 For every one that asketh receiveth; and he that seeketh findeth; and to him that knocketh it shall be opened.

11 If a son shall ask bread of any of you that is a father, will he give him a stone? or if he ask a fish, will he for a fish give him a serpent?
12 Or if he shall ask an egg, will he offer him a scorpion?
13 If ye then, being evil, know how to give good gifts unto your children: how much more shall your heavenly Father give the Holy Spirit to them that ask him?

The parallel verse to the passage quoted above is in Matthew 7:11, where Jesus says that the Father in Heaven will give good things to them that ask Him:

Matt 7:11 If ye then, being evil, know how to give good gifts unto your children, how much more shall your Father which is in heaven give good things to them that ask him?

While there are some who would interpret Jesus' comment here concerning good things as material things, we can see that He is talking about spiritual things, or things that we need to get by in life. The "good things" must be measured in the light of the One who is the Giver of those good things. Remember, Jesus taught us not to lay up treasures on earth, where moth and rust corrupt.

1 Corinthians 10: 24 tells us that our focus should be on seeing other's wealth be realized, and not our own. As we put other's needs before ours, God will take care of our needs. There is a principle of sowing and reaping.

1 Cor 10:24 Let no man seek his own, but every man another's wealth.

Luke 18:1 And he spake a parable unto them to this end, that men ought always to pray, and not to faint;
2 Saying, There was in a city a judge, which feared not God, neither regarded man:
3 And there was a widow in that city; and she came unto him, saying, Avenge me of mine adversary.
4 And he would not for a while: but afterward he said within himself, Though I fear not God, nor regard man;
5 Yet because this widow troubleth me, I will avenge her, lest by her continual coming she weary me.
6 And the Lord said, Hear what the unjust judge saith.
7 And shall not God avenge his own elect, which cry day and night unto him, though he bear long with them?
8 I tell you that he will avenge them speedily. Nevertheless when the Son of man cometh, shall he find faith on the earth?

Jesus prayed on behalf of others, knowing His prayers would be answered:

According to <Hebrews 11>, faith was already present in the experience of many people in the Old Testament as a key element of their spiritual lives. In this chapter, the various heroes of the Old Testament (Abel, Enoch, Noah, Abraham, Sarah, Isaac, Jacob, Joseph, and Moses) are described as living by faith. In addition, the Old Testament itself makes the same point. Abraham "believed in the Lord" <Gen. 15:6>; the Israelites "believed" <Ex. 4:31; 14:31>; and the prophet Habakkuk taught that "the just shall live by his faith" <Hab. 2:4>.

In the New Testament, "faith" covers various levels of personal commitment. Mere intellectual agreement to a truth is illustrated in <James 2:19>, where even demons are said to believe that there is one God. Obviously, however, they are not saved by this type of belief. Genuine saving faith is a personal attachment to Christ, best thought of as a combination of two ideas-- reliance on Christ and commitment to Him. Saving faith involves personally depending on the finished work of Christ's sacrifice as the only basis for forgiveness of sin and entrance into heaven. But saving faith is also a personal commitment of one's life to following Christ in obedience to His commands: "I know whom I have believed and am persuaded that He is able to keep what I have committed to Him until that Day" <2 Tim. 1:12>.

Faith is part of the Christian life from beginning to end. As the instrument by which the gift of

Luke 22:31 And the Lord said, Simon, Simon, behold, Satan hath desired to have you, that he may sift you as wheat:
32 But I have prayed for thee, that thy faith fail not: and when thou art converted, strengthen thy brethren.

Jesus sought the good of others, over His own good. He instructed the disciples that if they ask anything in His Name, it would be done for them. Yet we know that what we asked would be in accordance to the Will of God, and not according to our selfishness.

John 14:10 Believest thou not that I am in the Father, and the Father in me? the words that I speak unto you I speak not of myself: but the Father that dwelleth in me, he doeth the works.
11 Believe me that I am in the Father, and the Father in me: or else believe me for the very works' sake.
12 Verily, verily, I say unto you, He that believeth on me, the works that I do shall he do also; and greater works than these shall he do; because I go unto my Father.
13 And whatsoever ye shall ask in my name, that will I do, that the Father may be glorified in the Son.
14 If ye shall ask any thing in my name, I will do it.
15 If ye love me, keep my commandments.
16 And I will pray the Father, and he shall give you another Comforter, that he may abide with you for ever;
17 Even the Spirit of truth; whom the world cannot receive, because it seeth him not, neither knoweth him: but ye know him; for he dwelleth with you, and shall be in you.
18 I will not leave you comfortless: I will come to you.

See how Jesus prayed to the Father for His disciples:

John 17:1 These words spake Jesus, and lifted up his eyes to heaven, and said, Father, the hour is

come; glorify thy Son, that thy Son also may glorify thee:

2 As thou hast given him power over all flesh, that he should give eternal life to as many as thou hast given him.

3 And this is life eternal, that they might know thee the only true God, and Jesus Christ, whom thou hast sent.

4 I have glorified thee on the earth: I have finished the work which thou gavest me to do.

5 And now, O Father, glorify thou me with thine own self with the glory which I had with thee before the world was.

6 I have manifested thy name unto the men which thou gavest me out of the world: thine they were, and thou gavest them me; and they have kept thy word.

7 Now they have known that all things whatsoever thou hast given me are of thee.

8 For I have given unto them the words which thou gavest me; and they have received them, and have known surely that I came out from thee, and they have believed that thou didst send me.

9 I pray for them: I pray not for the world, but for them which thou hast given me; for they are thine.

10 And all mine are thine, and thine are mine; and I am glorified in them.

11 And now I am no more in the world, but these are in the world, and I come to thee. Holy Father, keep through thine own name those whom thou hast given me, that they may be one, as we are.

12 While I was with them in the world, I kept them in thy name: those that thou gavest me I have kept, and none of them is lost, but the son of perdition; that the scripture might be fulfilled.

13 And now come I to thee; and these things I speak in the world, that they might have my joy fulfilled in themselves.

14 I have given them thy word; and the world hath hated them, because they are not of the world, even as I am not of the world.

15 I pray not that thou shouldest take them out of the world, but that thou shouldest keep them from the evil.

16 They are not of the world, even as I am not of the world.

17 Sanctify them through thy truth: thy word is truth.

18 As thou hast sent me into the world, even so have I also sent them into the world.

19 And for their sakes I sanctify myself, that they also might be sanctified through the truth.

20 Neither pray I for these alone, but for them also which shall believe on me through their word;

21 That they all may be one; as thou, Father, art in me, and I in thee, that they also may be one in us: that the world may believe that thou hast sent me.

salvation is received <Eph. 2:8-9>, faith is thus distinct from the basis of salvation, which is grace, and and from the outworking of salvation, which is good works. The apostle Paul declared that salvation is through faith, not through keeping the works of the law <Eph. 2:8,9>.

Finally, in the New Testament, faith can refer to the teachings of the Bible, the faith which was once for all delivered to the saints <Jude 3>. In modern times, faith has been weakened in meaning so that some people use it to mean self-confidence. But in the Bible, true faith is confidence in God or Christ, not in oneself.   (from Nelson's Illustrated Bible Dictionary)(Copyright (C) 1986, Thomas Nelson Publishers)

Notes

_____
_____
_____
_____
_____
_____
_____
_____
_____
_____
_____
_____
_____
_____
_____
_____
_____
_____

22 And the glory which thou gavest me I have given them; that they may be one, even as we are one:
23 I in them, and thou in me, that they may be made perfect in one; and that the world may know that thou hast sent me, and hast loved them, as thou hast loved me.
24 Father, I will that they also, whom thou hast given me, be with me where I am; that they may behold my glory, which thou hast given me: for thou lovedst me before the foundation of the world.
25 O righteous Father, the world hath not known thee: but I have known thee, and these have known that thou hast sent me.
25 And I have declared unto them thy name, and will declare it: that the love wherewith thou hast loved me may be in them, and I in them. (KJV)

In this prayer, we can see that Jesus was concerned about the furtherance and the success of the disciple's ministry. Here He was, on the brink of the darkest hour of His Life, and instead of praying for His own well being, He prayed for their well being.

Also consider the fact that Jesus knew His Father, and that all things that He did was in Faith toward God. Jesus KNEW the Father would hear and Answer His prayer.

1) WHAT IS ONE CONDITION TO ANSWERED PRAYER ACCORDING TO MARK 11:25?

_____

_____

2) IT DOESN'T TAKE _____ TO FORGIVE SOMEONE.

3) WHAT IS ANOTHER CONDITION TO ANSWERED PRAYER ACCORDING TO 1 JOHN 5:14-

15?_____

4) A PRAYER OF FAITH SHOULD BE FOCUSED MORE ON _____
THAN _____

5) LIST SOME BIBLICAL EXAMPLES OF PRAYERS THAT WERE LIFTED UP TO
GOD

_____

6) WHAT DOES 1 CORINTHIANS 10:24 MEAN TO YOU?

_____

LESSON 7
BAPTISMS

WATER BAPTISM

Heb 6:1 Therefore leaving the principles of the doctrine of Christ, let us go on unto perfection; not laying again the foundation of repentance from dead works, and of faith toward God,
2 Of the doctrine of baptisms, and of laying on of hands, and of resurrection of the dead, and of eternal judgment.

WATER BAPTISM AND IT'S SIGNIFICANCE

Matt 3:1 In those days came John the Baptist, preaching in the wilderness of Judaea,
2 And saying, Repent ye: for the kingdom of heaven is at hand.
3 For this is he that was spoken of by the prophet Esaias, saying, The voice of one crying in the wilderness, Prepare ye the way of the Lord, make his paths straight.
4 And the same John had his raiment of camel's hair, and a leathern girdle about his loins; and his meat was locusts and wild honey.
5 Then went out to him Jerusalem, and all Judaea, and all the region round about Jordan,
6 And were baptized of him in Jordan, confessing their sins. (KJV)

Baptism wasn't merely a new thing that was instituted in the New Testament.

According to the Jewish Encyclopedia, BAPTISM was required of converts (Proselytes) to Judaism.

In some circles, baptism is frequently thought of as an act by which the believer enters the fellowship of the church through membership, but in actuality it is an act by which one enters into covenant with the Living God.

From the Jewish Encyclopedia:

"Immersion (tevilah) is a religious act specifically undertaken to achieve the ritual purity required for participation in certain religious ceremonials. Thus not only did the High Priest immerse himself before conducting the service on the Day of Atonement, but each priest who participated in the Temple service was also required to undergo immersion, beside washing his hands and feet from the laver. [ABLUTION]

"The biblical statement "he shall bathe his flesh in water" (Lev. 15:16) and its variants refer to total immersion of the body in a ritual bath (MIKVEH) or flowing river water. Ritual immersion alone is effective in ridding one of ritual impurity. In all cases of the immersion, the body must be scrupulously clean prior to the immersion. In modern Jewish Orthodox practice, the only manditory bodily immersion is that of the menstruating woman (NIDDAH), and the Proselyte. [IMMERSION]

To understand baptism, we need to understand the roots of this doctrine.

We can look at a number of passages to see that baptism is a form of cleansing.

We see that Naaman, a leper, underwent a sort of baptism to be cleansed of his leprosy:

II Ki 5:9 So Naaman came with his horses and with his chariot, and stood at the door of the house of Elisha.
10 And Elisha sent a messenger unto him, saying, Go and wash in Jordan seven times, and thy flesh shall come again to thee, and thou shalt be clean.
11 But Naaman was wroth, and went away, and said, Behold, I thought, He will surely come out to me, and stand, and call on the name of the LORD his God, and strike his hand over the place, and recover the leper.
12 Are not Abana and Pharpar, rivers of Damascus, better than all the waters of Israel? may I not wash in them, and be clean? So he turned and went away in a rage.
13 And his servants came near, and spake unto him, and said, My father, if the prophet had bid thee do some great thing, wouldest thou not have done it? how much rather then, when he saith to thee, Wash, and be clean?
14 Then went he down, and dipped himself seven times in Jordan, according to the saying of the man of God: and his flesh came again like unto the flesh of a little child, and he was clean.
15 And he returned to the man of God, he and all his company, and came, and stood before him: and he said, Behold, now I know that there is no God in all the earth, but in Israel: now therefore, I pray thee, take a blessing of thy servant.(KJV)

The Old Testament law for the leper involved cleansing with water

Lev 14:4 Then shall the priest command to take for him that is to be cleansed two birds alive and clean, and cedar wood, and scarlet, and hyssop:
5 And the priest shall command that one of the birds be killed in an earthen vessel over running water:
6 As for the living bird, he shall take it, and the cedar wood, and the scarlet, and the hyssop, and shall dip them and the living bird in the blood of the bird that was killed over the running water:
7 And he shall sprinkle upon him that is to be cleansed from the leprosy seven times, and shall pronounce him clean, and shall let the living bird loose into the open field. (KJV)

Num 19:17 And for an unclean person they shall take of the ashes of the burnt heifer of purification for sin, and running water shall be put thereto in a vessel:

18 And a clean person shall take hyssop, and dip it in the water, and sprinkle it upon the tent, and upon all the vessels, and upon the persons that were there, and upon him that touched a bone, or one slain, or one dead, or a grave:

19 And the clean person shall sprinkle upon the unclean on the third day, and on the seventh day: and on the seventh day he shall purify himself, and wash his clothes, and bathe himself in water, and shall be clean at even.

20 But the man that shall be unclean, and shall not purify himself, that soul shall be cut off from among the congregation, because he hath defiled the sanctuary of the LORD: the water of separation hath not been sprinkled upon him; he is unclean.

21 And it shall be a perpetual statute unto them, that he that sprinkleth the water of separation shall wash his clothes; and he that toucheth the water of separation shall be unclean until even.

22 And whatsoever the unclean person toucheth shall be unclean; and the soul that toucheth it shall be unclean until even. (KJV)

The people had to wash their clothes in preparation for the coming of the Lord in the wilderness:

Exod 19:10 And the LORD said unto Moses, Go unto the people, and sanctify them to day and to morrow, and let them wash their clothes,

11 And be ready against the third day: for the third day the LORD will come down in the sight of all the people upon mount Sinai.

12 And thou shalt set bounds unto the people round about, saying, Take heed to yourselves, that ye go not up into the mount, or touch the border of it: whosoever toucheth the mount shall be surely put to death:

13 There shall not an hand touch it, but he shall surely be stoned, or shot through; whether it be

beast or man, it shall not live: when the trumpet soundeth long, they shall come up to the mount.

14 And Moses went down from the mount unto the people, and sanctified the people; and they washed their clothes. (KJV)

Baptism is a form of purification. According to the book of Acts, Baptism results in washing away our sins....

Acts 22:10 And I said, What shall I do, Lord? And the Lord said unto me, Arise, and go into Damascus; and there it shall be told thee of all things which are appointed for thee to do.
11 And when I could not see for the glory of that light, being led by the hand of them that were with me, I came into Damascus.
12 And one Ananias, a devout man according to the law, having a good report of all the Jews which dwelt there,
13 Came unto me, and stood, and said unto me, Brother Saul, receive thy sight. And the same hour I looked up upon him.
14 And he said, The God of our fathers hath chosen thee, that thou shouldest know his will, and see that Just One, and shouldest hear the voice of his mouth.
15 For thou shalt be his witness unto all men of what thou hast seen and heard.
16 And now why tarriest thou? arise, and be baptized, and wash away thy sins, calling on the name of the Lord.

How would baptism wash away our sins? Galatians 3:24-29 gives us an answer. It is because we PUT ON Christ, when we are baptized.

Gal 3:24 Wherefore the law was our schoolmaster to bring us unto Christ, that we might be justified by faith.
25 But after that faith is come, we are no longer under a schoolmaster.
26 For ye are all the children of God by faith in Christ Jesus.
27 For as many of you as have been baptized into Christ have put on Christ.
28 There is neither Jew nor Greek, there is neither bond nor free, there is neither male nor female: for ye are all one in Christ Jesus.
29 And if ye be Christ's, then are ye Abraham's seed, and heirs according to the promise. (KJV)

Acts 2:38 Then Peter said unto them, Repent, and be baptized every one of you in the name of Jesus Christ for the remission of sins, and ye shall receive the gift of the Holy Ghost. (KJV)

So we can see that although baptism is sometimes performed as a ritual of membership into a specific denomination, this is not what Baptism entails. It is not baptism into the catholic church, or the church of Christ, or the Baptist or Lutheran church...it is baptism into Christ, MAKING A COVENANT WITH THE TRUE AND LIVING GOD.

There are three major positions on the nature of baptism:

The sacramental view.

The Covenantal view.

The symbolic view.

Various denominations within Christianity hold to one or the other of these views.

The Sacramental View:

Both Roman Catholics and Lutherans hold this view, namely that the person who goes through this rite receives remission of their sins, and is regenerated or given a new nature and an awakened or strengthened faith. According to this view, a person is "Born again" when they are baptized.

According to Roman Catholicism, baptism into the Church is essential for salvation. Oneness Pentecostals as well as many other denominations also hold this belief. According to Roman Catholicism, it is the rite itself that has the power to convey grace. It is not the water, but the sacrament as established by God and administered by the church that produces this change.

Lutherans maintain that it is the faith that is present in the person being baptized that saves him. Advocates of the sacramental view of baptism interpret John 3:5 as referring to water baptism.

John 3: 5 Jesus answered, Verily, verily, I say unto thee, Except a man be born of water and of the Spirit, he cannot enter into the kingdom of God.

Context of scripture is important to proper interpretation.

John 3:1 There was a man of the Pharisees, named Nicodemus, a ruler of the Jews:
2 The same came to Jesus by night, and said unto him, Rabbi, we know that thou art a teacher come from God: for no man can do these miracles that thou doest, except God be with him.

3 Jesus answered and said unto him, Verily, verily, I say unto thee, Except a man be born again, he cannot see the kingdom of God.
4 Nicodemus saith unto him, How can a man be born when he is old? can he enter the second time into his mother's womb, and be born?
5 Jesus answered, Verily, verily, I say unto thee, Except a man be born of water and of the Spirit, he cannot enter into the kingdom of God.
6 That which is born of the flesh is flesh; and that which is born of the Spirit is spirit.
7 Marvel not that I said unto thee, Ye must be born again.
8 The wind bloweth where it listeth, and thou hearest the sound thereof, but canst not tell whence it cometh, and whither it goeth: so is every one that is born of the Spirit.
9 Nicodemus answered and said unto him, How can these things be?

It has been said that Jesus completely sidestepped the statement that Nicodemus made when he came to Him, but I don't think that is the case. Jesus tackled Nicodemus' statement head on. Nicodemus was admitting that Jesus had to be from God, because He had done so many great miracles. What follows is Jesus' instruction to Nicodemus as to how a person can "see" the Kingdom of God.

Remember that Jesus once taught that the Kingdom of God is nothing that comes from observation...but that it is a Kingdom that is established IN us.

Luke 17: 20 And when he was demanded of the Pharisees, when the kingdom of God should come, he answered them and said, The kingdom of God cometh not with observation:
21 Neither shall they say, Lo here! or, lo there! for, behold, the kingdom of God is within you. (KJV)

From careful study of scripture, we can see that the Kingdom of God is a Kingdom which is to come, but we also see that the Kingdom of God is God's Rule established in us now, here on earth, and as His disciples we who are Christ's are to live our lives to further the Kingdom of God on this earth through our witness and ministry to others.

Jesus taught the disciples to pray "Thy Kingdom come, thy will be done, on earth, as it is in Heaven". This is a prayer of willing subjection to God to rule in our daily affairs, just as He rules in Heaven. The early church used to pray this prayer three times a day.

How is the Kingdom of God established IN us? Through faith, and inviting the One True God to have His Way in our lives.

Notes-

So Jesus tells Nicodemus that one must be born from above to enter into the Kingdom of God. "How can this be?" Nicodemus wonders. The subject at hand is BIRTH.

Nicodemus grapples with the concept of flesh being reborn. It is impossible, he says. He envisions a birth from the womb, and then wonders how a person could enter a second time into the womb. This is so foreign to a man who understands only the natural aspect of life.

So, Jesus instructs Nicodemus in what it is to be born again.

Jesus answered, *Verily, verily, I say unto thee, Except a man be born of water and of the Spirit, he cannot enter into the kingdom of God.*

Here is where I believe many people lose sight of the context of the conversation. They say that Jesus is speaking of water baptism here, when he spoke of being born of the water. I believe Jesus is explaining the difference between the first birth, and the second birth.

Everyone knows that the natural baby is in a water bag in the womb. Nicodemus was well aware of this, as well. Jesus is saying, first we need to be born naturally, and then we need to be born spiritually. I believe that verse 6 reiterates this point, when Jesus refers to the first birth (flesh) and then to the second birth (spirit).

That which is born of the flesh is flesh; and that which is born of the Spirit is spirit.

Next, we see that Jesus tells Nicodemus, "don't be surprised that I said you need to be born again".

Jn 3:7 Marvel not that I said unto thee, Ye must be born again.

ἄνωθεν anōthen
Thayer Definition:
1) from above, from a higher place
1a) of things which come from heaven or God
2) from the first, from the beginning, from the very first
3) anew, over again
Part of Speech: adverb
A Related Word by Thayer's/Strong's Number: from G507

Cult watch:

1) Catholics hold to a sacramental view of baptism. They believe that they are born again when they are baptized into the Church as infants. That is how they translate being born of the water; as baptism. Others including the Church of Christ interpret it this way as well. It will assist the Christian in his witness to Catholics in this instance to encourage them to read Jn 3:3 from the New American Bible Revised Edition, which they deem as a Catholic Bible:

Jesus answered and said to him, "Amen, amen, I say to you, no one can see the kingdom of God without being born from above."

In reading the context in the light of being "born from above", we can see that Jesus distinguishes from the fleshly birth and the spiritual birth.

The same approach can be used with the Church of Christ, but the problem is that most will accept nothing but the King James Version of the Bible. In this case, you need to demonstrate that the Greek word translated as "again" is better translated as "from above". That can be a challenge, but with much diligence and patience, the Christian laborer can plant a good seed at least.

The word translated as "again" is the Greek word "anothen", which would be better translated as "from above"[1], as we can see it used in John 3:31:

Joh 3:31 He that cometh from above is above all: he that is of the earth is earthly, and speaketh of the earth: he that cometh from heaven is above all.

The next verse in Jesus' initial dialogue with Nicodemus is a clear giveaway. You can see a natural birth. But you can't see a spiritual birth.

Jn 3:8 The wind bloweth where it listeth, and thou hearest the sound thereof, but canst not tell whence it cometh, and whither it goeth: so is every one that is born of the Spirit.

Remember here the passage we looked at in Luke 17:20

**Luke 17: 20 And when he was demanded of the Pharisees, when the kingdom of God should come, he answered them and said, The kingdom of God cometh not with observation:
21 Neither shall they say, Lo here! or, lo there! for, behold, the kingdom of God is within you.**

Nicodemus was still struggling with trying to comprehend a spiritual Truth from a carnal viewpoint.

John 3:9 Nicodemus answered and said unto him, How can these things be?

Then Jesus spoke about the catalyst of being born again...Belief in Jesus.

**John 3:14 And as Moses lifted up the serpent in the wilderness, even so must the Son of man be lifted up:
15 That whosoever believeth in him should not perish, but have eternal life.
16 For God so loved the world, that he gave his only begotten Son, that whosoever believeth in him should not perish, but have everlasting life.**

17 For God sent not his Son into the world to condemn the world; but that the world through him might be saved.
18 He that believeth on him is not condemned: but he that believeth not is condemned already, because he hath not believed in the name of the only begotten Son of God.
19 And this is the condemnation, that light is come into the world, and men loved darkness rather than light, because their deeds were evil.
20 For every one that doeth evil hateth the light, neither cometh to the light, lest his deeds should be reproved.
21 But he that doeth truth cometh to the light, that his deeds may be made manifest, that they are wrought in God.

This is in accordance with John 1:12, which also describes the New Birth:

John 1:11 He came unto his own, and his own received him not.
12 But as many as received him, to them gave he power to become the sons of God, even to them that believe on his name:
13 Which were born, not of blood, nor of the will of the flesh, nor of the will of man, but of God.

So we see that it is faith (as many as received Him) which is the instrument whereby we are Born Again, and not baptism.

Acts 8:36 And as they went on their way, they came unto a certain water: and the eunuch said, See, here is water; what doth hinder me to be baptized?
37 And Philip said, If thou believest with all thine heart, thou mayest. And he answered and said, I believe that Jesus Christ is the Son of God.
38 And he commanded the chariot to stand still: and they went down both into the water, both Philip and the eunuch; and he baptized him.

Eph 2:8 For by grace are ye saved through faith; and that not of yourselves: it is the gift of God:
9 Not of works, lest any man should boast.

Mar 16:16 He that believeth and is baptized shall be saved; but he that believeth not shall be damned.

Notice that the formula is that He that believeth and is baptized shall be saved...but he that believeth not shall be damned...it is faith that saves us. Baptism is the seal of that faith; the proof of one's embracing that faith - the act of cutting a covenant with God.

Titus 3:4 But after that the kindness and love of God our Saviour toward man appeared,
5 Not by works of righteousness which we have done, but according to his mercy he saved us, by the washing of regeneration, and renewing of the Holy Ghost;
6 Which he shed on us abundantly through Jesus Christ our Saviour;
7 That being justified by his grace, we should be made heirs according to the hope of eternal life.

The "washing of regeneration" could be translated as the "baptism of restoration".

The only other place in the New Testament where this word translated as "regeneration" is used is in Matthew 19:28, when Jesus mentions that time when the Son of man shall sit in the throne of his Glory, and while it is translated also as regeneration, the more accurate translation would be that Jesus is speaking of the restoration of the Kingdom of God on this earth.

Mat 19:28 And Jesus said unto them, Verily I say unto you, That ye which have followed me, in the regeneration when the Son of man shall sit in the throne of his glory, ye also shall sit upon twelve thrones, judging the twelve tribes of Israel.

Baptism is a restoration of our relationship with God, just as John's Baptism was a baptism of repentance in order to be restored to the Father, so the baptism for the Christian is also one of restoration to God through Jesus Christ.

To believe that it is the act of being immersed in water that saves us would put a "works oriented salvation" in the gospel. The act of obedience to the Word is what circumcises us to Christ or is a seal of the covenant that we have made with God the Father through Jesus Christ.

Covenental View:

But as we have seen, baptism does wash away our sins (Acts 22:16), but only if our heart is right when we are baptized. How? Because we are making a covenant with God, declaring that we have put our old man to death, and are living a life of separation toward God. Baptism serves the same purpose for New Testament believers that circumcision did for Old Testament believers.

Colossians 2:11-12: "In Him you were also circumcised with the circumcision made without hands, by putting off the body of the sins of the flesh, by the circumcision of Christ, buried with Him in baptism, in which you also were raised with Him through faith in the working of God, who raised Him from the dead."

The Old Testament Covenant was this:

**Gen 17:10 This is my covenant, which ye shall keep, between me and you and thy seed after thee; Every man child among you shall be circumcised.
11 And ye shall circumcise the flesh of your foreskin; and it shall be a token of the covenant betwixt me and you.
12 And he that is eight days old shall be circumcised among you, every man child in your generations, he that is born in the house, or bought with money of any stranger, which is not of thy seed.
13 He that is born in thy house, and he that is bought with thy money, must needs be circumcised: and my covenant shall be in your flesh for an everlasting covenant.
14 And the uncircumcised man child whose flesh of his foreskin is not circumcised, that soul shall be cut off from his people; he hath broken my covenant.**

In the covenantal view, baptism serves the same purpose for New Testament believers that circumcision did for Old Testament believers. For the Jews, circumcision was the external and visible sign that they were within the covenant that God had established with Abraham. The cutting of the foreskin was the most expressive way of declaring to the Lord that we were not going to be led by the lusts of our flesh, but rather, we would be faithful to Him, and heed the leading of His Will in our lives.

As we have seen earlier, converts to Judaism (or proselytes) also had to undergo this rite. But now under the new covenant, baptism instead of circumcision is required.

Circumcision refers to a cutting away of sin and a change of heart :

Deut 10:16 Circumcise therefore the foreskin of your heart, and be no more stiffnecked.

17 For the LORD your God is God of gods, and Lord of lords, a great God, a mighty, and a terrible, which regardeth not persons, nor taketh reward:

18 He doth execute the judgment of the fatherless and widow, and loveth the stranger, in giving him food and raiment.

19 Love ye therefore the stranger: for ye were strangers in the land of Egypt.

20 Thou shalt fear the LORD thy God; him shalt thou serve, and to him shalt thou cleave, and swear by his name.

In being baptized, the believer must understand what this act is. Romans 6 clearly explains to us what baptism is:

Rom 6:4 Therefore we are buried with him by baptism into death: that like as Christ was raised up from the dead by the glory of the Father, even so we also should walk in newness of life.

5 For if we have been planted together in the likeness of his death, we shall be also in the likeness of his resurrection:

6 Knowing this, that our old man is crucified with him, that the body of sin might be destroyed, that henceforth we should not serve sin.

7 For he that is dead is freed from sin.

8 Now if we be dead with Christ, we believe that we shall also live with him:

9 Knowing that Christ being raised from the dead dieth no more; death hath no more dominion over him.

10 For in that he died, he died unto sin once: but in that he liveth, he liveth unto God.

11 Likewise reckon ye also yourselves to be dead indeed unto sin, but alive unto God through Jesus Christ our Lord.

12 Let not sin therefore reign in your mortal body, that ye should obey it in the lusts thereof.

13 Neither yield ye your members as instruments of unrighteousness unto sin: but yield yourselves unto God, as those that are alive from the dead, and your members as instruments of righteousness unto God.

14 For sin shall not have dominion over you: for ye are not under the law, but under grace.

15 What then? shall we sin, because we are not under the law, but under grace? God forbid.

16 Know ye not, that to whom ye yield yourselves servants to obey, his servants ye are to whom ye obey; whether of sin unto death, or of obedience unto righteousness?

17 But God be thanked, that ye were the servants of sin, but ye have obeyed from the heart that form of doctrine which was delivered you.

18 Being then made free from sin, ye became the servants of righteousness.
19 I speak after the manner of men because of the infirmity of your flesh: for as ye have yielded your members servants to uncleanness and to iniquity unto iniquity; even so now yield your members servants to righteousness unto holiness.
20 For when ye were the servants of sin, ye were free from righteousness.
21 What fruit had ye then in those things whereof ye are now ashamed? for the end of those things is death.
22 But now being made free from sin, and become servants to God, ye have your fruit unto holiness, and the end everlasting life.
23 For the wages of sin is death; but the gift of God is eternal life through Jesus Christ our Lord.

The fact that the believer needs to understand the principal behind baptism in order to cut a covenant with the Lord negates the idea of infant baptism.

Matt 28: 19 Go ye therefore, and teach all nations, baptizing them in the name of the Father, and of the Son, and of the Holy Ghost:
20 Teaching them to observe all things whatsoever I have commanded you: and, lo, I am with you alway, even unto the end of the world. Amen.

You can't teach an infant to observe the things Jesus commanded us.

A covenant is made between two parties who understand the principles of a covenant as an agreement between both parties concerning a thing. But mere intellectual assent is not enough for a covenant between man and God.

The one who makes a covenant needs to have a sincere heart. The Bible tells us of a sorcerer named Simon, who believed, and was baptized.

Acts 8: 13 Then Simon himself believed also: and when he was baptized, he continued with Philip, and wondered, beholding the miracles and signs which were done.
14 Now when the apostles which were at Jerusalem heard that Samaria had received the word of God, they sent unto them Peter and John:
15 Who, when they were come down, prayed for them, that they might receive the Holy Ghost:
16 (For as yet he was fallen upon none of them: only they were baptized in the name of the Lord Jesus.)
17 Then laid they their hands on them, and they received the Holy Ghost.
18 And when Simon saw that through laying on of the apostles' hands the Holy Ghost was given, he offered them money,
19 Saying, Give me also this power, that on whomsoever I lay hands, he may receive the Holy Ghost.

20 But Peter said unto him, Thy money perish with thee, because thou hast thought that the gift of God may be purchased with money.
21 Thou hast neither part nor lot in this matter: for thy heart is not right in the sight of God.
22 Repent therefore of this thy wickedness, and pray God, if perhaps the thought of thine heart may be forgiven thee.
23 For I perceive that thou art in the gall of bitterness, and in the bond of iniquity.
24 Then answered Simon, and said, Pray ye to the Lord for me, that none of these things which ye have spoken come upon me.

Obviously the baptism wasn't what saved Simon the sorceror.

Salvation comes from a heart-felt desire to change the way we live, and to turn from our wickedness...we need someone to save us from our wicked desires, and the only One Who can save us is Jesus Christ, the Righteous One. Baptism is about *obedience,* not obeying a religious ordinance.

Acts 2:38 Then Peter said unto them, Repent, and be baptized every one of you in the name of Jesus Christ for the remission of sins, and ye shall receive the gift of the Holy Ghost.
39 For the promise is unto you, and to your children, and to all that are afar off, even as many as the Lord our God shall call.(KJV)

THE SYMBOLIC VIEW-

This view stresses the symbolic nature of baptism by emphasizing that baptism does not cause an inward change or alter a person's relationship to God in any way.

Baptism is a token, or an outward indication, of the inner change which has already occurred in the believer's life. It serves as a public identification of the person with Jesus Christ, and thus also as a public testimony of the change that has occurred. It is an act of initiation. It is baptism into the name of Jesus.

According to the symbolic view, baptism is not so much an initiation into the Christian life as into the Christian church. A distinction is drawn between the invisible or universal church, which consists of all believers in Christ, and the visible or local church, a gathering of believers in a specific place.

This position explains that the church practices baptism and the believer submits to it because Jesus commanded that this be done and He gave us the example by being baptized Himself. Thus, baptism is an act of obedience, commitment, and proclamation.

According to this understanding of baptism, no spiritual benefit occurs because of baptism. Rather than producing REGENERATION of faith, baptism always comes after faith and the salvation that faith produces. The only spiritual value of baptism is that it establishes membership in the church and exposes the believer to the values of this type of fellowship.

There is a controversy which rages among Christian circles as to "what Name we are to be baptized" into:

I believe one would be best served by being baptized in obedience to the Words of our Lord Jesus Christ:

Matt 28: 18 And Jesus came and spake unto them, saying, All power is given unto me in heaven and in earth.
19 Go ye therefore, and teach all nations, baptizing them in the name of the Father, and of the Son, and of the Holy Ghost:
20 Teaching them to observe all things whatsoever I have commanded you: and, lo, I am with you alway, even unto the end of the world. Amen.

For the purpose of this study, we must draw the conclusion that the act of baptism is an act of entering into covenant with the One True God.

It is sacramental in that Jesus Christ commanded that it be observed.

It is symbolic in that we are symbolically buried with Christ under the water, and are raised up out of the watery grave to live with Christ.

But the true essence of baptism is that it is covenantal in nature. In our obedience to His Command, we are declaring to the Lord and to the world that we are putting an end to the old man who was lost in sin, and we are serving the One True God from now on.

Baptism is a form of

_____

When we are baptized, we put off the _____, and put on

_____

How is the Kingdom of God established IN us?

_____

_____

Baptism is an outward demonstration of making a _____ with God.

What passage of scripture explains the doctrine of baptism?

_____

Lesson 8

BAPTISM:
IN THE NAME OF THE FATHER, THE SON AND THE HOLY GHOST, OR IN THE NAME OF JESUS ONLY?

The Question is frequently asked by an anti-trinitarian:

"What is the name of the Father, or of the Holy Spirit, if we are to baptize in their NAME?"

The question I like to ask any son or daughter is this...what do you call your natural father? If you love him, and honor him, and respect him, though you may know him to be named Bill or Fred or John or Joseph; to you, his name will always be "father", or dad, or pa, or papa, or daddy, or some other term of intimacy. Earlier we saw that one of the Names of God is "Abba".

The Son is Jesus Christ or Yeshuah, Ha Maschiah. And the Holy Spirit is Holy Spirit, or Ruach Ha Kodesh. Father, Son, and Holy Spirit are not merely *titles* for the one true God, they are Who He is... They are His Names.

See how Jesus personalized the Holy Spirit by saying "he" and "himself", instead of "it":

John 15:26   But when the Comforter is come, whom I will send unto you from the Father, even the Spirit of truth, which proceedeth from the Father, he shall testify of me: (KJV)

He proceeds from the Father just as Jesus does...They are ONE. Of the same substance, co-eternal and co-equal with one another. See another place where the word "He" is used in describing the Holy Spirit, denoting personality, instead of some impersonal active force as the Jehovah's Witnesses teach:

John 16:13 Howbeit when he, the Spirit of truth, is come, he will guide you into all truth: for he shall not speak of himself; but whatsoever he shall hear, that shall he speak: and he will shew you things to come. (KJV)

So when we baptize in the Name of the Father, the Son, and the Holy Spirit, we can see that this is the correct formula. It is important to note how Jesus commissioned the disciples and those who would come after them:

Matt 28:18 And Jesus came and spake unto them, saying, All power is given unto me in heaven and in earth.
19 Go ye therefore, and teach all nations, baptizing them in the name of the Father, and of the Son, and of the Holy Ghost:
20 Teaching them to observe all things whatsoever I have commanded you: and, lo, I am with you alway, even unto the end of the world. Amen. (KJV)

Notice that He said that they were to teach them to observe all things whatsoever He had commanded them.

My question to those who baptize in the NAME OF JESUS ONLY is this: did not our Lord just command His disciples to baptize in the NAME OF THE FATHER, AND OF THE SON, AND OF THE HOLY GHOST? It seems that those who insist in baptizing in the Name of Jesus only are in direct violation of the commandment of Jesus recorded in Matthew 28:18-20.

The next question would be *"if all this is true, then why do we not see this formula used in the book of Acts, or anywhere else?"*

The classic argument for baptism in the Name of Jesus Only is based on what Peter says in Acts 2:28. Peter told the group of people he was preaching to to be baptized *in the Name of Jesus Christ for the remission of sins*. He did not say to be baptized in the Name of the Father, of the Son, and of the Holy Ghost:

Acts 2:37 Now when they heard this, they were pricked in their heart, and said unto Peter and to the rest of the apostles, Men and brethren, what shall we do?
38 Then Peter said unto them, Repent, and be baptized every one of you in the name of Jesus Christ for the remission of sins, and ye shall receive the gift of the Holy Ghost. (KJV)

There are other passages that seem to support the argument for the baptism in the Name of Jesus only, and I intend to deal with each one that I am aware of, but I will address them one at a time. There is a common thread to be seen in each of these passages.

First, we need to know who this group is that are being spoken to here. The Bible tells us that they were *"devout"* Jews:

Acts 2:5 And there were dwelling at Jerusalem Jews, devout men, out of every nation under heaven.
6 Now when this was noised abroad, the multitude came together, and were confounded, because that every man heard them speak in his own language.

According to Thayer's, "Devout" is translated thus:

2126 eulabes-
1) taking hold well a) carefully and surely b) cautiously 2) reverencing God, pious, religious

Notes

_____
_____
_____
_____
_____
_____
_____
_____
_____
_____
_____
_____
_____
_____
_____
_____
_____
_____
_____
_____
_____
_____
_____

7 And they were all amazed and marvelled, saying one to another, Behold, are not all these which speak Galilaeans?
8 And how hear we every man in our own tongue, wherein we were born?
9 Parthians, and Medes, and Elamites, and the dwellers in Mesopotamia, and in Judaea, and Cappadocia, in Pontus, and Asia,
10 Phrygia, and Pamphylia, in Egypt, and in the parts of Libya about Cyrene, and strangers of Rome, Jews and proselytes,
11 Cretes and Arabians, we do hear them speak in our tongues the wonderful works of God.
12 And they were all amazed, and were in doubt, saying one to another, What meaneth this?
13 Others mocking said, These men are full of new wine. (KJV)

So we can see that those whom Peter was addressing were already those who had reverenced God. They knew the Father. But they did not know Jesus, and they did not know the Holy Spirit.

It is important to be mindful that the occasion for Peter's preaching was that the Holy Spirit had just been poured out on the disciples, and these devout Jews were wondering what had occurred.

See what those who had been assembled in the upper room had been told by Jesus, prior to this taking place:

Acts 1:1 The former treatise have I made, O Theophilus, of all that Jesus began both to do and teach,
2 Until the day in which he was taken up, after that he through the Holy Ghost had given commandments unto the apostles whom he had chosen:
3 To whom also he shewed himself alive after his passion by many infallible proofs, being seen of them forty days, and speaking of the things pertaining to the kingdom of God:
4 And, being assembled together with them, commanded them that they should not depart from Jerusalem, but wait for the promise of the Father, which, saith he, ye have heard of me.

5 For John truly baptized with water; but ye shall be baptized with the Holy Ghost not many days hence. (KJV)

In this passage, we see the Father (verse 4), the Son (verse 1), and the Holy Ghost (verse 2, and verse 5) all mentioned. The disciples had been baptized by John in the waters of repentance toward the Father, and they had received Jesus as the One through Whom they would receive the remission of sins. The only person of the Triune God these in the upper room had yet to receive was the Holy Ghost, and so they were instructed to wait for this to happen. This was accomplished in Acts 2:1-4.

The sermon Peter preaches to these *devout* Jews is about the Lord Jesus Christ and the Holy Spirit. They already knew the Father and they worshipped Him. That is what made them "devout". In verse 16-21, Peter addresses the issue of the Holy Spirit, showing that it was the prophecy of Joel which had come to pass. Verses 22-32 tell us of the role of the Messiah Jesus, according to the fulfillment of prophecy. Again, in verse 33, we see the Father, the Son and the Holy Ghost all mentioned at once:

Acts 2:33   Therefore being by the right hand of God exalted, and having received of the Father the promise of the Holy Ghost, he hath shed forth this, which ye now see and hear. (KJV)

Acts 2:36 Therefore let all the house of Israel know assuredly, that God hath made that same Jesus, whom ye have crucified, both Lord and Christ. (KJV)

They worshipped God. But they needed to know Who the Christ was. Here, in Peter's discourse, they learn that God made Jesus both Lord and Christ. The proof of it laid in the fact that the Holy Spirit had fallen upon these disciples, and the Jews who were present witnessed it. Having heard and received the Truth spoken by Peter, we read that they were pricked in their heart:

Acts 2:37 Now when they heard this, they were pricked in their heart, and said unto Peter and to the rest of the apostles, Men and brethren, what shall we do?
38 Then Peter said unto them, Repent, and be baptized every one of you in the name of Jesus Christ for the remission of sins, and ye shall receive the gift of the Holy Ghost.
39 For the promise is unto you, and to your children, and to all that are afar off, even as many as the Lord our God shall call. (KJV)

Though we read relatively little concerning John the Baptist, we do know that his ministry was a ministry of baptism of repentance. Through considering that which was written about him, we can tell that his ministry was one that impacted Judea and the area around it. Multitudes were baptized by him:

Mark 1:4 John did baptize in the wilderness, and preach the baptism of repentance for the remission of sins

5 And there went out unto him all the land of Judaea, and they of Jerusalem, and were all baptized of him in the river of Jordan, confessing their sins. (KJV)

Luke 7:28 For I say unto you, Among those that are born of women there is not a greater prophet than John the Baptist: but he that is least in the kingdom of God is greater than he.
29 And all the people that heard him, and the publicans, justified God, being baptized with the baptism of John.
30 But the Pharisees and lawyers rejected the counsel of God against themselves, being not baptized of him. (KJV)

It would be safe to assume that these "devout" men who were witnesses of this phenomenon in Acts chapter two had also been baptized by John's baptism of repentance toward the Father. It remained for them to be baptized into Jesus (the Son), and the Holy Spirit. I believe that as we study the various passages concerning those who had been baptized in the book of Acts, that we will find this common link: that they were *devout* people who knew the Father. It only remained for the Son and the Holy Spirit to be introduced to them.

Phillip preached Jesus in Samaria. If the reader will recall the dialogue between Jesus and the Samaritan woman at the well in John 4, we see that the Samaritans worshipped the God of Jacob, the Father (John 4:12).

So again, we see that it was Jesus Who needed to be preached in Samaria. No doubt because of the woman at the well, some seeds had already been planted regarding this man called Jesus, causing the Samaritans to be open to Philip's preaching concerning Jesus Christ. According to the Word of God, John baptized those who were in Jerusalem, all Judea, and all the region round about Jordan (Matt. 3:5) If you look at a map, you can see that this would have included Samaria.

So we see that in our account in Acts chapter 8, the people of Samaria were baptized in the Name of Jesus (the Son), but the baptism was still not complete - they needed the baptism of the Holy Spirit, which is not done with water:

1) There are those Christians who believe in a "modalism" of God, that the ONE God was revealed in three modes; the first being the Father of the Old Testament and as Jesus revealed Him to Israel.

Jesus, Who was that same God manifested in the flesh revealed Himself as the Son of the Father while He walked on the earth, but once He died and resurrected, He is no longer the Son.

Some Apostolic Pentecostals will not pray to the Father; they only address Jesus in their prayer because of this modalist or "Oneness" theology.

But what took place in Acts 8:37 happened after the resurrection of Jesus and His ascension, and the Ethiopian eunuch's confession unto salvation was that Jesus is the Son of God, not was the Son of God.

1Jn 5:6 This is he that came by water and blood, even Jesus Christ; not by water only, but by water and blood. And it is the Spirit that beareth witness, because the Spirit is truth.
7 For there are three that bear record in heaven, the Father, the Word, and the Holy Ghost: and these three are one.
8 And there are three that bear witness in earth, the Spirit, and the water, and the blood: and these three agree in one.

Acts 8:15 Who, when they were come down, prayed for them, that they might receive the Holy Ghost:
16 (For as yet he was fallen upon none of them: only they were baptized in the name of the Lord Jesus.)
17 Then laid they their hands on them, and they received the Holy Ghost. (KJV)

Next we see the story of the Ethiopian Eunuch. Obviously, the eunuch was already a believer in the God of Israel. He was studying Isaiah's prophecy of the coming Messiah in Isa. 53:7. Philip then revealed to him Jesus, and the Eunuch understood his need for baptism.

Acts 8:36 And as they went on their way, they came unto a certain water: and the eunuch said, See, here is water; what doth hinder me to be baptized? 37 And Philip said, If thou believest with all thine heart, thou mayest. And he answered and said, I believe that Jesus Christ is the Son of God. (KJV)

DON'T LET THIS FACT SLIP BY YOU:

Notice the requirement that Phillip gave the eunuch was *that he must believe that Jesus was the Son of God*[1]. The eunuch already knew the Father. *He needed to know the Son.* Not the Father, nor the Holy Spirit. The eunuch's profession of faith was that Jesus Christ is (present tense) the Son of God. Not *was* the Son of God, or acted like the Son of God.

Jesus had died, was buried, and rose again, and now the Son of God sits on the right hand of God the Father.

A lot of people stumble at this because it seems to teach that there are three Gods, but the fact is Jesus prayed to someone in the Garden, and He called Him Father. He also acknowledged that He was with Him in the beginning, and that they were One with each other (read His prayer in John 17). In the New Testament we see the term "Godhead" (Rom 1:20, and Col 2:9), and 1 John 5:6-11 reveals that Triune Nature of God.

Again, in Acts chapter 10, we see another account of baptism in the Name of Jesus.

1Jn 5:9 If we receive the witness of men, the witness of God is greater: for this is the witness of God which he hath testified of his Son.
10 He that believeth on the Son of God hath the witness in himself: he that believeth not God hath made him a liar; because he believeth not the record that God gave of his Son.
11 And this is the record, that God hath given to us eternal life, and this life is in his Son.
12 He that hath the Son hath life; and he that hath not the Son of God hath not life.

Notes

Acts 10:47 Can any man forbid water, that these should not be baptized, which have received the Holy Ghost as well as we?
48 And he commanded them to be baptized in the name of the Lord. Then prayed they him to tarry certain days. (KJV)

Who were these who were baptized? In verse two of Chapter 10, we read that Cornelius was a "*devout*" man, and one who feared God with all his house. Obviously, he already worshipped the Father. He already knew the baptism of John (repentance toward the Father):

Acts 10:37 That word, I say, ye know, which was published throughout all Judaea, and began from Galilee, after the baptism which John preached;(KJV)

He was a *devout* man, so we can be safe in deducing that he had been baptized with John's baptism already. The Holy Spirit fell on Cornelius and his house as Peter spoke, and then they were baptized in the Name of the Lord Jesus.

Again, in Acts 19:1, we see that they found disciples who had been baptized unto John's baptism (repentance toward the Father). They still needed to be baptized in the Name of Jesus (the Son), and in the Name of the Holy Ghost. After they had been baptized in the Name of the Lord Jesus, they then received the baptism of the Holy Ghost through Laying on of hands.

Acts 19:2 He said unto them, Have ye received the Holy Ghost since ye believed? And they said unto him, We have not so much as heard whether there be any Holy Ghost.
3 And he said unto them, Unto what then were ye baptized? And they said, Unto John's baptism.
4 Then said Paul, John verily baptized with the baptism of repentance, saying unto the people, that they should believe on him which should come after him, that is, on Christ Jesus.
5 When they heard this, they were baptized in the name of the Lord Jesus.
6 And when Paul had laid his hands upon them, the Holy Ghost came on them; and they spake with tongues, and prophesied. (KJV)

I believe that in each instance of baptism in Jesus' name, we can see that those who had been baptized were already believers in the God of Israel (the Father). The evidence points to the fact that they had already been baptized into John's baptism, which was done in the Name of the Father, and the only thing that remained was to be baptized in the Name of Jesus, and of the Holy Ghost.

Those who insist on baptism in the Name of Jesus Only are anti-trinitarians, yet I believe that Bible shows ample evidence for the Trinity.

Those who preach Jesus Only say that Jesus was the Son only while He walked the earth. But remember the profession of faith made by the Ethiopian eunuch. He said *"I believe that Jesus IS the Son of God."* (Acts 3:13,26)

After Paul's conversion, he preached that Jesus Christ IS (not was) the Son of God:

1 Cor 1:9 God is faithful, by whom ye were called unto the fellowship of his Son Jesus Christ our Lord.
10 Now I beseech you, brethren, by the name of our Lord Jesus Christ, that ye all speak the same thing, and that there be no divisions among you; but that ye be perfectly joined together in the same mind and in the same judgment. (KJV)

Gal 4:6 And because ye are sons, God hath sent forth the Spirit of his Son into your hearts, crying, Abba, Father. (KJV)

Heb 4:14 Seeing then that we have a great high priest, that is passed into the heavens, Jesus the Son of God, let us hold fast our profession. (KJV)

I Jn 1:3 That which we have seen and heard declare we unto you, that ye also may have fellowship with us: and truly our fellowship is with the Father, and with his Son Jesus Christ. (KJV)

I believe that the "Baptism in Jesus' Name Only" doctrine is a doctrine which creates division and strife among the Body of Christ. Taking it even a step farther, I would even go so far as to say that biblically, Oneness theology and Jehovah Witness type theology as well as the theology of Islam is an antichrist theology:

I Jn 2:22 Who is a liar but he that denieth that Jesus is the Christ? He is antichrist, that denieth the Father and the Son.
23 Whosoever denieth the Son, the same hath not the Father: (but) he that acknowledgeth the Son hath the Father also.
24 Let that therefore abide in you, which ye have heard from the beginning. If that which ye have heard from the beginning shall remain in you, ye also shall continue in the Son, and in the Father. (KJV)

The Word declares that God loved the world so much that He sent His Only Begotten Son.

This is the Truth of the Christ, the Messiah.

Not that the Father died for us, but that He gave His only begotten Son. It would be far easier for me to give my life in place of my son. But to give my son so someone else may live?

Jesus is at the right hand of the Father, according to the gospel which is preached in the Word of God. The only way around this for Jesus Only teachers is to allegorize it.

I Jn 2:22 Who is a liar but he that denieth that Jesus is the Christ? He is antichrist, that denieth the Father and the Son.
23 Whosoever denieth the Son, the same hath not the Father: (but) he that acknowledgeth the Son hath the Father also.
24 Let that therefore abide in you, which ye have heard from the beginning. If that which ye have heard from the beginning shall remain in you, ye also shall continue in the Son, and in the Father. (KJV)

HE IS ANTICHRIST, THAT DENIETH THE FATHER AND THE SON.

The proper teaching is that the Father sent the Son to be the Saviour of the world, not that the Father became the Son to become the saviour of the world:

I Jn 4:14 14 And we have seen and do testify that the Father sent the Son to be the Saviour of the world. (KJV)

The fact of the matter is that the fellowship a true Child of God has is with the Father, and with the Son.

I Jn 1:3 3 That which we have seen and heard declare we unto you, that ye also may have fellowship with us: and truly our fellowship is with the Father, and with his Son Jesus Christ. (KJV)

Born Again Christians don't deny the Son ship of the Lord Jesus Christ. We don't deny the Fatherhood of the Almighty God, and we don't deny the deity of the Holy Spirit.

Yet we do not profess there are three Gods.

We worship the Father as the Father.

We Worship the Son as the Son, and we Worship the Holy Spirit Who guides us into all Truth as the Holy Spirit.

And we declare them to be ONE.

I have no hang up with this, because I know that God is God, and I am not.

I understand that His Ways are far above my own ways.

If He wants to manifest Himself as three persons to me, and wants me to acknowledge Him as the Father, the Son and the Holy Spirit, I have no problem with that.

We were created in His Image as one person, but yet a threefold being consisting of Body, Soul and Spirit.

I acknowledge my Father in Heaven.

I acknowledge my Lord Jesus Christ, the only Begotten Son of the Father.

And I acknowledge the work of the Holy Spirit in my Life. According to the Word of God, I have fellowship with the Father, and with His Son, Jesus Christ.

1 Pet 1:3 Blessed be the God and Father of our Lord Jesus Christ, which according to his abundant mercy hath begotten us again unto a lively hope by the resurrection of Jesus Christ from the dead, (KJV)

2 Pet 1:16 For we have not followed cunningly devised fables, when we made known unto you the power and coming of our Lord Jesus Christ, but were eyewitnesses of his majesty.
17 For he received from God the Father honour and glory, when there came such a voice to him from the excellent glory, This is my beloved Son, in whom I am well pleased.(KJV)

Heb 1: 5 For unto which of the angels said he at any time, Thou art my Son, this day have I begotten thee? And again, I will be to him a Father, and he shall be to me a Son? (KJV)

The problem with the Jehovah witnesses and the Oneness Pentecostals and adherents to Islam is that they either are missing the Son, or the Father, and are walking in the spirit of antiChrist.

Their doctrine is based on antichrist principles, and moves them to error in other doctrines.

Oneness Pentecostals are generally immersed in legalism, like the Pharisees, and the Jehovah Witnesses deny a Hell and perpetrate a soul-sleep doctrine like the Saducees.

The words of Jesus Himself in the Book of Revelation speak loudly enough to dispel the notion that Jesus is the Father, OR that we are not to worship Jesus but the Father Only:

Rev 2: 26 And he that overcometh, and keepeth my works unto the end, to him will I give power over the nations:
27 And he shall rule them with a rod of iron; as the vessels of a potter shall they be broken to shivers: even as I received of my Father. (KJV)

Rev 3:5 He that overcometh, the same shall be clothed in white raiment; and I will not blot out his name out of the book of life, but I will confess his name before my Father, and before his angels. (KJV)

In the Book of Revelation Jesus Himself is still declaring that He is the SON of God. Nothing changed in that respect after His resurrection.

Rev 3:21 To him that overcometh will I grant to sit with me in my throne, even as I also overcame, and am set down with my Father in his throne.
22 He that hath an ear, let him hear what the Spirit saith unto the churches.
(KJV)

Those who deny the Deity of Jesus Christ need to understand that it will be Jesus who blots out the names.

That it is Jesus Who grants us Power, and that it is Jesus who permits the overcomer to sit with Him in His throne.

Those Who deny the Trinity need to see that Jesus received His Rule from His Father, and Jesus will confess the overcomers before the Father, and Jesus is seated with His Father.

I say let every man be a liar, but God's Word is True!

What was the common factor between all those who were baptized in Jesus' Name in the book of Acts? -

What does "devout" mean?_____

What was Jesus' Commandment in Matthew 28:19?

_____
_____
_____

What is the definition of Anti Christ according to 1 John 2:22?

_____
_____

LESSON 9
BAPTISM OF THE HOLY SPIRIT

Heb 6:1 Therefore leaving the principles of the doctrine of Christ, let us go on unto perfection; not laying again the foundation of repentance from dead works, and of faith toward God,
2 Of the doctrine of baptisms, and of laying on of hands, and of resurrection of the dead, and of eternal judgment.

The baptism of the Holy Spirit and the baptism in water are two different BAPTISMS. Both are to be experienced by the new believer.

Acts 8:14 Now when the apostles which were at Jerusalem heard that Samaria had received the word of God, they sent unto them Peter and John:
15 Who, when they were come down, prayed for them, that they might receive the Holy Ghost:
16 (For as yet he was fallen upon none of them: only they were baptized in the name of the Lord Jesus.)
17 Then laid they their hands on them, and they received the Holy Ghost.

John baptized with water unto repentance, but Jesus will baptize us with the Holy Spirit and with fire.

Matt 3:11 I indeed baptize you with water unto repentance: but he that cometh after me is mightier than I, whose shoes I am not worthy to bear: he shall baptize you with the Holy Ghost, and with fire:
12 Whose fan is in his hand, and he will throughly purge his floor, and gather his wheat into the garner; but he will burn up the chaff with unquenchable fire.

The Holy Spirit purges us of our sinful nature, and our desires become one with God.

Acts 1: 4 And, being assembled together with them, commanded them that they should not depart from Jerusalem, but wait for the promise of the Father, which, saith he, ye have heard of me.
5 For John truly baptized with water; but ye shall be baptized with the Holy Ghost not many days hence.
6 When they therefore were come together, they asked of him, saying, Lord, wilt thou at this time restore again the kingdom to Israel?
7 And he said unto them, It is not for you to know the times or the seasons, which the Father hath put in his own power.

8 But ye shall receive power, after that the Holy Ghost is come upon you: and ye shall be witnesses unto me both in Jerusalem, and in all Judaea, and in Samaria, and unto the uttermost part of the earth. (KJV)

Just like the disciples, we receive the ability (power) to witness about Jesus after we receive the Holy Ghost. That is not to say that one cannot witness about Jesus without the Holy Spirit. But it is the Holy Spirit which transcends us beyond that which is philosophical and religious, to that which is empowering and emboldening.

It is the Holy Spirit which gives us boldness.

Act 4:29 And now, Lord, behold their threatenings: and grant unto thy servants, that with all boldness they may speak thy word,
30 By stretching forth thine hand to heal; and that signs and wonders may be done by the name of thy holy child Jesus.
31 And when they had prayed, the place was shaken where they were assembled together; and they were all filled with the Holy Ghost, and they spake the word of God with boldness.

It is the Holy Spirit that gives us ability to witness:

Mat 10:17 But beware of men: for they will deliver you up to the councils, and they will scourge you in their synagogues;
18 And ye shall be brought before governors and kings for my sake, for a testimony against them and the Gentiles.
19 But when they deliver you up, take no thought how or what ye shall speak: for it shall be given you in that same hour what ye shall speak.
20 For it is not ye that speak, but the Spirit of your Father which speaketh in you.

In the Old Testament Book of Joel, we see that the Lord prophesied the baptism of the Holy Spirit.

Joel 2:28 And it shall come to pass afterward, that I will pour out my spirit upon all flesh; and your sons and your daughters shall prophesy, your old men shall dream dreams, your young men shall see visions: 29And also upon the servants and upon the handmaids in those days will I pour out my spirit. (KJV)

Why would God pour out His Spirit upon all flesh? So that He would be testified of, and that His Name would be made known. Sons and daughters shall prophesy, old men shall dream dreams, young men shall see visions.

The baptism of the Holy Spirit is given to empower the believer to further the Kingdom of God.

Mar 16:15 And he said unto them, Go ye into all the world, and preach the gospel to every creature.
16 He that believeth and is baptized shall be saved; but he that believeth not shall be damned.
17 And these signs shall follow them that believe; In my name shall they cast out devils; they shall speak with new tongues;
18 They shall take up serpents; and if they drink any deadly thing, it shall not hurt them; they shall lay hands on the sick, and they shall recover.

But the baptism of the Holy Spirit is not just about empowering...Jesus bypassed what the disciples said about the power they had received...He said the important thing was that their names were written in the book of Life.

Luke 10:17 And the seventy returned again with joy, saying, Lord, even the devils are subject unto us through thy name.
18 And he said unto them, I beheld Satan as lightning fall from heaven.
19 Behold, I give unto you power to tread on serpents and scorpions, and over all the power of the enemy: and nothing shall by any means hurt you.
20 Notwithstanding in this rejoice not, that the spirits are subject unto you; but rather rejoice, because your names are written in heaven.

In the Book of Acts, we see an instance when a man was rebuked for desiring the power of the Holy Spirit.

Acts 8:9 But there was a certain man, called Simon, which beforetime in the same city used sorcery, and bewitched the people of Samaria, giving out that himself was some great one:
10 To whom they all gave heed, from the least to the greatest, saying, This man is the great power of God.

11 And to him they had regard, because that of long time he had bewitched them with sorceries.

12 But when they believed Philip preaching the things concerning the kingdom of God, and the name of Jesus Christ, they were baptized, both men and women.

13 Then Simon himself believed also: and when he was baptized, he continued with Philip, and wondered, beholding the miracles and signs which were done.

14 Now when the apostles which were at Jerusalem heard that Samaria had received the word of God, they sent unto them Peter and John:

15 Who, when they were come down, prayed for them, that they might receive the Holy Ghost:

16 (For as yet he was fallen upon none of them: only they were baptized in the name of the Lord Jesus.)

17 Then laid they their hands on them, and they received the Holy Ghost.

18 And when Simon saw that through laying on of the apostles' hands the Holy Ghost was given, he offered them money,

19 Saying, Give me also this power, that on whomsoever I lay hands, he may receive the Holy Ghost.

20 But Peter said unto him, Thy money perish with thee, because thou hast thought that the gift of God may be purchased with money.

21 Thou hast neither part nor lot in this matter: for thy heart is not right in the sight of God.

22 Repent therefore of this thy wickedness, and pray God, if perhaps the thought of thine heart may be forgiven thee.

23 For I perceive that thou art in the gall of bitterness, and in the bond of iniquity.

Witches and sorcerers set their mind on supernatural power. A child of God is to set his mind on the furtherance of the Kingdom of God. The supernatural power of the Holy Spirit will naturally follow as the Gifts of the Holy Spirit flow through him or her. The power of the Holy Spirit is not meant to demonstrate what a man or woman of God we are, but is intended to result in the furtherance of the Kingdom of God on this earth.

The baptism of the Holy Spirit is primarily given to believers to testify of Jesus Christ.

John 16:7 Nevertheless I tell you the truth; It is expedient for you that I go away: for if I go not away, the Comforter will not come unto you; but if I depart, I will send him unto you.

8 And when he is come, he will reprove the world of sin, and of righteousness, and of judgment:

9 Of sin, because they believe not on me;

10 Of righteousness, because I go to my Father, and ye see me no more;

11 Of judgment, because the prince of this world is judged.
12 I have yet many things to say unto you, but ye cannot bear them now.
13 Howbeit when he, the Spirit of truth, is come, he will guide you into all truth: for he shall not speak of himself; but whatsoever he shall hear, that shall he speak: and he will shew you things to come.
14 He shall glorify me: for he shall receive of mine, and shall shew it unto you. (KJV)

When we are baptized with the Holy Spirit, we are baptized into one body, the Body of Christ. We are given Gifts by the Holy Spirit, in which we are to operate corporately, to further the Kingdom of God. Again, it is not for our glory, but for the glory of God.

1 Cor 12:11 But all these worketh that one and the selfsame Spirit, dividing to every man severally as he will.
12 For as the body is one, and hath many members, and all the members of that one body, being many, are one body: so also is Christ.
13 For by one Spirit are we all baptized into one body, whether we be Jews or Gentiles, whether we be bond or free; and have been all made to drink into one Spirit.
14 For the body is not one member, but many.

John 1:32 And John bare record, saying, I saw the Spirit descending from heaven like a dove, and it abode upon him.
33 And I knew him not: but he that sent me to baptize with water, the same said unto me, Upon whom thou shalt see the Spirit descending, and remaining on him, the same is he which baptizeth with the Holy Ghost.
34 And I saw, and bare record that this is the Son of God. (KJV)

No man can baptize with the Holy Ghost - only Jesus, Who promised He would send the Comforter after He went away.

Another Comforter
(*allon paraklēton*).

Another of like kind (*allon*, not *heteron*), besides Jesus who becomes our Paraclete, Helper, Advocate, with the Father (1Jo 2:1, Cf. Rom 8:26.). This old word (Demosthenes), from *parakaleō*, was used for legal assistant, pleader, advocate, one who pleads another's cause (Josephus, Philo, in illiterate papyrus), in N.T. only in John's writings, though the idea of it is in Rom 8:26-34. Cf. Deissmann, *Light,* etc., p. 336. So the Christian has Christ as his Paraclete with the Father, the Holy Spirit as the Father's Paraclete with us (Joh 14:16, Joh 14:26; Joh 15:26; Joh 16:7; 1Jo 2:1).

(Robertson's Word Pictures)

Notes

_____
_____
_____
_____
_____
_____
_____
_____
_____
_____
_____
_____

John 14:15 If ye love me, keep my commandments.
16 And I will pray the Father, and he shall give you another Comforter, that he may abide with you for ever;
17 Even the Spirit of truth; whom the world cannot receive, because it seeth him not, neither knoweth him: but ye know him; for he dwelleth with you, and shall be in you.
18 I will not leave you comfortless: I will come to you.
19 Yet a little while, and the world seeth me no more; but ye see me: because I live, ye shall live also.
20 At that day ye shall know that I am in my Father, and ye in me, and I in you.

In John 14:16, we see the Holy Spirit is another (Gr. ALLOS) Comforter, of the SAME KIND AS CHRIST WAS.

Greek: allos, AS OPPOSED TO THE GREEK WORD HETEROS, WHICH MEANS ANOTHER OF A DIFFERENT KIND: we can see these two Greek words used in Galatians 1:

Gal 1: 6 I marvel that ye are so soon removed from him that called you into the grace of Christ unto another (HETEROS) gospel:
7 Which is not another (ALLOS); but there be some that trouble you, and would pervert the gospel of Christ.

John 14:16 speaks of the Triune nature of God...One God revealed in Three persons. The Holy Spirit is of the same substance of Jesus and the Father, because He is God, as are they.

At Christ's baptism, we see that the Holy Spirit descended on Him like a dove, and the Father gave His endorsement by declaring Him to be His beloved Son. Jesus walked and operated in the fullness of the Holy Spirit. Jesus declared that He only spoke the things that the Father showed Him. Now He would have to depart, if the Holy Spirit was to be given to others.

John 14:25 These things have I spoken unto you, being yet present with you.
26 But the Comforter, which is the Holy Ghost, whom the Father will send in my name, he shall teach you all things, and bring all things to your remembrance, whatsoever I have said unto you.
27 Peace I leave with you, my peace I give unto you: not as the world giveth, give I unto you. Let not your heart be troubled, neither let it be afraid.
28 Ye have heard how I said unto you, I go away, and come again unto you. If ye loved me, ye would rejoice, because I said, I go unto the Father: for my Father is greater than I. (KJV)

THE PURPOSE OF THE BAPTISM OF THE HOLY SPIRIT

1) TO ENABLE US TO WALK ACCORDING TO THE WILL OF GOD

Ezek 36:24 For I will take you from among the heathen, and gather you out of all countries, and will bring you into your own land.
25 Then will I sprinkle clean water upon you, and ye shall be clean: from all your filthiness, and from all your idols, will I cleanse you.
26 A new heart also will I give you, and a new spirit will I put within you: and I will take away the stony heart out of your flesh, and I will give you an heart of flesh.
27 And I will put my spirit within you, and cause you to walk in my statutes, and ye shall keep my judgments, and do them.

2) TO EMPOWER US TO DO HIS WILL

John 16: 7 Nevertheless I tell you the truth; It is expedient for you that I go away: for if I go not

away, the Comforter will not come unto you; but if I depart, I will send him unto you.

8 And when he is come, he will reprove the world of sin, and of righteousness, and of judgment:

9 Of sin, because they believe not on me;

10 Of righteousness, because I go to my Father, and ye see me no more;

11 Of judgment, because the prince of this world is judged.

12 I have yet many things to say unto you, but ye cannot bear them now.

13 Howbeit when he, the Spirit of truth, is come, he will guide you into all truth: for he shall not speak of himself; but whatsoever he shall hear, that shall he speak: and he will shew you things to come.

14 He shall glorify me: for he shall receive of mine, and shall shew it unto you.

15 All things that the Father hath are mine: therefore said I, that he shall take of mine, and shall shew it unto you.

Notice the Work of the Holy Spirit. When He is come, He will reprove the world of sin, of righteousness, and of judgment. How? When we yield to Him in obedience, and minister as He leads us.

In Micah, 3:8, we see that this was the purpose of the Holy Spirit in the Old Testament as well.

Micah 3:8 But truly I am full of power by the spirit of the LORD, and of judgment, and of might, to declare unto Jacob his transgression, and to Israel his sin.

3) Through every Born again Believer, He will reprove the world of sin, because the world doesn't believe in Jesus, and yet right before their eyes is a walking miracle; a Born Again child of God. This person professes to a lost and dying world the Truth of Who Jesus is, and that Jesus came to set them free from the bondage of sin. We are all living epistles of the reality of God. No longer do we do the things we once did, because the Holy Spirit enables us to be separate from the world.

Notes

1651 elegcho- 1) to convict, to refute, to confute
a) generally with a suggestion of shame of the person convicted
b) by conviction to bring to the light, to expose
to find fault with, correct
a) by word:
1) to reprehend severely, to chide, to admonish, to reprove
2) to call to account, to show one his fault, to demand an explanation
b) by deed: to chasten, to punish

Notes

Pet 4:1 Forasmuch then as Christ hath suffered for us in the flesh, arm yourselves likewise with the same mind: for he that hath suffered in the flesh hath ceased from sin;
2 That he no longer should live the rest of his time in the flesh to the lusts of men, but to the will of God.
3 For the time past of our life may suffice us to have wrought the will of the Gentiles, when we walked in lasciviousness, lusts, excess of wine, revellings, banquetings, and abominable idolatries:
4 Wherein they think it strange that ye run not with them to the same excess of riot, speaking evil of you:
5 Who shall give account to him that is ready to judge the quick and the dead.

4) Through the believer, the Holy Spirit reproves the world of righteousness.

The word "reprove" means rebuke, or convict.

This one who had previously spent his life in unrighteousness now lives a life set apart from the way things are done in the world. He doesn't just speak it, but through the Holy Spirit, he is able to live it. The world cannot see Jesus any longer, but they can see His effect in the Believer's life.

5) Through the believer, the Holy Spirit reproves the world of the Judgment to come. The prince of this world and his grip on the believer has been defeated. Sin and its' awful consequences are unveiled. The Holy Spirit is given to every believer to this end...to demonstrate the Power of God in a person's life. Just as the Holy Spirit worked mightily through Jesus, so He seeks to do the same through each and every believer today.

Titus 3: 3 For we ourselves also were sometimes foolish, disobedient, deceived, serving divers

lusts and pleasures, living in malice and envy, hateful, and hating one another.

4 But after that the kindness and love of God our Saviour toward man appeared,

5 Not by works of righteousness which we have done, but according to his mercy he saved us, by the washing of regeneration, and renewing of the Holy Ghost;

6 Which he shed on us abundantly through Jesus Christ our Saviour;

7 That being justified by his grace, we should be made heirs according to the hope of eternal life.

6) The Holy Spirit works in and through the yielded believer to bring light to the world. See how this worked through Peter:

Acts 2:1 And when the day of Pentecost was fully come, they were all with one accord in one place.

2 And suddenly there came a sound from heaven as of a rushing mighty wind, and it filled all the house where they were sitting.

3 And there appeared unto them cloven tongues like as of fire, and it sat upon each of them.

4 And they were all filled with the Holy Ghost, and began to speak with other tongues, as the Spirit gave them utterance.

5 And there were dwelling at Jerusalem Jews, devout men, out of every nation under heaven.

6 Now when this was noised abroad, the multitude came together, and were confounded, because that every man heard them speak in his own language.

7 And they were all amazed and marvelled, saying one to another, Behold, are not all these which speak Galilaeans?

8 And how hear we every man in our own tongue, wherein we were born?

9 Parthians, and Medes, and Elamites, and the dwellers in Mesopotamia, and in Judaea, and Cappadocia, in Pontus, and Asia,

10 Phrygia, and Pamphylia, in Egypt, and in the parts of Libya about Cyrene, and strangers of Rome, Jews and proselytes,

11 Cretes and Arabians, we do hear them speak in our tongues the wonderful works of God.

12 And they were all amazed, and were in doubt, saying one to another, What meaneth this?

13 Others mocking said, These men are full of new wine.

14 But Peter, standing up with the eleven, lifted up his voice, and said unto them, Ye men of Judaea, and all ye that dwell at Jerusalem, be this known unto you, and hearken to my words:

15 For these are not drunken, as ye suppose, seeing it is but the third hour of the day.

16 But this is that which was spoken by the prophet Joel;

Joe 2:28 And it shall come to pass afterward, that I will pour out my spirit upon all flesh; and your sons and your daughters shall prophesy, your old men shall dream dreams, your young men shall see visions:

29 And also upon the servants and upon the handmaids in those days will I pour out my spirit.

30 And I will shew wonders in the heavens and in the earth, blood, and fire, and pillars of smoke.

31 The sun shall be turned into darkness, and the moon into blood, before the great and the terrible day of the LORD come.

32 And it shall come to pass, that whosoever shall call on the name of the LORD shall be delivered: for in mount Zion and in Jerusalem shall be deliverance, as the LORD hath said, and in the remnant whom the LORD shall call.

Notes

_____
_____
_____
_____
_____
_____
_____
_____
_____
_____
_____
_____
_____
_____
_____
_____

17 And it shall come to pass in the last days, saith God, I will pour out of my Spirit upon all flesh: and your sons and your daughters shall prophesy, and your young men shall see visions, and your old men shall dream dreams:

18 And on my servants and on my handmaidens I will pour out in those days of my Spirit; and they shall prophesy:

19 And I will shew wonders in heaven above, and signs in the earth beneath; blood, and fire, and vapour of smoke:

20 The sun shall be turned into darkness, and the moon into blood, before that great and notable day of the Lord come:

21 And it shall come to pass, that whosoever shall call on the name of the Lord shall be saved.

He convicts men of Righteousness by holding up the Standard of Christ:

22 Ye men of Israel, hear these words; Jesus of Nazareth, a man approved of God among you by miracles and wonders and signs, which God did by him in the midst of you, as ye yourselves also know:

He convicts men of Sin and points out their guilt:

23 Him, being delivered by the determinate counsel and foreknowledge of God, ye have taken, and by wicked hands have crucified and slain:

He convicts them of Judgment To Come:

24 Whom God hath raised up, having loosed the pains of death: because it was not possible that he should be holden of it.

25 For David speaketh concerning him, I foresaw the Lord always before my face, for he is on my right hand, that I should not be moved:

26 Therefore did my heart rejoice, and my tongue was glad; moreover also my flesh shall rest in hope:

27 Because thou wilt not leave my soul in hell, neither wilt thou suffer thine Holy One to see corruption.

28 Thou hast made known to me the ways of life; thou shalt make me full of joy with thy countenance.

29 Men and brethren, let me freely speak unto you of the patriarch David, that he is both dead and buried, and his sepulchre is with us unto this day.

30 Therefore being a prophet, and knowing that God had sworn with an oath to him, that of the fruit of his loins, according to the flesh, he would raise up Christ to sit on his throne;

31 He seeing this before spake of the resurrection of Christ, that his soul was not left in hell, neither his flesh did see corruption.

32 This Jesus hath God raised up, whereof we all are witnesses.

33 Therefore being by the right hand of God exalted, and having received of the Father the promise of the Holy Ghost, he hath shed forth this, which ye now see and hear.

Judgment:

34 For David is not ascended into the heavens: but he saith himself, The LORD said unto my Lord, Sit thou on my right hand,

35 Until I make thy foes thy footstool.

36 Therefore let all the house of Israel know assuredly, that God hath made that same Jesus, whom ye have crucified, both Lord and Christ.

Conviction from the Holy Spirit brings results:

37 Now when they heard this, they were pricked in their heart, and said unto Peter and to the rest of the apostles, Men and brethren, what shall we do?

Conviction from the Holy Spirit results in men turning from Sin to Righteousness:

38 Then Peter said unto them, Repent, and be baptized every one of you in the name of Jesus Christ for the remission of sins, and ye shall receive the gift of the Holy Ghost.

39 For the promise is unto you, and to your children, and to all that are afar off, even as many as the Lord our God shall call.

Conviction from the power of the Holy Spirit: Sin, Righteousness, And Judgment To Come:

40 And with many other words did he testify and exhort, saying, Save yourselves from this untoward generation.

41 Then they that gladly received his word were baptized: and the same day there were added unto them about three thousand souls.

42 And they continued stedfastly in the apostles' doctrine and fellowship, and in breaking of bread, and in prayers.

43 And fear came upon every soul: and many wonders and signs were done by the apostles.

44 And all that believed were together, and had all things common;

45 And sold their possessions and goods, and parted them to all men, as every man had need.

46 And they, continuing daily with one accord in the temple, and breaking bread from house to house, did eat their meat with gladness and singleness of heart,

47 Praising God, and having favour with all the people. And the Lord added to the church daily such as should be saved.

We can see this pattern of the Holy Spirit's work in and through a believer's life:

Acts 10:34 Then Peter opened his mouth, and said, Of a truth I perceive that God is no respecter of persons:

Sin, Righteousness

35 But in every nation he that feareth him, and worketh righteousness, is accepted with him.

36 The word which God sent unto the children of Israel, preaching peace by Jesus Christ: (he is Lord of all:)

37 That word, I say, ye know, which was published throughout all Judaea, and began from Galilee, after the baptism which John preached;

38 How God anointed Jesus of Nazareth with the Holy Ghost and with power: who went about doing good, and healing all that were oppressed of the devil; for God was with him.

Testifying About Jesus

39 And we are witnesses of all things which he did both in the land of the Jews, and in Jerusalem; whom they slew and hanged on a tree:
40 Him God raised up the third day, and shewed him openly;
41 Not to all the people, but unto witnesses chosen before of God, even to us, who did eat and drink with him after he rose from the dead.

Judgment:

42 And he commanded us to preach unto the people, and to testify that it is he which was ordained of God to be the Judge of quick and dead.
43 To him give all the prophets witness, that through his name whosoever believeth in him shall receive remission of sins.
44 While Peter yet spake these words, the Holy Ghost fell on all them which heard the word.
45 And they of the circumcision which believed were astonished, as many as came with Peter, because that on the Gentiles also was poured out the gift of the Holy Ghost.
46 For they heard them speak with tongues, and magnify God. Then answered Peter,
47 Can any man forbid water, that these should not be baptized, which have received the Holy Ghost as well as we?
48 And he commanded them to be baptized in the name of the Lord. Then prayed they him to tarry certain days.

To further illustrate our case, we will look at another instance where the Holy Spirit did the work He is intended to do through His servants:

Acts 4:7 And when they had set them in the midst, they asked, By what power, or by what name, have ye done this?
8 Then Peter, filled with the Holy Ghost, said unto them, Ye rulers of the people, and elders of Israel,

Righteousness

9 If we this day be examined of the good deed done to the impotent man, by what means he is made whole;

Sin

10 Be it known unto you all, and to all the people of Israel, that by the name of Jesus Christ of Nazareth, whom ye crucified, whom God raised from the dead, even by him doth this man stand here before you whole.
11 This is the stone which was set at nought of you builders, which is become the head of the corner.

Judgment To Come

12 Neither is there salvation in any other: for there is none other name under heaven given among men, whereby we must be saved.
13 Now when they saw the boldness of Peter and John, and perceived that they were unlearned and ignorant men, they marvelled; and they took knowledge of them, that they had been with Jesus.

Righteousness

14 And beholding the man which was healed standing with them, they could say nothing against it.
15 But when they had commanded them to go aside out of the council, they conferred among themselves,
16 Saying, What shall we do to these men? for that indeed a notable miracle hath been done by them is manifest to all them that dwell in Jerusalem; and we cannot deny it.
17 But that it spread no further among the people, let us straitly threaten them, that they speak henceforth to no man in this name.
18 And they called them, and commanded them not to speak at all nor teach in the name of Jesus.

Righteousness

19 But Peter and John answered and said unto them, Whether it be right in the sight of God to hearken unto you more than unto God, judge ye.
20 For we cannot but speak the things which we have seen and heard.
21 So when they had further threatened them, they let them go, finding nothing how they might punish them, because of the people: for all men glorified God for that which was done.

1 WHAT DID JESUS TELL THE DISCIPLES WOULD HAPPEN WHEN THEY RECEIVED THE HOLY GHOST?

_____

_____

2. IN THE BOOK OF JOEL, WHAT ARE WE TOLD WOULD HAPPEN WHEN THE HOLY SPIRIT CAME UPON MANKIND IN THE LAST DAYS?

_____

_____

3. WHAT WOULD BE THE PURPOSE OF THIS?

_____

_____

_____

4. WHY DO YOU THINK JESUS SAID:

Luke 10: 20 Notwithstanding in this rejoice not, that the spirits are subject unto you; but rather rejoice, because your names are written in heaven.

5. IN JOHN 16:13-14, JESUS TELLS THE DISCIPLES THAT WHEN THE HOLY SPIRIT COMES, HE WILL...

_____

_____

6. IN JOHN 16:8, WE SEE THAT THE HOLY SPIRIT WILL

_____

_____

7. HOW DOES THIS OCCUR?

_____

_____

BASIC DOCTRINES

BAPTISMS

LESSON 9

EVIDENCE OF THE BAPTISM OF THE HOLY SPIRIT

Heb 6:1 Therefore leaving the principles of the doctrine of Christ, let us go on unto perfection; not laying again the foundation of repentance from dead works, and of faith toward God,
2 Of the doctrine of baptisms, and of laying on of hands, and of resurrection of the dead, and of eternal judgment.

Is the Baptism of the Holy Spirit with the evidence of speaking in tongues a biblical doctrine, or a church doctrine?

Acts 2: 2 And suddenly there came a sound from heaven as of a rushing mighty wind, and it filled all the house where they were sitting.
3 And there appeared unto them cloven tongues like as of fire, and it sat upon each of them.
4 And they were all filled with the Holy Ghost, and began to speak with other tongues, as the Spirit gave them utterance.

Acts 10:46 For they heard them speak with tongues, and magnify God. Then answered Peter,

Acts 19:6 And when Paul had laid his hands upon them, the Holy Ghost came on them; and they spake with tongues, and prophesied.

Acts 8:15 Who, when they were come down, prayed for them, that they might receive the Holy Ghost:
16 (For as yet he was fallen upon none of them: only they were baptized in the name of the Lord Jesus.)
17 Then laid they their hands on them, and they received the Holy Ghost.
18 And when Simon saw that through laying on of the apostles' hands the Holy Ghost was given, he offered them money,
19 Saying, Give me also this power, that on whomsoever I lay hands, he may receive the Holy Ghost.

Notice that the account in chapter 8 does not mention the gift of tongues being manifested. That is not to say that they did or they didn't manifest themselves on this day; and the fact that Simon "saw" that through laying on of the

_____
_____
_____
_____
_____
_____
_____
_____
_____
_____
_____
_____
_____
_____
_____
_____
_____
_____

1Co 12:4 Now there are diversities of gifts, but the same Spirit.
5 And there are differences of administrations, but the same Lord.
6 And there are diversities of operations, but it is the same God which worketh all in all.
7 But the manifestation of the Spirit is given to every man to profit withal.
8 For to one is given by the Spirit the word of wisdom; to another the word of knowledge by the same Spirit;
9 To another faith by the same Spirit; to another the gifts of healing by the same Spirit;
10 To another the working of miracles; to another prophecy; to another discerning of spirits; to another divers kinds of tongues; to another the interpretation of tongues:
11 But all these worketh that one and the selfsame Spirit, dividing to every man severally as he will.

apostles' hands the Holy Ghost was given, would seem to indicate that they were speaking in tongues.

What was it that Simon saw? We really cannot say, because the Scripture is silent about it, but I would speculate that the external evidence of them having received the Holy Spirit may well have been that they were speaking in tongues.

On the other hand, they could have been acting like they were drunk, as had happened at Pentecost. It is my personal conviction that the scripture account is silent here in regards to the manifestation of the Spirit through the gift of tongues, because WHILE TONGUES ARE AN EVIDENCE OF THE BAPTISM OF THE HOLY SPIRIT, tongues aren't the ONLY means of evidence of the baptism of the Holy Spirit.

Nor does the fact that a person speaks in tongues prove that he or she is baptized in the Holy Spirit.

Satan is a counterfeit, and any Satanist or other practitioner of the occult can tell you that they also have a "tongues" that they speak. It is important to rightly divide the Word of Truth to avoid falling into doctrinal error. The adage "baptism of the Holy Spirit with the evidence of speaking in tongues" is NOWHERE found in Scripture. Again, the gift of tongues CAN be evidence that one is baptized in the Holy Spirit, but it is not THE evidence.

I believe that operating in any of the Gifts listed in 1 Cor 12 would be an evidence that one has been baptized in the Holy Spirit.

Speaking of counterfeits, Satan also has diviners, or those who operate in the prophetic (see Deuteronomy 13:1-2).

Deu 13:1 If there arise among you a prophet, or a dreamer of dreams, and giveth thee a sign or a wonder,

2 And the sign or the wonder come to pass, whereof he spake unto thee, saying, Let us go after other gods, which thou hast not known, and let us serve them;
3 Thou shalt not hearken unto the words of that prophet, or that dreamer of dreams: for the LORD your God proveth you, to know whether ye love the LORD your God with all your heart and with all your soul.

There are witches and shamans and "treaters" who practice faith healing.

There are those in the occult arts who can give a personal word of knowledge.

Pharoah's magicians duplicated most of the miracles that God worked through Moses. It is for this very reason that many in the church discredit the Work of the Holy Spirit, and attribute all that which is supernatural to the devil. This is also a mistake. We are told that we must covet earnestly the best gifts (1 Cor 12:31).

We must always understand that God is Sovereign, and He will give to every man the Gift that He chooses according to His Own Will, and we should be open to receiving those Gifts that He wishes us to have.

1Co 12:11 But all these worketh that one and the selfsame Spirit, dividing to every man severally as he will.

I personally believe this doctrine of "*Baptism of the Holy Spirit with the evidence of speaking in tongues*" is simply a man-made doctrine. The phrase is found nowhere in scripture.

That is not to discredit or to minimize the spiritual gift of tongues. Every believer should desire every spiritual gift.

Paul said "I would that ye all spake in tongues" (1 Cor 14:5). I believe that chapter 14 of 1 Corinthians was written to address this very issue. We will look at that chapter a little later. For now, we should look at the various gifts of the Holy Spirit as Paul addresses them in 1 Corinthians 12:

A careful reading of 1 Corinthians 12 (particularly verses 28-30) shows us that obviously, not all have the gift of healing, or the gift of tongues, or prophecy.

Let's look closer at the spiritual gifts:

1 Cor 12: 1 Now concerning spiritual gifts, brethren, I would not have you ignorant.
2 Ye know that ye were Gentiles, carried away unto these dumb idols, even as ye were led.

Paul addressed a serious problem that existed in the Church of Corinth when he wrote chapters 12-14 in his first letter to the 1 Corinthians.

The Christians in Corinth were putting more emphasis on the POWER of the Holy Spirit's gifts, than they were on the PRESENCE of the Holy Spirit's refining work in their lives.

If we put more emphasis on the Gifts of the Holy Spirit than on the Giver, then we may well fall for the counterfeits that Satan would put in the Church in an attempt to lead us astray.

He opened his teaching by mentioning idolatry in relation with spiritual gifts, and putting more emphasis on the gifts than on the Giver of the Gifts is akin to spiritual idolatry.

Personally, I believe that Paul was dealing with a situation in the church quite similar to that which we see today - I believe that there was a fascination with the gift of tongues or any other of the gifts of the Holy Spirit that prevailed in the church, while the people of God were neglecting the responsibility of walking in obedience to the Word.

Many were operating in the Power of the Holy Spirit, yet there was immorality and division in the Church. One of the things that was happening was that a man committed adultery with his stepmother (his father's wife), and a lot of people in the church talked about it (gossip), but did nothing to stop it, and yet the Gifts of the Holy Spirit were at work in that church.

1Co 5:1 It is reported commonly *that there is* fornication among you, and such fornication as is not so much as named among the Gentiles, that one should have his father's wife.

There was a divisive spirit akin to denominationalism

1Co 12:1 Now concerning spiritual *gifts,* brethren, I would not have you ignorant.
2 Ye know that ye were Gentiles, carried away unto these dumb idols, even as ye were led.

that was at work in the Corinthian church, and yet the Gifts of the Holy Spirit were at work in the church:

1Co 3:3 **For ye are yet carnal: for whereas *there is* among you envying, and strife, and divisions, are ye not carnal, and walk as men?**
4 **For while one saith, I am of Paul; and another, I *am* of Apollos; are ye not carnal?**

2Co 12:20 **For I fear, lest, when I come, I shall not find you such as I would, and *that* I shall be found unto you such as ye would not: lest *there be* debates, envyings, wraths, strifes, backbitings, whisperings, swellings, tumults:**

I believe that in 1 Co 12:1-3 Paul is pointing out the fact that man has a tendency to idolize the supernatural, rather than walking in obedience to the Word of God.

It is interesting that Paul used some very important words when he began his teaching on Spiritual gifts in 1 Corinthians 12.

Paul began his teaching by saying "*I would not have you ignorant...*" Just as in Paul's day, many Christians today stand in awe of the gifts of the Holy Spirit more than they do the GIVER of the gift.

So what if I have a gift of healing, so that all kinds of people are healed in my ministry? If I am not walking in the *fruit* of the spirit, these gifts will profit me nothing. Am I the one that is doing the healing? Or is it God doing the healing through me?

I can love the Gift more than God, Who gave the gift. Sorcerers and witches, fortune tellers and "treaters" love their supernatural abilities more than they love God. The proof of where my affections are lies in my personal walk with the Lord. I can fool every person, but I can't fool God, Who knows my innermost being.

1 Cor 12:3 Wherefore I give you to understand, that no man speaking by the Spirit of God calleth Jesus accursed: and that no man can say that Jesus is the Lord, but by the Holy Ghost.

4 Now there are diversities of gifts, but the same Spirit.

5 And there are differences of administrations, but the same Lord.

6 And there are diversities of operations, but it is the same God which worketh all in all.

7 But the manifestation of the Spirit is given to every man to profit withal.

8 For to one is given by the Spirit the word of wisdom; to another the word of knowledge by the same Spirit;

9 To another faith by the same Spirit; to another the gifts of healing by the same Spirit;

10 To another the working of miracles; to another prophecy; to another discerning of spirits; to another divers kinds of tongues; to another the interpretation of tongues:

11 But all these worketh that one and the selfsame Spirit, dividing to every man severally as he will.

12 For as the body is one, and hath many members, and all the members of that one body, being many, are one body: so also is Christ.

13 For by one Spirit are we all baptized into one body, whether we be Jews or Gentiles, whether we be bond or free; and have been all made to drink into one Spirit.

14 For the body is not one member, but many.

15 If the foot shall say, Because I am not the hand, I am not of the body; is it therefore not of the body?

16 And if the ear shall say, Because I am not the eye, I am not of the body; is it therefore not of the body?

17 If the whole body were an eye, where were the hearing? If the whole were hearing, where were the smelling?

18 But now hath God set the members every one of them in the body, as it hath pleased him.

19 And if they were all one member, where were the body?

20 But now are they many members, yet but one body.

21 And the eye cannot say unto the hand, I have no need of thee: nor again the head to the feet, I have no need of you.

22 Nay, much more those members of the body, which seem to be more feeble, are necessary:

23 And those members of the body, which we think to be less honourable, upon these we bestow more abundant honour; and our uncomely parts have more abundant comeliness.

24 For our comely parts have no need: but God hath tempered the body together, having given more abundant honour to that part which lacked:

25 That there should be no schism in the body; but that the members should have the same care one for another.

26 And whether one member suffer, all the members suffer with it; or one member be honoured, all the members rejoice with it.
27 Now ye are the body of Christ, and members in particular.
28 And God hath set some in the church, first apostles, secondarily prophets, thirdly teachers, after that miracles, then gifts of healings, helps, governments, diversities of tongues.
29 Are all apostles? are all prophets? are all teachers? are all workers of miracles?
30 Have all the gifts of healing? do all speak with tongues? do all interpret?
31 But covet earnestly the best gifts: and yet shew I unto you a more excellent way.

Let us look closer at verses 28-30 and the questions that Paul asks in verses 29 and 30:

1 Cor 12: 28 And God hath set some in the church, first apostles, secondarily prophets, thirdly teachers, after that miracles, then gifts of healings, helps, governments, diversities of tongues.
29 Are all apostles? are all prophets? are all teachers? are all workers of miracles?
30 Have all the gifts of healing? do all speak with tongues? do all interpret?

The obvious answer to all of these questions is a resounding NO. Not all are apostles. Not all are prophets. Not all are teachers. Not all are workers of miracles. Not all have the gifts of healing. Not all speak with tongues. And not all interpret.

A lot of emphasis is placed on the gift of tongues in the Charismatic/Pentecostal circles today. But notice what 1 Cor. 13:1 says about the gift of tongues or for that matter, what the rest of the chapter says about any of the gifts.

1 Cor 13:1 Though I speak with the tongues of men and of angels, and have not charity, I am become as sounding brass, or a tinkling cymbal. (KJV)

Love is a fruit of the Spirit. Operating in the GIFTS of the Spirit without the FRUIT of the Spirit is possible, but it is to no avail. We are all familiar with Matthew 7:21-25:

Matt 7:21 Not every one that saith unto me, Lord, Lord, shall enter into the kingdom of heaven; but he that doeth the will of my Father which is in heaven.

22 Many will say to me in that day, Lord, Lord, have we not prophesied in thy name? and in thy name have cast out devils? and in thy name done many wonderful works?
23 And then will I profess unto them, I never knew you: depart from me, ye that work iniquity.
24 Therefore whosoever heareth these sayings of mine, and doeth them, I will liken him unto a wise man, which built his house upon a rock:
25 And the rain descended, and the floods came, and the winds blew, and beat upon that house; and it fell not: for it was founded upon a rock.(KJV)

Hebrews 2:2-4 seems to echo this:

Heb 2: 2 For if the word spoken by angels was stedfast, and every transgression and disobedience received a just recompence of reward;
3 How shall we escape, if we neglect so great salvation; which at the first began to be spoken by the Lord, and was confirmed unto us by them that heard him;
4 God also bearing them witness, both with signs and wonders, and with divers miracles, and gifts of the Holy Ghost, according to his own will?

The Gifts of the Spirit are given to the believer through the Holy Spirit.

The fruit of the Spirit are the result of patient continuance in obedience to the Word of God, *WHICH CAN ONLY BE DONE THROUGH THE ABIDING OF THE HOLY SPIRIT IN ONE'S LIFE.*

1 Cor 12:8 For to one is given by the Spirit the word of wisdom; to another the word of knowledge by the same Spirit;
9 To another faith by the same Spirit; to another the gifts of healing by the same Spirit;
10 To another the working of miracles; to another prophecy; to another discerning of spirits; to another divers kinds of tongues; to another the interpretation of tongues:
11 But all these worketh that one and the selfsame Spirit, dividing to every man severally as he will.

Mark 16:17 And these signs shall follow them that believe; In my name shall they cast out devils; they shall speak with new tongues;
18 They shall take up serpents; and if they drink any deadly thing, it shall not hurt them; they shall lay hands on the sick, and they shall recover.

The questions to be asked here are these: Will every person who believes cast out devils? Will every person speak with new tongues? Will every person take up serpents, or pray for the sick and see them recover? We read of only one

Joh 15:1 I am the true vine, and my Father is the husbandman.
2 Every branch in me that beareth not fruit he taketh away: and every branch that beareth fruit, he purgeth it, that it may bring forth more fruit.
3 Now ye are clean through the word which I have spoken unto you.
4 Abide in me, and I in you. As the branch cannot bear fruit of itself, except it abide in the vine; no more can ye, except ye abide in me.
5 I am the vine, ye are the branches: He that abideth in me, and I in him, the same bringeth forth much fruit: for without me ye can do nothing.
6 If a man abide not in me, he is cast forth as a branch, and is withered; and men gather them, and cast them into the fire, and they are burned.
7 If ye abide in me, and my words abide in you, ye shall ask what ye will, and it shall be done unto you.
8 Herein is my Father glorified, that ye bear much fruit; so shall ye be my disciples.
9 As the Father hath loved me, so have I loved you: continue ye in my love.
10 If ye keep my commandments, ye shall abide in my love; even as I have kept my Father's commandments, and abide in his love.

Notes

_____
_____
_____
_____
_____
_____
_____
_____
_____
_____
_____
_____
_____

instance where a person was bitten by a serpent, and nothing happened to him (Paul, in the book of Acts. 28:3-6). I believe the answer is to be found in 1 Corinthians 12:11, which says the Holy Spirit divides the gifts "severally as He will".

The Gift of Tongues edifies the one who prays in tongues.

1Co 14:2 For he that speaketh in an *unknown* tongue speaketh not unto men, but unto God: for no man understandeth *him;* howbeit in the spirit he speaketh mysteries.
3 But he that prophesieth speaketh unto men *to* edification, and exhortation, and comfort.
4 He that speaketh in an *unknown* tongue edifieth himself; but he that prophesieth edifieth the church.
5 I would that ye all spake with tongues, but rather that ye prophesied: for greater *is* he that prophesieth than he that speaketh with tongues, except he interpret, that the church may receive edifying.

In John chapter 15, the Lord tells His disciples that if they ABIDE in Him, they will bear much fruit, If they don't, they will be withered and cast forth as a worthless branch.

A more precise measurement of whether a person is baptized in the Holy Spirit, is whether or not the Fruit of the Spirit are manifesting themselves in the believer's life.

Gal 5:22 But the fruit of the Spirit is love, joy, peace, longsuffering, gentleness, goodness, faith,
23 Meekness, temperance: against such there is no law.
24 And they that are Christ's have crucified the flesh with the affections and lusts.
25 If we live in the Spirit, let us also walk in the Spirit.
26 Let us not be desirous of vain glory, provoking one another, envying one another.

Is there evidence of Love in that person's life?

Is there evidence of Patience in a person's life?

Is there evidence of Meekness in a person's life?

Is there evidence of Joy permeating that person's being?

Is there evidence of an attitude of longsuffering toward other people?

Is there a Gentle spirit that lives in this person?

Does this person live his life in Goodness?

Is this person a person of unwavering faith?

Is he or she temperate in all things?

These evidences in a person's life are surer signs of the baptism of the Holy Spirit than any gifts they may or may not have.

If someone is operating in the gifts and the calling of God, but yet without the fruit of the Spirit, it will avail him or her nothing in that day when they stand before God.

CONCERNING THE PREMISE THAT THE SPIRITUAL GIFTS HAVE CEASED IN THE LIGHT OF 1 CORINTHIANS 13:8:

1 Cor 13:8 Charity never faileth: but whether there be prophecies, they shall fail; whether there be tongues, they shall cease; whether there be knowledge, it shall vanish away.

The word "cease" here was also used in several other places, but to demonstrate our point, I will point out one passage where the word was used in the gospels:

1) Many of the cults as well as some "main stream" Christian denominations hold to the doctrine of Cessationism. Cessationists teach that the Gifts of the Holy Spirit as outlined in 1 Corinthians 12 and Romans 12 have ceased once the original apostles died. The thought is that the Gifts of the Holy Spirit were given to give credence to the Gospel of the Kingdom of God, but when the New Testament was written ("that which is perfect", referred to in 1Co 13:10), the Gifts were no longer needed.

1 Co 13:8 Charity never faileth: but whether there be prophecies, they shall fail; whether there be tongues, they shall cease; whether there be knowledge, it shall vanish away.
9 For we know in part, and we prophesy in part.
10 But when that which is perfect is come, then that which is in part shall be done away.

But in contest, the entire 13th chapter of 1Corinthians is referring to Love. When one grows from selfishness to selflessness, then they begin to understand fully the things of the Spirit. Without Love, all the Gifts are just things for show. Immature Christians seek power to testify of their spirituality. But the mature Christian demonstrates power as an outgrowth of his or her Love.

1 Cor 13:11 When I was a child, I spake as a child, I understood as a child, I thought as a child: but when I became a man, I put away childish things.
12 For now we see through a glass, darkly; but then face to face: now I know in part; but then shall I know even as also I am known.
13 And now abideth faith, hope, charity, these three; but the greatest of these is charity.

Luke 5: 4 Now when he had *left* speaking, he said unto Simon, Launch out into the deep, and let down your nets for a draught.

Obviously, that wasn't the last time Jesus ever spoke. I believe that 1 Cor. 13:8 is saying that we won't constantly pray in tongues, just as we won't constantly speak in our natural language.

1 Cor 13: 8 Charity never faileth: but whether there be prophecies, they shall fail; whether there be tongues, they shall cease; whether there be knowledge, it shall vanish away.
9 For we know in part, and we prophesy in part.
10 But when that which is perfect is come, then that which is in part shall be done away.
11 When I was a child, I spake as a child, I understood as a child, I thought as a child: but when I became a man, I put away childish things.
12 For now we see through a glass, darkly; but then face to face: now I know in part; but then shall I know even as also I am known.
13 And now abideth faith, hope, charity, these three; but the greatest of these is charity.

The point being made in verse 8 is defined by context in what follows. In this walk with Christ, we are constantly learning, but we never achieve the Big Picture until we actually are with Him. We only know in part. We only prophesy to the degree which we can understand.

The prophetic will eventually come to pass, and after that it is of no use. It is now *history* instead of something that we look forward to[1].

Knowledge is only good as far as it is applied. My knowledge as an electrical engineer may have little or no value when I need to repair a leaking pipe. The things that never change, but always remain, are FAITH, HOPE, AND LOVE...AND THE GREATEST OF THESE THREE IS LOVE. Love and faith are identified as fruit of the Spirit in Galatians 5:22.

Nowhere in the Bible does it teach that the Spiritual Gifts would be done away. Those who teach such a doctrine are philosophers at best. The Word of God aptly refers to these teachers who would come in the last days:

2Ti 3:1 This know also, that in the last days perilous times shall come. 2 For men shall be lovers of their own selves, covetous, boasters, proud, blasphemers, disobedient to parents, unthankful, unholy, 3 Without natural affection, trucebreakers, false accusers, incontinent, fierce, despisers of those that are good, 4 Traitors, heady, highminded, lovers of pleasures more than lovers of God; 5 Having a form of godliness, but denying the power thereof: from such turn away. 6 For of this sort are they which creep into houses, and lead captive silly women laden with sins, led away with divers lusts, 7 Ever learning, and never able to come to the knowledge of the truth.

......5 Having a form of godliness, but denying the power thereof: from such turn away.

Verse five shows us that Paul was warning Timothy of how it would be in the Church in the Last Days. They would have a form of godliness but deny the Power thereof, which is exactly what Cessationism does.

2Ti 3:13 But evil men and seducers shall wax worse and worse, deceiving, and being deceived. 14 But continue thou in the things which thou hast learned and hast been assured of, knowing of whom thou hast learned them; 15 And that from a child thou hast known the holy scriptures, which are able to make thee wise unto salvation through faith which is in Christ Jesus.

Remember, the word translated as Hope signifies "confidence" in the Greek.

1 Cor 14:1 Follow after charity, and desire spiritual gifts, but rather that ye may prophesy. 2 For he that speaketh in an unknown tongue speaketh not unto men, but unto God: for no man understandeth him; howbeit in the spirit he speaketh mysteries. 3 But he that prophesieth speaketh unto men to edification, and exhortation, and comfort. 4 He that speaketh in an unknown tongue edifieth himself; but he that prophesieth edifieth the church. 5 I would that ye all spake with tongues, but rather that ye prophesied: for greater is he that prophesieth than he that speaketh with tongues, except he interpret, that the church may receive edifying. 6 Now, brethren, if I come unto you speaking with tongues, what shall I profit you, except I shall speak to you either by revelation, or by knowledge, or by prophesying, or by doctrine? 7 And even things without life giving sound, whether pipe or harp, except they give a distinction in the sounds, how shall it be known what is piped or harped? 8 For if the trumpet give an uncertain sound, who shall prepare himself to the battle? 9 So likewise ye, except ye utter by the tongue words easy to be understood, how shall it be known what is spoken? for ye shall speak into the air. 10 There are, it may be, so many kinds of voices in the world, and none of them is without signification. 11 Therefore if I know not the meaning of the voice, I shall be unto him that speaketh a barbarian, and he that speaketh shall be a barbarian unto me. 12 Even so ye, forasmuch as ye are zealous of spiritual gifts, seek that ye may excel to the edifying of the church. 13 Wherefore let him that speaketh in an unknown tongue pray that he may interpret.

16 All scripture is given by inspiration of God, and is profitable for doctrine, for reproof, for correction , for instruction in righteousness:
17 That the man of God may be perfect, throughly furnished unto all good works.

All Scripture. Including all the verses that speak of the Baptism of the Holy Spirit, and the Gifts of the Spirit Are given to us so that the man of God may be perfect (mature), thoroughly furnished unto all good works.

Without the Baptism of the Holy Spirit and preaching the Word of God void of the evidence of His Power through His Gifts in operation in the work of the Ministry, the Church becomes just a spectator oriented house of philosophers who bandy about words to no profit.

If you have not yet been baptized in the Holy Spirit, now is the time for you to begin to seek that wonderful Gift from God.

1Co 2:4 And my speech and my preaching was not with enticing words of man's wisdom, but in demonstration of the Spirit and of power:
5 That your faith should not stand in the wisdom of men, but in the power of God.

Notes

14 For if I pray in an unknown tongue, my spirit prayeth, but my understanding is unfruitful.
15 What is it then? I will pray with the spirit, and I will pray with the understanding also: I will sing with the spirit, and I will sing with the understanding also.
16 Else when thou shalt bless with the spirit, how shall he that occupieth the room of the unlearned say Amen at thy giving of thanks, seeing he understandeth not what thou sayest?
17 For thou verily givest thanks well, but the other is not edified.
18 I thank my God, I speak with tongues more than ye all:
19 Yet in the church I had rather speak five words with my understanding, that by my voice I might teach others also, than ten thousand words in an unknown tongue.
20 Brethren, be not children in understanding: howbeit in malice be ye children, but in understanding be men.
21 In the law it is written, With men of other tongues and other lips will I speak unto this people; and yet for all that will they not hear me, saith the Lord.
22 Wherefore tongues are for a sign, not to them that believe, but to them that believe not: but prophesying serveth not for them that believe not, but for them which believe.
23 If therefore the whole church be come together into one place, and all speak with tongues, and there come in those that are unlearned, or unbelievers, will they not say that ye are mad?
24 But if all prophesy, and there come in one that believeth not, or one unlearned, he is convinced of all, he is judged of all:
25 And thus are the secrets of his heart made manifest; and so falling down on his face he will worship God, and report that God is in you of a truth.
26 How is it then, brethren? when ye come together, every one of you hath a psalm, hath a doctrine, hath a tongue, hath a revelation, hath

an interpretation. Let all things be done unto edifying.

27 If any man speak in an unknown tongue, let it be by two, or at the most by three, and that by course; and let one interpret.
28 But if there be no interpreter, let him keep silence in the church; and let him speak to himself, and to God.
29 Let the prophets speak two or three, and let the other judge.
30 If any thing be revealed to another that sitteth by, let the first hold his peace.
31 For ye may all prophesy one by one, that all may learn, and all may be comforted.
32 And the spirits of the prophets are subject to the prophets.
For God is not the author of confusion, but of peace, as in all churches of the saints. (KJV)

Paul was showing the Church in chapter 14 that while tongues are a viable gift of the Spirit, they are not the most important of the gifts...He says:

Cor. 14:1 Follow after charity, and desire spiritual gifts, but rather that ye may prophesy.

For the next several verses, Paul contrasts the gift of Prophecy to the gift of tongues. His main point is that the gifts of God should be used for building up and encouraging the church. Notice that he also puts the priority in the right perspective: PURSUE AFTER LOVE (the fruit first) and desire spiritual gifts (second).

Also notice that Paul emphasized desiring to prophesy, and he didn't mention desiring tongues. But in the church today, the emphasis is put on speaking in tongues.

1 Cor 14:38 But if any man be ignorant, let him be ignorant.
39 Wherefore, brethren, covet to prophesy, and forbid not to speak with tongues.
40 Let all things be done decently and in order.

Let's look once more at an example of a person who wanted the gift without the fruit of the Spirit:

Acts 8:14 Now when the apostles which were at Jerusalem heard that Samaria had received the word of God, they sent unto them Peter and John:
15 Who, when they were come down, prayed for them, that they might receive the Holy Ghost:
16 (For as yet he was fallen upon none of them: only they were baptized in the name of the Lord Jesus.)

17 Then laid they their hands on them, and they received the Holy Ghost.
18 And when Simon saw that through laying on of the apostles' hands the Holy Ghost was given, he offered them money,
19 Saying, Give me also this power, that on whomsoever I lay hands, he may receive the Holy Ghost.
20 But Peter said unto him, Thy money perish with thee, because thou hast thought that the gift of God may be purchased with money.
21 Thou hast neither part nor lot in this matter: for thy heart is not right in the sight of God.
22 Repent therefore of this thy wickedness, and pray God, if perhaps the thought of thine heart may be forgiven thee.
23 For I perceive that thou art in the gall of bitterness, and in the bond of iniquity.
24 Then answered Simon, and said, Pray ye to the Lord for me, that none of these things which ye have spoken come upon me.
25 And they, when they had testified and preached the word of the Lord, returned to Jerusalem, and preached the gospel in many villages of the Samaritans.

We are not to idolize the Gifts of the Holy Spirit. Those who do this have their hearts in the wrong place. Having said that, we are to covet earnestly the best gifts, but we should never lose sight of the fact that the gifts of God are for Glorifying Him and furthering His Kingdom, and building up and encouraging the Body of Christ.

Every Christian should desire to speak in tongues. It is a spiritual Gift from God. But they shouldn't limit their desire to only tongues.

The doctrine of Cessationism is probably taught in some denominations because of the abuse and the exploitation of the Gifts in many Pentecostal/Charismatic churches. Satan even has his puppets in the pulpits and on so called Christian programming. A lot of what is done in the Name of Jesus is simply "Simony", using the gifts of God for personal gain, just as the Simon the sorcerer thought to do. But just because there are abuses in the Church doesn't mean we should neglect the Gifts of God. We just need to balance the operation of the Gifts with the Word of God.

Many Christians in the church today speak in tongues, but rarely do they have the boldness to testify of Jesus and His Presence in their lives. The Primary Purpose of the Baptism of the Holy Spirit is not to be "slain in the spirit", to speak in tongues in the midst of the congregation, to run around the sanctuary, or to feel goose bumps, but to empower the Christian to be a witness of Jesus.

The true evidence that one is baptized in the Holy Spirit will be the presence of the fruit of the Spirit in one's life, and that they will be genuinely desirous to witness to others about Jesus Christ wherever they go:

Act 1:8 But ye shall receive power, after that the Holy Ghost is come upon you: and ye shall be witnesses unto me both in Jerusalem, and in all Judea, and in Samaria, and unto the uttermost part of the earth.

The man made doctrine of "Baptism Of The Holy Spirit With Evidence Of Speaking In Tongues" has become a smoke screen to lull the Christian into complacency concerning the commission of the Lord to go and preach the gospel to every creature, and to make them feel good about themselves despite their lack of evidence of the Fruit of the Spirit in their lives.

When one prays to receive the baptism of the Holy Spirit, he or she should desire whatever gift or gifts the Holy Spirit chooses to impart to them. Only focusing on the gift of tongues has the tendency to minimize the importance of the other gifts of the Holy Spirit.

The teachers insist that all should speak in tongues, but they don't teach that all should heal, or prophesy or do miraculous signs. They teach that only certain people can do that, which leads to men who operate in those gifts to be highly esteemed among the "laity". If all are to speak in tongues, then all are to heal, to prophesy, and to do miraculous signs.

The truth is that the Gifts of the spirit are given to every man "severally as He will", and they are given in order to further the Gospel of the Kingdom of God, not to line a celebrity's pockets.

WHAT IS THE EVIDENCE THAT ONE HAS BEEN BAPTIZED IN THE HOLY SPIRIT? -

_____

WHAT IS THE PRIMARY PURPOSE FOR THE BAPTISM OF THE HOLY SPIRIT?

_____

_____

WHAT ARE THE FRUIT OF THE SPIRIT?_____
_____

WHAT IS THE PURPOPSE OF THE GIFTS OF THE SPIRIT?

_____
_____

WHAT DOES 1 CORINTHIANS 13:1-3 TELL ME ABOUT THE GIFTS?
_____
_____

WHAT ARE THE ATTRIBUTES OF LOVE? (1 COR 13:4-8)
_____
_____

THE BIBLE SAYS TO COVET EARNESTLY THE BEST GIFTS. CAN YOU HAVE THE GIFTS WITHOUT THE BAPTISM OF THE HOLY SPIRIT?

_____

AGAIN, THE BIBLE SAYS TO COVET EARNESTLY THE BEST GIFTS. THE GIFT OF TONGUES IS ONE OF THOSE GIFTS. PAUL SAID "I WOULD THAT YOU ALL _____ "

WERE THE GIFTS OF THE HOLY SPIRIT DONE AWAY WITH?_____

HOW WOULD YOU ANSWER A CESSATIONIST?
_____
_____
_____
_____

BASIC DOCTRINES

LESSON 10

LAYING ON OF HANDS

Heb 6:1 Therefore leaving the principles of the doctrine of Christ, let us go on unto perfection; not laying again the foundation of repentance from dead works, and of faith toward God,
2 Of the doctrine of baptisms, and of laying on of hands, and of resurrection of the dead, and of eternal judgment.

The doctrine of the laying on of hands is rarely taught in the Church today, but according to Hebrews 6, it is a foundational doctrine, and as such, needs to be taught, and put into practice, not as a ritual, but as a regular function of the Body of Christ.

When the priests offered sacrifice for themselves and for the people, they laid their hands on the head of a goat, confessing their sins, and the sins of the people; and let the goat go into the wilderness, in this way transferring their sin to the scapegoat.

Lev 16:20 And when he hath made an end of reconciling the holy place, and the tabernacle of the congregation, and the altar, he shall bring the live goat:
21 And Aaron shall lay both his hands upon the head of the live goat, and confess over him all the iniquities of the children of Israel, and all their transgressions in all their sins, putting them upon the head of the goat, and shall send him away by the hand of a fit man into the wilderness:
22 And the goat shall bear upon him all their iniquities unto a land not inhabited: and he shall let go the goat in the wilderness.

Jesus Christ bore our sins once and for all, so there is no need any longer for sacrifice or transference of our sin to another.

Forgiveness of sin

The laying on of hands can represent forgiveness of iniquities *(avon = perversity, moral evil, depravity, and the guilt associated with those things), transgressions (pesha = rebellion, against God primarily, as well as authorities placed over us), and sin (chattah _= habitual sinfulness, offenses committed by a person on a daily basis..."missing the mark" - Adam Clark)*

Cult Watch:

1) Seventh Day Adventists teach that the scapegoat spoken of in Leviticus 16 was not a type of Christ, but of Satan, which misses the point of the atonement of Christ, which removes our sin completely away from us. Christ bore our sins, and died as an atonement for us.

Lev 16:7 And he shall take the two goats, and present them before the LORD at the door of the tabernacle of the congregation.
8 And Aaron shall cast lots upon the two goats; one lot for the LORD, and the other lot for the scapegoat.
9 And Aaron shall bring the goat upon which the LORD'S lot fell, and offer him for a sin offering.
10 But the goat, on which the lot fell to be the scapegoat, shall be presented alive before the LORD, to make an atonement with him, and to let him go for a scapegoat into the wilderness.
11 And Aaron shall bring the bullock of the sin offering, which is for himself, and shall make an atonement for himself, and for his house, and shall kill the bullock of the sin offering which is for himself: .....
15 Then shall he kill the goat of the sin offering, that is for the people, and bring his blood within the vail, and do with that blood as he did with the blood of the bullock, and sprinkle it upon the mercy seat, and before the mercy seat:
16 And he shall make an atonement for the holy place, because of the uncleanness of the children of Israel, and because of their transgressions in all their sins: and so shall he do for the tabernacle of the congregation, that remaineth among them in the midst of their uncleanness.
congregation of Israel.

According to Albert Barnes and Adam Clarke: *"Maimonides (Jewish rabbi, scholar of the Torah, and philosopher during the 10th century) gives us the confession that the priest was to say over the goat in the following words: -*

"O Lord, thy people, the house of Israel, have sinned and done iniquity, and trespassed before thee. O Lord, make atonement now for the iniquities and transgressions and sins that thy people, the house of Israel, have sinned and transgressed against thee; as it is written in the law of Moses thy servant, saying: That in this day he shall make atonement for you, to cleanse you from all your sins before the Lord, and ye shall be clean." - See the Mishna, vol. ii., p. 329

The picture is of Christ, Who took our sins upon Himself, bore our sins, no matter how bad or evil they were, and as such they are no longer imputed to us. In the laying on of hands, the minister is confirming the forgiveness of Christ toward those to whom he ministers.

Understanding the atoning sacrifice of Christ will make it easier for some to receive healing.

In Mark 16:18, Jesus said those who believe would lay hands on the sick and they would recover. Sometimes the healing is prevented through a sense of unworthiness on the part of the one who is being prayed for.

Some people think that their sickness is a result of the chastisement of the Lord because of some real or imagined sin he or she may have committed. Through laying on of hands to administer healing, the minister is not just tending to the physical need, but to the spiritual need as well. It must be understood that Christ bore our sins, so we don't have to.[1]

17 And there shall be no man in the tabernacle of the congregation when he goeth in to make an atonement in the holy place, until he come out, and have made an atonement for himself, and for his household, and for all the congregation of Israel.

18 And he shall go out unto the altar that is before the LORD, and make an atonement for it; and shall take of the blood of the bullock, and of the blood of the goat, and put it upon the horns of the altar round about.

19 And he shall sprinkle of the blood upon it with his finger seven times, and cleanse it, and hallow it from the uncleanness of the children of Israel.

20 And when he hath made an end of reconciling the holy place, and the tabernacle of the congregation, and the altar, he shall bring the live goat:

21 And Aaron shall lay both his hands upon the head of the live goat, and confess over him all the iniquities of the children of Israel, and all their transgressions in all their sins, putting them upon the head of the goat, and shall send him away by the hand of a fit man into the wilderness:

22 And the goat shall bear upon him all their iniquities unto a land not inhabited: and he shall let go the goat in the wilderness.

Jesus bore our sins, and He atoned for our sins. To ascribe any of this type and shadows to the devil as the Seventh Day Adventists do is grave error.

═══════════

Notes

_____
_____
_____
_____
_____
_____
_____
_____

═══════════

Mar 16:17 And these signs shall follow them that believe; In my name shall they cast out devils; they shall speak with new tongues; 18 They shall take up serpents; and if they drink any deadly thing, it shall not hurt them; they shall lay hands on the sick, and they shall recover

Joh 20:22 And when he had said this, he breathed on them, and saith unto them, Receive ye the Holy Ghost: 23 Whose soever sins ye remit, they are remitted unto them; and whose soever sins ye retain, they are retained.

Mat 16:19 And I will give unto thee the keys of the kingdom of heaven: and whatsoever thou shalt bind on earth shall be bound in heaven: and whatsoever thou shalt loose on earth shall be loosed in heaven.

Mat 18:18 Verily I say unto you, Whatsoever ye shall bind on earth shall be bound in heaven: and whatsoever ye shall loose on earth shall be loosed in heaven. 19 Again I say unto you, That if two of you shall agree on earth as touching any thing that they shall ask, it shall be done for them of my Father which is in heaven. 20 For where two or three are gathered together in my name, there am I in the midst of them.

The priests laid their hands on those animals that were to be sacrificed on behalf of the people.

Exo 29:10 And thou shalt cause a bullock to be brought before the tabernacle of the congregation: and Aaron and his sons shall put their hands upon the head of the bullock. 11 And thou shalt kill the bullock before the LORD, by the door of the tabernacle of the congregation.

Notes

Lev 4:13 And if the whole congregation of Israel sin through ignorance, and the thing be hid from the eyes of the assembly, and they have done somewhat against any of the commandments of the LORD concerning things which should not be done, and are guilty;
14 When the sin, which they have sinned against it, is known, then the congregation shall offer a young bullock for the sin, and bring him before the tabernacle of the congregation.
15 And the elders of the congregation shall lay their hands upon the head of the bullock before the LORD: and the bullock shall be killed before the LORD.

Again, we have Jesus, Who was sacrificed once and for all for us. There is no more need of a sacrifice for our sin, other than the one Jesus made for us.

We are called to the ministry of reconciliation - reconciling mankind to God.

2Co 5:17 Therefore if any man be in Christ, he is a new creature: old things are passed away; behold, all things are become new.
18 And all things are of God, who hath reconciled us to himself by Jesus Christ, and hath given to us the ministry of reconciliation;
19 To wit, that God was in Christ, reconciling the world unto himself, not imputing their trespasses unto them; and hath committed unto us the word of reconciliation.

The ministry of forgiveness or remitting of sin through the shed Blood of Jesus Christ is of the utmost importance to the minister of God and the recipient. Healing is found in forgiveness. We will discuss this more a little later in our study.

Some Christians are hesitant to have others lay their hands on them because they are fearful of receiving a curse or a transference of sin. But the Word of God assures us that He Who is in us (the Holy Spirit) is greater than he that is in the world (Satan) [1 Jn

4:4]. The only power Satan has is what you give him through your fear or submission to him.

By the same kind of reasoning, some people think that 1 Timothy 5:22 warns us not to be too hasty in laying our hands on someone to pray for them, because we might catch an evil spirit or something.

1Ti 5:22 Lay hands suddenly on no man, neither be partaker of other men's sins: keep thyself pure.

As I mentioned before, the Holy Spirit that is inside of us is greater than the god of this world. So we need not be fearful of laying our hands on someone to pray for them.

Ordination to Ministry

Contextually that the laying on of hands spoken of in 1 Timothy is referring to the act of conferring a ministry on some one. If read in context, we can see that 1 Timothy 5 is addressing church discipline and order. Ordination to a ministerial office is not something to be taken lightly.

In the Old Testament, the Laying on of hands was also performed on occasions of consecration to a ministerial office:

Num 8:10 And thou shalt bring the Levites before the LORD: and the children of Israel shall put their hands upon the Levites: 11 And Aaron shall offer the Levites before the LORD for an offering of the children of Israel, that they may execute the service of the LORD.

Num 27:22 And Moses did as the LORD commanded him: and he took Joshua, and set him before Eleazar the priest, and before all the congregation:
23 And he laid his hands upon him, and gave him a charge, as the LORD commanded by the hand of Moses.

Deu 34:8 And the children of Israel wept for Moses in the plains of Moab thirty days: so the days of weeping and mourning for Moses were ended. 9 And Joshua the son of Nun was full of the spirit of wisdom; for Moses had laid his hands upon him: and the children of Israel hearkened unto him, and did as the LORD commanded Moses.

The ordination of people to ministry wasn't simply an Old Testament ordinance; it is also an ordinance which applies in the Church today.

Act 6:1 And in those days, when the number of the disciples were multiplied, there arose a murmuring of the Grecians against the Hebrews, because their widows were neglected in the daily ministration.
2 Then the twelve called the multitude of the disciples unto them, and said, It is not reason that we should leave the word of God, and serve tables.
3 Wherefore, brethren, look ye out among you seven men of honest report, full of the Holy Ghost and wisdom, whom we may appoint over this business.
4 But we will give ourselves continually to prayer, and to the ministry of the word.
5 And the saying pleased the whole multitude: and they chose Stephen, a man full of faith and of the Holy Ghost, and Philip, and Prochorus, and Nicanor, and Timon, and Parmenas, and Nicolas a proselyte of Antioch:
6 Whom they set before the apostles: and when they had prayed, they laid their hands on them.

Laying on of hands is performed in the commissioning of a person or persons to perform a specific mission.

Act 13:2 As they ministered to the Lord, and fasted, the Holy Ghost said, Separate me Barnabas and Saul for the work whereunto I have called them.
3 And when they had fasted and prayed, and laid their hands on them, they sent them away.
4 So they, being sent forth by the Holy Ghost, departed unto Seleucia; and from thence they sailed to Cyprus.

Blessing

In the Old Testament, we see that the laying on of hands was performed in the act of conferring a blessing upon a person (Gen 48:13-20). We see the same principle in the New Testament, as well when the people brought their children to be blessed by Jesus.

Mat 19:13 Then were there brought unto him little children, that he should put his hands on them, and pray: and the disciples rebuked them.
14 But Jesus said, Suffer little children, and forbid them not, to come unto me: for of such is the kingdom of heaven.
15 And he laid his hands on them, and departed thence.

The Impartation of the Holy Spirit

The impartation of the Holy Spirit can be given through the laying on of hands.

Act 8:14 Now when the apostles which were at Jerusalem heard that Samaria had received the word of God, they sent unto them Peter and John:
15 Who, when they were come down, prayed for them, that they might receive the Holy Ghost:
16 (For as yet he was fallen upon none of them: only they were baptized in the name of the Lord Jesus.)
17 Then laid they their hands on them, and they received the Holy Ghost.

Act 19:1 And it came to pass, that, while Apollos was at Corinth, Paul having passed through the upper coasts came to Ephesus: and finding certain disciples,
2 He said unto them, Have ye received the Holy Ghost since ye believed? And they said unto him, We have not so much as heard whether there be any Holy Ghost.
3 And he said unto them, Unto what then were ye baptized? And they said, Unto John's baptism.
4 Then said Paul, John verily baptized with the baptism of repentance, saying unto the people, that they should believe on him which should come after him, that is, on Christ Jesus.
5 When they heard this, they were baptized in the name of the Lord Jesus.
6 And when Paul had laid his hands upon them, the Holy Ghost came on them; and they spake with tongues, and prophesied.
7 And all the men were about twelve.

At this point, I believe it is necessary to point out that the impartation of the Holy Spirit is not exclusively received only through the laying on of hands. In Acts 2:1-4 and Acts 10:44 we see that the impartation of the Holy Spirit was exclusively through the Sovereign move of God.

Impartation of Spiritual Gifts

In the laying on of hands, a person may receive a spiritual gift such as those listed in 1 Corinthians 12-14.

Rom 1:11 For I long to see you, that I may impart unto you some spiritual gift, to the end ye may be established;
12 That is, that I may be comforted together with you by the mutual faith both of you and me.

Paul exhorted Timothy to stir up the spiritual gift that he had received through the laying on of Paul's hands. Some believe that Paul was simply referring to the gift of the baptism of the Holy Spirit, but I believe he was referring to a particular spiritual gift. I believe that at the time of this epistle, there was beginning to be severe persecution against the Church, and anyone who would dare to minister in the gifts of the Holy Spirit would likely attract attention to themselves and open themselves up to the possibility of imprisonment or even death.

2Ti 1:6 Wherefore I put thee in remembrance that thou stir up the gift of God, which is in thee by the putting on of my hands.
7 For God hath not given us the spirit of fear; but of power, and of love, and of a sound mind.
8 Be not thou therefore ashamed of the testimony of our Lord, nor of me his prisoner: but be thou partaker of the afflictions of the gospel according to the power of God;

Healing the Sick

Finally, we are instructed to put into practice the laying on of hands in praying for the sick.

Mar 16:17 And these signs shall follow them that believe; In my name shall they cast out devils; they shall speak with new tongues;
18 They shall take up serpents; and if they drink any deadly thing, it shall not hurt them; they shall lay hands on the sick, and they shall recover.

We see that Jesus laid His Hands on people who were sick:

Mar 6:5 And he could there do no mighty work, save that he laid his hands upon a few sick folk, and healed them.

Mat 9:18 While he spake these things unto them, behold, there came a certain ruler, and worshiped him, saying, My daughter is even now dead: but come and lay thy hand upon her, and she shall live.

Mar 7:31 And again, departing from the coasts of Tyre and Sidon, he came unto the sea of Galilee, through the midst of the coasts of Decapolis.
32 And they bring unto him one that was deaf, and had an impediment in his speech; and they beseech him to put his hand upon him.
33 And he took him aside from the multitude, and put his fingers into his ears, and he spit, and touched his tongue;
34 And looking up to heaven, he sighed, and saith unto him, Ephphatha, that is, Be opened.
35 And straightway his ears were opened, and the string of his tongue was loosed, and he spake plain.

Mar 8:22 And he cometh to Bethsaida; and they bring a blind man unto him, and besought him to touch him.
23 And he took the blind man by the hand, and led him out of the town; and when he had spit on his eyes, and put his hands upon him, he asked him if he saw ought.
24 And he looked up, and said, I see men as trees, walking.
25 After that he put his hands again upon his eyes, and made him look up: and he was restored, and saw every man clearly.

Throughout the book of Acts, we can see the practice of laying on of hands to heal the sick:

Act 9:17 And Ananias went his way, and entered into the house; and putting his hands on him said, Brother Saul, the Lord, even Jesus, that appeared unto thee in the way as thou camest, hath sent me, that thou mightest receive thy sight, and be filled with the Holy Ghost. 18 And immediately there fell from his eyes as it had been scales: and he received sight forthwith, and arose, and was baptized.

Act 28:8 And it came to pass, that the father of Publius lay sick of a fever and of a bloody flux: to whom Paul entered in, and prayed, and laid his hands on him, and healed him.

Jam 5:13 Is any among you afflicted? let him pray. Is any merry? let him sing psalms.
14 Is any sick among you? let him call for the elders of the church; and let them pray over him, anointing him with oil in the name of the Lord:
15 And the prayer of faith shall save the sick, and the Lord shall raise him up; and if he have committed sins, they shall be forgiven him.
16 Confess your faults one to another, and pray one for another, that ye may be healed. The effectual fervent prayer of a righteous man availeth much.

Through the anointing with oil there must by implication be the laying on of hands by those who are doing the anointing.

To sum the whole of this study up, the laying on of hands is practiced in the Christian church for these reasons:

Primarily, to administer the assurance of forgiveness to a person, which will open the way for the opportunity to:

To bestow blessings upon a person.

To impart the Baptism of the Holy Spirit.

To bestow upon a person a specific spiritual gift.

To ordain a person to a specific ministerial office.

To send a person or people out on a mission for God.

To heal the sick.

Mar 16:17 And these signs shall follow them that believe; In my name shall they cast out devils; they shall speak with new tongues; 18 They shall take up serpents; and if they drink any deadly thing, it shall not hurt them; they shall lay hands on the sick, and they shall recover.

1) Who is qualified to minister healing to a sick person?

_____

2) What is the most common way for the ministry of healing to be performed?

_____

3) Understanding the extent of the atonement of Christ is important to understand the extent to which God wants us to be _____ and healed.

4) What does "Lay hands suddenly on no man mean"?

_____

BASIC DOCTRINES

THAT WHICH IS TO COME

LESSON 11

RESURRECTION OF THE DEAD

Heb 6:1 Therefore leaving the principles of the doctrine of Christ, let us go on unto perfection; not laying again the foundation of repentance from dead works, and of faith toward God,
2 Of the doctrine of baptisms, and of laying on of hands, and of resurrection of the dead, and of eternal judgment.

Many questions and much speculation arise concerning the resurrection, and what it will be like after we die.

Since the day death entered into the world, I suppose the questions have prevailed: "Will I ever see my loved ones again?" or "is there life after death?" Philosophers and poets have spoken and written volumes on the subject.

Although the Bible has much to say regarding the resurrection, there are still a lot of questions that have gone unanswered. For the purpose of DOCTRINAL studies, I will attempt to present only that which the Bible speaks clearly on.

First of all, I must assure the reader right up front that there IS a day in which the dead will rise. The Resurrection is a very real tenet of the Christian faith. When Jesus walked the earth, there were two major schools of thought in the Jewish religion concerning what was to happen after we die.

One group, the Pharisees, affirmed that there was a resurrection after one died.

The other group, the Sadducees, denied the doctrine of the resurrection. Let's see how Jesus dealt with this group.

Mat 22:23 The same day came to him the Sadducees, which say that there is no resurrection, and asked him,
24 Saying, Master, Moses said, If a man die, having no children, his brother shall marry his wife, and raise up seed unto his brother.
25 Now there were with us seven brethren: and the first, when he had married a wife, deceased, and, having no issue, left his wife unto his brother:

210

Notes

Gen 16:7 And the angel of the LORD found her by a fountain of water in the wilderness, by the fountain in the way to Shur. 8 And he said, Hagar, Sarai's maid, whence camest thou? and whither wilt thou go? And she said, I flee from the face of my mistress Sarai.

Notes

---

26 Likewise the second also, and the third, unto the seventh.
27 And last of all the woman died also.
28 Therefore in the resurrection whose wife shall she be of the seven? for they all had her.
29 Jesus answered and said unto them, Ye do err, not knowing the Scriptures, nor the power of God.
30 For in the resurrection they neither marry, nor are given in marriage, but are as the angels of God in heaven.
31 But as touching the resurrection of the dead, have ye not read that which was spoken unto you by God, saying,
32 I am the God of Abraham, and the God of Isaac, and the God of Jacob God is not the God of the dead, but of the living.
33 And when the multitude heard this, they were astonished at his doctrine.
34 But when the Pharisees had heard that he had put the Sadducees to silence, they were gathered together.

The first thing we see here in Jesus' teaching is that in the resurrection there is no marriage, but all who are resurrected into the Kingdom of God are like the angels.

I don't believe this teaches that angels are gender neutral as some teachers maintain. In many places, we see angles being referred to as "he" or "him", which would indicate a gender (**Gen 16:8**). Never do we see an angel referred to as an "it".

The purpose of the man and woman and the institution of marriage was to procreate and to populate the earth. In Heaven or in the new earth, we will no longer procreate, but will be as the angels in heaven.

Hebrews tells us that angels are ministering spirits ((Hebrews 1:7, Psalm 104:4). We will live to serve in the Presence of our Holy God, and will be sent by the Most High God to carry out specific tasks. What those tasks will be I cannot specifically say, other than what the Bible says regarding the thousand year reign of the saints of God, which we will look at in a moment, but if we will be like the angels, we can be assured that we will be about the Lord's business.

While we will be LIKE the angels, we will not be angels, because there is a distinction between angels and men.

In the Word of God, we see that angels are instruments of God's Judgment (see Genesis 19, 2 Sam 24:16, 2 Kings 19:35, as well as the book of Revelation).

The Word of God tells us that we will also be in a position where we will judge angels. Undoubtedly this is speaking of the devil and his angels. This would explain some of why he hates us so, and is intent on destroying humanity and bringing us down to his level, and why he is called the accuser of the brethren.

Although we were made a little lower than the angels, yet God has put us in a position that is above the angels. To none of the angels had He given authority over the world, yet He commissioned His creation Adam to bring the world into subjection to himself. This should be incentive for us to live holy lives before the Lord God Almighty, because the one who is guilty of ungodliness cannot rightly judge another who is guilty of the same crime.

1Co 6:2 Do ye not know that the saints shall judge the world? and if the world shall be judged by you, are ye unworthy to judge the smallest matters?
3 Know ye not that we shall judge angels? how much more things that pertain to this life?

The Word of God reveals to us that angels are God's messengers, sent to proclaim God's Word to His

Psa 34:7 The angel of the LORD encampeth round about them that fear him, and delivereth them.

Psa 91:11 For he shall give his angels charge over thee, to keep thee in all thy ways

Notes

_____
_____
_____
_____
_____
_____
_____
_____
_____
_____
_____
_____
_____
_____
_____
_____
_____
_____
_____
_____
_____
_____
_____
_____
_____
_____

people, as in the case of Daniel who was visited by an angel, as well as Abraham and others who had multiple encounters with angels (Gen 22:11-15).

We are told that the angels are protectors of those who fear God (Ps 34:7, 91:11). So we will be like the angels, but we will not *be* angels.

At this point in our study, I think it is necessary to point out that the Word of God speaks of TWO resurrections. The first resurrection will be after the great tribulation spoken of by our Lord Jesus Christ in Matthew 24.

During this time, those who had not worshipped the beast, nor his image, neither had received the mark of the beast spoken of in Revelation 13, and who have died because of their testimony for Jesus in the face of great persecution shall live and reign with Jesus Christ for a thousand years.

Rev 20:4 And I saw thrones, and they sat upon them, and judgment was given unto them: and I saw the souls of them that were beheaded for the witness of Jesus, and for the word of God, and which had not worshiped the beast, neither his image, neither had received his mark upon their foreheads, or in their hands; and they lived and reigned with Christ a thousand years. 5 But the rest of the dead lived not again until the thousand years were finished. This is the first resurrection.
6 Blessed and holy is he that hath part in the first resurrection: on such the second death hath no power, but they shall be priests of God and of Christ, and shall reign with him a thousand years.

Obviously, there will be a class of people who live on the earth who are not reigning with God, and who those who have taken part in the first resurrection will rule over, and will judge.

Who these people are is left open to speculation. Although this may not be a politically correct thing to say, I personally believe that these people could be unconverted Israel, those who have not yet accepted Jesus Christ as the Messiah. I don't believe they will only be Jews, but people from all nations and tribes and tongues who are descendants of those tribes that were scattered throughout the world. In Romans 10 and 11, Paul discusses God's Plan for Israel, and it is not that He has just written them off.

Rom 11:1 I say then, Hath God cast away his people? God forbid. For I also am an Israelite, of the seed of Abraham, of the tribe of Benjamin.
2 God hath not cast away his people which he foreknew. Wot ye not what the Scripture saith of Elijah? how he maketh intercession to God against Israel, saying,
3 Lord, they have killed thy prophets, and digged down thine altars; and I am left alone, and they seek my life.
4 But what saith the answer of God unto him? I have reserved to myself seven thousand men, who have not bowed the knee to the image of Baal.
5 Even so then at this present time also there is a remnant according to the election of grace.
6 And if by grace, then is it no more of works: otherwise grace is no more grace. But if it be of works, then is it no more grace: otherwise work is no more work.
7 What then? Israel hath not obtained that which he seeketh for; but the election hath obtained it, and the rest were blinded.
8 (According as it is written, God hath given them the spirit of slumber, eyes that they should not see, and ears that they should not hear;) unto this day.
9 And David saith, Let their table be made a snare, and a trap, and a stumblingblock, and a recompense unto them:
10 Let their eyes be darkened, that they may not see, and bow down their back always.
11 I say then, Have they stumbled that they should fall? God forbid: but rather through their fall salvation is come unto the Gentiles, for to provoke them to jealousy.
12 Now if the fall of them be the riches of the world, and the diminishing of them the riches of the Gentiles; how much more their fullness?
13 For I speak to you Gentiles, inasmuch as I am the apostle of the Gentiles, I magnify mine office:
14 If by any means I may provoke to emulation them which are my flesh, and might save some of them.
15 For if the casting away of them be the reconciling of the world, what shall the receiving of them be, but life from the dead?
16 For if the firstfruit be holy, the lump is also holy: and if the root be holy, so are the branches.

17 And if some of the branches be broken off, and thou, being a wild olive tree, wert grafted in among them, and with them partakest of the root and fatness of the olive tree;

18 Boast not against the branches. But if thou boast, thou bearest not the root, but the root thee.

19 Thou wilt say then, The branches were broken off, that I might be grafted in.

20 Well; because of unbelief they were broken off, and thou standest by faith. Be not highminded, but fear:

21 For if God spared not the natural branches, take heed lest he also spare not thee.

22 Behold therefore the goodness and severity of God: on them which fell, severity; but toward thee, goodness, if thou continue in his goodness: otherwise thou also shalt be cut off.

23 And they also, if they abide not still in unbelief, shall be grafted in: for God is able to graft them in again.

24 For if thou wert cut out of the olive tree which is wild by nature, and wert grafted contrary to nature into a good olive tree: how much more shall these, which be the natural branches, be grafted into their own olive tree?

25 For I would not, brethren, that ye should be ignorant of this mystery, lest ye should be wise in your own conceits; that blindness in part is happened to Israel, until the fullness of the Gentiles be come in.

26 And so all Israel shall be saved: as it is written, There shall come out of Zion the Deliverer, and shall turn away ungodliness from Jacob:

27 For this is my covenant unto them, when I shall take away their sins.

28 As concerning the gospel, they are enemies for your sakes: but as touching the election, they are beloved for the fathers' sakes.

29 For the gifts and calling of God are without repentance.

30 For as ye in times past have not believed God, yet have now obtained mercy through their unbelief:

31 Even so have these also now not believed, that through your mercy they also may obtain mercy.

32 For God hath concluded them all in unbelief, that he might have mercy upon all.

33 O the depth of the riches both of the wisdom and knowledge of God! how unsearchable are his judgments, and his ways past finding out!

34 For who hath known the mind of the Lord? or who hath been his counselor?

35 Or who hath first given to him, and it shall be recompensed unto him again?

36 For of him, and through him, and to him, are all things: to whom be glory forever. Amen.

After the thousand year reign, Satan will be loosed out of his prison where he had been shut up at the time of the Coming of the Lord for His saints, and will be given a short season to deceive the nations.

Rev 20:7 And when the thousand years are expired, Satan shall be loosed out of his prison,
8 And shall go out to deceive the nations which are in the four quarters of the earth, Gog and Magog, to gather them together to battle: the number of whom is as the sand of the sea.
9 And they went up on the breadth of the earth, and compassed the camp of the saints about, and the beloved city: and fire came down from God out of heaven, and devoured them.

He will gather together his armies to fight against the saints of God who are reigning with Jesus Christ, and the Lord will devour them with fire from Heaven. It isn't going to be a long battle at all, and the devil will be thrown into the lake of fire. After this, the rest of the dead will be resurrected, and will be judged according to their works.

Rev 20:11 And I saw a great white throne, and him that sat on it, from whose face the earth and the heaven fled away; and there was found no place for them.
12 And I saw the dead, small and great, stand before God; and the books were opened: and another book was opened, which is the book of life: and the dead were judged out of those things which were written in the books, according to their works.
13 And the sea gave up the dead which were in it; and death and hell delivered up the dead which were in them: and they were judged every man according to their works.
14 And death and hell were cast into the lake of fire. This is the second death.
15 And whosoever was not found written in the book of life was cast into the lake of fire.

Those who have taken part in the first resurrection will not stand before the Great White Throne of Judgment. On such as these, we are told that the second death has no power (Rev 20:6).

Another thing Jesus told those Sadducees who came to question Him about the resurrection, was that they cannot die any more (Luke 20:36), which is confirmed in Rev 20:6.

There are differences of opinion as to whether we go immediately to be with the Lord as soon as we die, or whether we sleep until the time of the resurrection.

Rev 20:5 But the rest of the dead lived not again until the thousand years were finished. This is the first resurrection.
6 Blessed and holy is he that hath part in the first resurrection: on such the second death hath no power, but they shall be priests of God and of Christ, and shall reign with him a thousand years.
7 And when the thousand years are expired, Satan shall be loosed out of his prison,

Luk 20:35 But they which shall be accounted worthy to obtain that world, and the resurrection from the dead, neither marry, nor are given in marriage:
36 Neither can they die any more: for they are equal unto the angels; and are the children of God, being the children of the resurrection.

Notes

Again, looking at Jesus' reply to the Sadducees, we can see an important statement concerning the state of the dead:

Luk 20:37 Now that the dead are raised, even Moses showed at the bush, when he calleth the Lord the God of Abraham, and the God of Isaac, and the God of Jacob.
38 For he is not a God of the dead, but of the living: for all live unto him.

The fact that God said *"I Am (PRESENT TENSE) the God of Abraham, Isaac, and Jacob"* showed the people that Abraham, Isaac and Jacob were still alive, despite the fact that their bodies were long decayed. Had it not been so, God would have said I WAS the God of Abraham, Isaac, and Jacob, and the scribes recognized this difference, and acknowledged it.

Luk 20:39 Then certain of the scribes answering said, Master, thou hast well said.
40 And after that they durst not ask him any question at all.

See another example where Jesus spoke of the state of those who die.

Joh 11:24 Martha saith unto him, I know that he shall rise again in the resurrection at the last day.
25 Jesus said unto her, I am the resurrection, and the life: he that believeth in me, though he were dead, yet shall he live:
26 And whosoever liveth and believeth in me shall never die. Believest thou this?

Prior to the resurrection of Jesus Christ, the righteous dead such as Abraham, Isaac, and Jacob went to a place of rest called Paradise or later, in Jesus' time, Abraham's Bosom. The wicked went to a place called Hades, where there was awareness of torment as they awaited and

Cult watch:

Rev 6:9 And when he had opened the fifth seal, I saw under the altar the souls of them that were slain for the word of God, and for the testimony which they held:
10 And they cried with a loud voice, saying, How long, O Lord, holy and true, dost thou not judge and avenge our blood on them that dwell on the earth?
11 And white robes were given unto every one of them; and it was said unto them, that they should rest yet for a little season, until their fellowservants also and their brethren, that should be killed as they were, should be fulfilled.

Notes
___

still await the Judgment of God. See Luke 16 and the account of Lazarus and the rich man.

On the cross, Jesus promised the penitent thief that he would be with Him in Paradise that very day (Luke 23:43).

In Revelation we see that the dead in Christ are conscious of their surroundings as they stand in the presence of God, petitioning Him for His Righteous Judgment upon the earth.

Rev 6:9 And when he had opened the fifth seal, I saw under the altar the souls of them that were slain for the word of God, and for the testimony which they held:
10 And they cried with a loud voice, saying, How long, O Lord, holy and true, dost thou not judge and avenge our blood on them that dwell on the earth?
11 And white robes were given unto every one of them; and it was said unto them, that they should rest yet for a little season, until their fellow servants also and their brethren, that should be killed as they were, should be fulfilled.

Again, we can see another example of those who had died in Christ during the period of the Great tribulation (verse 14) standing before God, conscious of their surroundings, and praising and worshipping God[1].

Whereas prior to the death, burial and resurrection of Christ, those who were God's people were preserved in a place called Abraham's Bosom (read Luke 16:19-31), now after Christ's Resurrection, those who die in Christ are immediately in His Presence. Hence, Paul could confidently write this statement:
Php 1:21 For to me to live *is* Christ, and to die *is* gain.

22 But if I live in the flesh, this *is* the fruit of my labour: yet what I shall choose I wot not.

23 For I am in a strait betwixt two, having a desire to depart, and to be with Christ; which is far better:

24 Nevertheless to abide in the flesh *is* more needful for you.

Rev 7:9 After this I beheld, and, lo, a great multitude, which no man could number, of all nations, and kindreds, and people, and tongues, stood before the throne, and before the Lamb, clothed with white robes, and palms in their hands;

10 And cried with a loud voice, saying, Salvation to our God which sitteth upon the throne, and unto the Lamb.

11 And all the angels stood round about the throne, and about the elders and the four beasts, and fell before the throne on their faces, and worshiped God,

12 Saying, Amen: Blessing, and glory, and wisdom, and thanksgiving, and honor, and power, and might, be unto our God forever and ever. Amen.

13 And one of the elders answered, saying unto me, What are these which are arrayed in white robes? and whence came they?

14 And I said unto him, Sir, thou knowest. And he said to me, These are they which came out of great tribulation, and have washed their robes, and made them white in the blood of the Lamb.

15 Therefore are they before the throne of God, and serve him day and night in his temple: and he that sitteth on the throne shall dwell among them.

16 They shall hunger no more, neither thirst any more; neither shall the sun light on them, nor any heat.

17 For the Lamb which is in the midst of the throne shall feed them, and shall lead them unto living fountains of waters: and God shall wipe away all tears from their eyes.

Joh 20:27 Then saith he to Thomas, Reach hither thy finger, and behold my hands; and reach hither thy hand, and thrust it into my side: and be not faithless, but believing.

Joh 20:14 And when she had thus said, she turned herself back, and saw Jesus standing, and knew not that it was Jesus.

Joh 20:19 Then the same day at evening, being the first day of the week, when the doors were shut where the disciples were assembled for fear of the Jews, came Jesus and stood in the midst, and saith unto them, Peace be unto you.
20 And when he had so said, he shewed unto them his hands and his side. Then were the disciples glad, when they saw the Lord.

Luk 24:38 And he said unto them, Why are ye troubled? and why do thoughts arise in your hearts?
39 Behold my hands and my feet, that it is I myself: handle me, and see; for a spirit hath not flesh and bones, as ye see me have.
40 And when he had thus spoken, he shewed them his hands and his feet.

Notes
_____
_____
_____
_____
_____
_____
_____
_____
_____
_____
_____
_____

According to Jesus, those of us who believe on Him, shall not stand before Him in condemnation for our sins, but have passed from death unto life.

Joh 5:22 For the Father judgeth no man, but hath committed all judgment unto the Son:
23 That all men should honor the Son, even as they honor the Father. He that honoreth not the Son honoreth not the Father which hath sent him.
24 Verily, verily, I say unto you, He that heareth my word, and believeth on him that sent me, hath everlasting life, and shall not come into condemnation; but is passed from death unto life.
25 Verily, verily, I say unto you, The hour is coming, and now is, when the dead shall hear the voice of the Son of God: and they that hear shall live.
26 For as the Father hath life in himself; so hath he given to the Son to have life in himself;
27 And hath given him authority to execute judgment also, because he is the Son of man.

There will come a time when our dead bodies will be reunited with our souls, and we will be resurrected bodily from the grave.

Jn 5:28 Marvel not at this: for the hour is coming, in the which all that are in the graves shall hear his voice,
29 And shall come forth; they that have done good, unto the resurrection of life; and they that have done evil, unto the resurrection of damnation.

As we have seen, the resurrection of life and the resurrection of damnation are a thousand years apart from each other.

Rom 6:5 For if we have been planted together in the likeness of his death, we shall be also in the likeness of his resurrection:

Jesus' Body was buried in a tomb.

During the time it was in the tomb, he went in the spirit to preach to those who were in Hades (1 Peter 3:19, 20; 1 Peter 4:6)[2].

So just as Jesus was conscious to preach to the spirits who were in Hades, the spirits themselves had to be conscious to hear Him preach! The doctrine of "soul sleep" that some teach is an obvious lie from the weight of the Scriptures that prove otherwise.

When Jesus' body was resurrected, it was basically the same body, since it had the nail prints and the wound in His side (Jn 20:27), but it was a Glorified Body. He must have appeared somewhat differently, as many of the people who saw Him did not recognize Him at first (Jn 20:14).

His Body was not subject to the natural laws that our physical bodies are subject to, since he passed through a wall (Jn 20:19), yet His body was indeed physical, because He told His disciples to touch Him so they could see that He wasn't a spirit (Luke 24:39).

1 Corinthians 15 contains some of the most wonderful insights concerning the resurrection. Concerning what we will be like, we read:

1 Cor 15:35 But some man will say, How are the dead raised up? and with what body do they come?
36 Thou fool, that which thou sowest is not quickened, except it die:
37 And that which thou sowest, thou sowest not that body that shall be, but bare grain, it may chance of wheat, or of some other grain:
38 But God giveth it a body as it hath pleased him, and to every seed his own body.
39 All flesh is not the same flesh: but there is one kind of flesh of men, another flesh of beasts, another of fishes, and another of birds.
40 There are also celestial bodies, and bodies terrestrial: but the glory of the celestial is one, and the glory of the terrestrial is another.
41 There is one glory of the sun, and another glory of the moon, and another glory of the stars: for one star differeth from another star in glory.
42 So also is the resurrection of the dead. It is sown in corruption; it is raised in incorruption:

3) Mormons teach that all human beings were first born as spirit beings and then were given a body to be born into on earth, where they would live and work out their salvation, one day becoming gods of their own planets.

1 Cor 15:46 plainly says *Howbeit that was not first which is spiritual, but that which is natural; and afterward that which is spiritual*

We are born in this flesh, and later in life we become born of the spirit of God if we receive Jesus Christ as our personal Lord and Savior.

Notes

43 It is sown in dishonor; it is raised in glory: it is sown in weakness; it is raised in power:
44 It is sown a natural body; it is raised a spiritual body. There is a natural body, and there is a spiritual body.
45 And so it is written, The first man Adam was made a living soul; the last Adam was made a quickening spirit.
46 Howbeit that was not first which is spiritual, but that which is natural; and afterward that which is spiritual[3].
47 The first man is of the earth, earthy: the second man is the Lord from heaven.
48 As is the earthy, such are they also that are earthy: and as is the heavenly, such are they also that are heavenly.
49 And as we have borne the image of the earthy, we shall also bear the image of the heavenly.

As we saw in Romans 6:5, we will be in the likeness of His resurrection. We will have a glorified body, incorruptible. No more wrinkles, no more infirmities, but perfect as God had intended it to be.

1 Cor 15:50 Now this I say, brethren, that flesh and blood cannot inherit the kingdom of God; neither doth corruption inherit incorruption.
51 Behold, I show you a mystery; We shall not all sleep, but we shall all be changed,
52 In a moment, in the twinkling of an eye, at the last trump: for the trumpet shall sound, and the dead shall be raised incorruptible, and we shall be changed.
53 For this corruptible must put on incorruption, and this mortal must put on immortality.
54 So when this corruptible shall have put on incorruption, and this mortal shall have put on immortality, then shall be brought to pass the saying that is written, Death is swallowed up in victory.
55 O death, where is thy sting? O grave, where is thy victory?
56 The sting of death is sin; and the strength of sin is the law.

Php 1:21 For to me to live is Christ, and to die is gain.
22 But if I live in the flesh, this is the fruit of my labour: yet what I shall choose I wot not.
23 For I am in a strait betwixt two, having a desire to depart, and to be with Christ; which is far better:
24 Nevertheless to abide in the flesh is more needful for you.

Notes
_____
_____
_____
_____
_____
_____
_____
_____
_____
_____
_____
_____
_____
_____
_____
_____
_____
_____
_____
_____
_____
_____
_____
_____
_____
_____
_____
_____
_____
_____
_____

The question is sometimes asked: What about our loved ones who died in their sins? What about our children or our spouses, or our parents or siblings who turned away from God and died without giving their lives to Jesus? How will we be able spend eternity in the Presence of God knowing that they are burning in Hell? In Revelation 21:3-5, we can see the answer:

Rev 21:3 And I heard a great voice out of heaven saying, Behold, the tabernacle of God is with men, and he will dwell with them, and they shall be his people, and God himself shall be with them, and be their God.
4 And God shall wipe away all tears from their eyes; and there shall be no more death, neither sorrow, nor crying, neither shall there be any more pain: for the former things are passed away.
5 And he that sat upon the throne said, Behold, I make all things new. And he said unto me, Write: for these words are true and faithful.

In verse 4, we see that God will wipe away all tears from their eyes, and there would be no more death, no more sorrow, nor crying, nor pain, because the former things were passed away. Since there will be no more pain or sorrow or crying, we can only conclude that we won't remember anything about those who have gone to Hell.

CONCERNING THE PHARISEES AND THE SADDUCEES, WHAT POSITIONS DID EACH PARTY TAKE CONCERNING THE RESURRECTION?

_____
_____
_____

DESCRIBE THE FIRST RESURRECTION AND THE SECOND RESURRECTION

_____
_____
_____

_____

_____

_____

_____

WHAT IS THE DIFFERENCE BETWEEN THOSE WHO DIED BEFORE CHRIST'S RESURRECTION AND THOSE WHO DIE AFTER HIS RESURRECTION?

_____

_____

_____

_____

WHY DOESN'T THE DOCTRINE OF "SOUL SLEEP" WORK?

_____

_____

_____

BASIC DOCTRINES

LESSON 12

THE JUDGMENT TO COME

Heb 6:1 Therefore leaving the principles of the doctrine of Christ, let us go on unto perfection; not laying again the foundation of repentance from dead works, and of faith toward God,
2 Of the doctrine of baptisms, and of laying on of hands, and of resurrection of the dead, and of eternal judgment.

One cannot study the doctrine of the resurrection without encountering references to the impending Judgment of God upon the world.

Indeed, Hebrews 9:27 tells us that it is appointed once for a man to die, and after that, the judgment.

Heb 9:27 And as it is appointed unto men once to die, but after this the judgment:
28 So Christ was once offered to bear the sins of many; and unto them that look for him shall he appear the second time without sin unto salvation.

Acts 17:31 also mentions the fact that God has appointed a day in which He will judge the world in the Person of Jesus Christ[1]:

Act 17:30 And the times of this ignorance God winked at; but now commandeth all men every where to repent:
31 Because he hath appointed a day, in the which he will judge the world in righteousness by that man whom he hath ordained; whereof he hath given assurance unto all men, in that he hath raised him from the dead.

And in Romans 14, we are once more assured that we will all stand before the Judgment seat of Christ:

Mat 25:31 When the Son of man shall come in his glory, and all the holy angels with him, then shall he sit upon the throne of his glory:
32 And before him shall be gathered all nations: and he shall separate them one from another, as a shepherd divideth his sheep from the goats:
33 And he shall set the sheep on his right hand, but the goats on the left.
34 Then shall the King say unto them on his right hand, Come, ye blessed of my Father, inherit the kingdom prepared for you from the foundation of the world:
35 For I was an hungred, and ye gave me meat: I was thirsty, and ye gave me drink: I was a stranger, and ye took me in:
36 Naked, and ye clothed me: I was sick, and ye visited me: I was in prison, and ye came unto me.
37 Then shall the righteous answer him, saying, Lord, when saw we thee an hungred, and fed thee? or thirsty, and gave thee drink?
38 When saw we thee a stranger, and took thee in? or naked, and clothed thee?
39 Or when saw we thee sick, or in prison, and came unto thee?
40 And the King shall answer and say unto them, Verily I say unto you, Inasmuch as ye have done it unto one of the least of these my brethren, ye have done it unto me.
41 Then shall he say also unto them on the left hand, Depart from me, ye cursed, into everlasting fire, prepared for the devil and his angels:
42 For I was an hungred, and ye gave me no meat: I was thirsty, and ye gave me no drink:
43 I was a stranger, and ye took me not in: naked, and ye clothed me not: sick, and in prison, and ye visited me not.
44 Then shall they also answer him, saying, Lord, when saw we thee an hungred, or athirst, or a stranger, or naked, or sick, or in prison, and did not minister unto thee?

Rom 14:9 For to this end Christ both died, and rose, and revived, that he might be Lord both of the dead and living.
10 But why dost thou judge thy brother? or why dost thou set at naught thy brother? for we shall all stand before the judgment seat of Christ.
11 For it is written, As I live, saith the Lord, every knee shall bow to me, and every tongue shall confess to God.
12 So then every one of us shall give account of himself to God.

Understanding that there will be a day when all men will stand before Jesus Christ should give us an urgency to warn those who have rejected Jesus Christ by proclaiming His message of the Gospel of repentance and the necessity of being Born again.

2Co 5:10 For we must all appear before the judgment seat of Christ; that every one may receive the things done in his body, according to that he hath done, whether it be good or bad.
11 Knowing therefore the terror of the Lord, we persuade men; but we are made manifest unto God; and I trust also are made manifest in your consciences.

Jesus said that unless a man is Born again, he cannot see the Kingdom of God. This is a serious charge. See page 137-141 for an explanation of what being "Born Again" actually means.

2Ti 4:1 I charge thee therefore before God, and the Lord Jesus Christ, who shall judge the quick and the dead at his appearing and his kingdom;
2 Preach the word; be instant in season, out of season; reprove, rebuke, exhort with all longsuffering and doctrine.

Jud 1:14 And Enoch also, the seventh from Adam, prophesied of these, saying, Behold, the Lord cometh with ten thousands of his saints,
15 To execute judgment upon all, and to convince all that are ungodly among them of all

Seventh Day Adventists and Jehovah's Witnesses adhere to a doctrine of Annihilation; that there isn't an eternal Hell. But Jesus Himself told about a future resurrection of damnation. Those who have done good will attain to the resurrection of life; those who lived evil lives unto a resurrection of damnation. To resurrect means to come alive. One would have eternal life, one would be resurrected to damnation.

Damnation:

G2920

κρίσις   krisis   *kree'-sis* (Subjectively or objectively, for or against); by extension a *tribunal*; by implication *justice* (specifically divine *law*): - accusation, condemnation, damnation, judgment

There is no indication in this definition that annihilation is involved here.

Notes

_____

their ungodly deeds which they have ungodly committed, and of all their hard speeches which ungodly sinners have spoken against him.

Rev 20:11 And I saw a great white throne, and him that sat on it, from whose face the earth and the heaven fled away; and there was found no place for them.
12 And I saw the dead, small and great, stand before God; and the books were opened: and another book was opened, which is the book of life: and the dead were judged out of those things which were written in the books, according to their works.
13 And the sea gave up the dead which were in it; and death and hell delivered up the dead which were in them: and they were judged every man according to their works.
14 And death and hell were cast into the lake of fire. This is the second death.
15 And whosoever was not found written in the book of life was cast into the lake of fire.

Jesus taught about His Coming and the resurrection of the dead and His Judgment which will follow.

Joh 5:25 Verily, verily, I say unto you, The hour is coming, and now is, when the dead shall hear the voice of the Son of God: and they that hear shall live.
26 For as the Father hath life in himself; so hath he given to the Son to have life in himself;
27 And hath given him authority to execute judgment also, because he is the Son of man.
28 Marvel not at this: for the hour is coming, in the which all that are in the graves shall hear his voice,
29 And shall come forth; they that have done good, unto the resurrection of life; and they that have done evil, unto the resurrection of damnation.

WHAT IS THE RESURRECTION OF DAMNATION?

WHAT IS THE DOCTRINE OF ANNIHILATION, AND WHY DOESN'T IT HOLD UP TO SCRIPTURE?

BASIC DOCTRINES
THE JUDGMENT

CHAPTER 13

THE DOCTRINE OF HELL

A REFUTATION OF THOSE WHO SAY THERE IS NO HELL

Heb 6:1 Therefore leaving the principles of the doctrine of Christ, let us go on unto perfection; not laying again the foundation of repentance from dead works, and of faith toward God,
2 Of the doctrine of baptisms, and of laying on of hands, and of resurrection of the dead, and of eternal judgment.

There is a teaching out there that is embraced by many cults such as the Jehovah's Witnesses and the Seventh Day Adventists and Universalists that maintains that there is not a place of literal eternal torment where the unbelievers go.

As is the case with most who wrestle with the scriptures in an attempt to make them say what they want them to say, those who teach this doctrine appeal to the reader's emotional side rather than merely abiding by what the Word of God says.

Like the Serpent in the Garden when he tempted Eve - he also appealed to Eve's emotions...These false teachers would ask the unlearned: "Did Jesus REALLY teach about HELL in LUKE 16? Does it make sense that a loving God would allow a saintly mother to view her son in torment through all eternity?" Satan asked Eve: "Did God REALLY say that you would DIE? NO, He actually knows that you will be like Him when you eat that fruit!"

RIGHT UP FRONT, I NEED TO CLARIFY THAT I AM NOT INFERRING THAT EVERYONE WHO TEACHES AGAINST THE DOCTRINE OF A LITERAL HELL IS IN LEAGUE WITH SATAN TO DECEIVE PEOPLE.

But the same type of faulty reasoning used by the serpent is used by these teachers. Here is a typical argument used by these false teachers concerning the story of Lazarus and the rich man:

"Before we see what the story says consider this scenario: A saintly

Luk 16:19 There was a certain rich man, which was clothed in purple and fine linen, and fared sumptuously every day:

20 And there was a certain beggar named Lazarus, which was laid at his gate, full of sores,

21 And desiring to be fed with the crumbs which fell from the rich man's table: moreover the dogs came and licked his sores.

22 And it came to pass, that the beggar died, and was carried by the angels into Abraham's bosom: the rich man also died, and was buried;

23 And in hell he lift up his eyes, being in torments, and seeth Abraham afar off, and Lazarus in his bosom.

24 And he cried and said, Father Abraham, have mercy on me, and send Lazarus, that he may dip the tip of his finger in water, and cool my tongue; for I am tormented in this flame.

25 But Abraham said, Son, remember that thou in thy lifetime receivedst thy good things, and likewise Lazarus evil things: but now he is comforted, and thou art tormented.

26 And beside all this, between us and you there is a great gulf fixed: so that they which would pass from hence to you cannot; neither can they pass to us, that would come from thence.

27 Then he said, I pray thee therefore, father, that thou wouldest send him to my father's house:

28 For I have five brethren; that he may testify unto them, lest they also come into this place of torment.

29 Abraham saith unto him, They have Moses and the prophets; let them hear them.

30 And he said, Nay, father Abraham: but if one went unto them from the dead, they will repent.

31 And he said unto him, If they hear not Moses and the prophets, neither will they be persuaded, though one rose from the dead.

mother dies and goes to heaven. Her son, for whom she has shed many tears during his life of debauchery, goes to hell. She loves her son and longs to have him with her, but there's no way either can pass to the other.

If the usual interpretation of Lazarus and the rich man is true, those who preach a heaven-hell theory have to admit the mother can see her son forever tormented in the inferno of hell, and hear his unbearable screams of agony, and be helpless to do anything for him. That doesn't seem like a nice way to spend eternity."

The flaw in this "logic" that the false teachers present should be obvious to any thinking person. In the story of Lazarus and the rich man, we see that the rich man is painfully aware of Lazarus' position of rest in Abraham's Bosom, but *there is no indication that Lazarus is aware of the rich man's plight.*

The account is about what the rich man was experiencing, not Lazarus. Notice that the dialogue is between Abraham and the rich man, and that Lazarus was merely the subject of the discussion, but not involved in the discussion. The picture that the Lord intended to show was that even in Hell, the Rich man was unrepentant and thought that Lazarus could serve him.

The saintly mother won't be aware of the torment her ungodly son is experiencing. There are no tears in Heaven. There is no memory of those things that are wicked and vile, so there won't be any memory of her son. Whether he is burning in Hell or annihilated forever, if there was any memory in heaven of those things, there would be tears that would be shed. A mother's loss for her son, however it occurs is an occasion for grief. A mother who spent eternity realizing she will never ever see her son would shed many tears, as well.

Teachers who wrestle with the scriptures to get them to say what their "reasoning" would have them to say, fail to think the whole matter through. They end their arguments with statements like we have just seen: *"That doesn't seem like a nice way to spend eternity."* The simple fact of the matter is that in Hell, part of the torment will be that these eternal souls who had rejected the Truth of the Lord Jesus Christ will be painfully aware of all they have forfeited in exchange for their momentary pleasures on earth.

It doesn't matter what seems nice or unpleasant to us...the fact is that God declares unequivocally,

Isa 55:7 Let the wicked forsake his way, and the unrighteous man his thoughts: and let him return unto the LORD, and he will have mercy upon him; and to our God, for he will abundantly pardon.
8 For my thoughts are not your thoughts, neither are your ways my ways, saith the LORD.
9 For as the heavens are higher than the earth, so are my ways higher than your ways, and my thoughts than your thoughts.

So often men try to recreate God in their own image, and they try to measure His Justice by their own twisted idea of what justice is; or they try to measure His Grace by what they think it should be, or they try to define His Love by their warped idea of what love should be.

That is the problem that these false teachers are confronted with. They don't understand the Absolute Sovereignty of God. If He warns us against spending eternity in Hell fire and torment, we shouldn't wrestle with the idea...we should hear Him and respond. These false teachers cause people to judge God and to declare that if there is a place of eternal torment, then God isn't the God of Love that He says He is.

A more fitting scripture cannot be found for these teachers than this:

Rom 9:20 Nay but, O man, who art thou that repliest against God? Shall the thing formed say to him that formed it, Why hast thou made me thus?

"And it came to pass that...the rich man also died and was buried. And in hell he lifted up his eyes being in torments, and saw Abraham afar off and Lazarus in his bosom (Luke 16:22-23)."

The first thing I would like the reader to consider is that Jesus Christ referred to Himself as the Way, the Truth and the Life. If He is TRUTH personified as He claimed Himself to be, why would he tell stories that would cause multitudes of people to believe in a place that does not exist?

If the Bible is true, why would it speak of torment associated with a place called Hades, Gehenna, or the Lake of fire, if it was not intended to be understood as such? There is a simplicity here that must not be overlooked.

Anyone reading the gospels and the teaching of the Bible in Mark 9:43-47, Matthew 5:22-30, Matthew 10:28, Matthew 18:9, Matt 23:15,33, Luke 12:5, Luke 16:19-31, James 3:6, 2 Pet 2:4, as they refer to Hell would walk away with the understanding that there is a place of eternal torment that awaits the unrepentant sinner after he or she dies, but there are numerous cults who would twist the scriptures to read otherwise.

**2Co 11:3 But I fear, lest by any means, as the serpent beguiled Eve through his subtlety, so your minds should be corrupted from the simplicity that is in Christ.
4 For if he that cometh preacheth another Jesus, whom we have not preached, or if ye receive another spirit, which ye have not received, or another gospel, which ye have not accepted, ye might well bear with him.**

1Ti 4:1 Now the Spirit speaketh expressly, that in the latter times some shall depart from the faith, giving heed to seducing spirits, and doctrines of devils; (Mormonism's lies)
2 Speaking lies in hypocrisy (Jehovah's witnesses – in altering the Bible)**; having their conscience seared with a hot iron** (Unconditional Eternal Securitists)**;**
3 Forbidding to marry, (Catholism) **and commanding to abstain from meats** (Catholicism and Seventh Day Adventism)**, which God hath created to be received with thanksgiving of them which believe and know the truth.**

4 For every creature of God is good, and nothing to be refused, if it be received with thanksgiving:
5 For it is sanctified by the word of God and prayer.
6 If thou put the brethren in remembrance of these things, thou shalt be a good minister of Jesus Christ, nourished up in the words of faith and of good doctrine, whereunto thou hast attained.

These teachers generally make a statement like this:

Every Old Testament reference to hell comes from the Hebrew word <sheol> meaning the world of the dead, the grave, a pit.

It is correct that Every Old Testament reference to Hell comes from the Hebrew word "Sheol", and Strong's concordance defines this word as the grave, or the pit, as well as Hell, or the world of the dead.

What the false teachers fail to advise the reader is that there are a few words in the Old Testament that are used regarding the final destination of those who die. Sheol is only one of those words.

The false teachers would have the reader to believe that every place the word "Sheol" is translated as "hell", it should be better translated as "grave". But they don't supply the earnest seeker of truth with all the facts.

The fact is that in 62 verses of the Old Testament, another Hebrew Word is used to denote the grave, or a specific place of burial <qeber>.

In 13 more places, we see the root of the word previously mentioned used to denote the grave <qeburah>. So in 75 places in the Old Testament, we can see that there is a specific word used to denote a grave or a burial place.

The false teachers don't ever seem to mention those facts. They try to keep the reader focused on the word Sheol, and infer through their omission of facts that Sheol is the exclusive word for "Grave". They will point the reader to several places in the Old Testament where Sheol is translated as "Grave", such as these:

1Ki 2:6 Do therefore according to thy wisdom, and let not his hoar head go down to the grave in peace.

Job 7:9 As the cloud is consumed and vanisheth away: so he that goeth down to the grave shall come up no more.

Job 21:13 They spend their days in wealth, and in a moment go down to the grave.

In each instance, they will show you that the word translated as "grave" is the Hebrew word "Sheol", and then they will proceed to insist that "grave" is all Sheol really means.

They will dance the unsuspecting Christian around a host of Greek words, like Hades, Gehenna, and Tartarus, and explain that none of them actually mean "Hell" as they have been represented to mean. Never will the word "Queburah" or the word "Qeber" (the true Hebrew words meaning "grave" or a place of burial) come into the discussion, and after showing a lot of scriptures where sheol is translated as "grave" in the bible, they will then proceed to appeal to your emotional side, and tell you that a God of Love would never sentence a person to spend eternity in torment.

But if they truly did stick to the formula of "precept upon precept, line upon line", they would understand that the Love of God is what caused Him to humble Himself and take upon Himself the form of a servant and to dwell among us, so that He could warn us about the fact that we are eternal souls, created in His Image, and are destined to live forever.

He didn't come to fill us full of fairy tales about places that don't really exist, and events that will never happen...He came to warn us to choose wisely in this life where we are going to spend eternity. THAT'S THE LOVE OF GOD!

Our two newly discovered Hebrew words are defined as follows:

H6900
קבורה / קברה
qebu ra h
BDB Definition: 1) grave, burial, burial site
1a) grave
1b) burial

H6913
קבר / קברה
qeber / qibra h
BDB Definition: 1) grave, sepulchre, tomb

What is really wonderful about these words is that there is never any "gray area" as to what is meant when they are used. When you read the passages in which they are used, you have no doubt that they are speaking of the grave or a graveyard or a tomb. Here are a few examples of where they are used.

Num 19:16 And whosoever toucheth one that is slain with a sword in the open fields, or a dead body, or a bone of a man, or a grave, shall be unclean seven days.

Jdg 8:32 And Gideon the son of Joash died in a good old age, and was buried in the sepulcher of Joash his father, in Ophrah of the Abi-ezrites.

2Sa 3:32 And they buried Abner in Hebron: and the king lifted up his voice, and wept at the grave of Abner; and all the people wept.

So we can see that the "grave" in the Old Testament is a different place than the place referred to as Sheol.

Generally, after they have laid the foundation for their lie with the word "Sheol", the false teachers will then proceed to the New Testament Greek and deal with the Greek words "Hades", "Gehenna", and "Tarturos", each of which are translated in various places as "Hell".

They will jump from the Old Testament and declare that "Hades" is the Greek equivalent of the word "Sheol", and fabricate a story of how the word "Hades" originated. They will ascribe this teaching of Hades as a place of punishment as deriving from the apocrypha, from Persian writings, and from the Italian poet, Dante Alighieri (1265-1321) who wrote "The Divine Comedy".

I don't know how this would escape any thinking person, but the Italian Poet Dante Alighieri was not the first to "popularize the concept"... Jesus taught and warned His listeners about Hell 1200+ years before Dante ever lived! Mark, Luke, Matthew, James, 2 Peter, Jude, and Revelation are NOT the apocrypha, nor are they writings from Persia, and each one of these books of the New Testament deal with Hell as being a place of punishment.

Here is an actual example of how one false teacher deals with the story of Lazarus and the rich man:

"We also know the rich man is not in a place reserved for the devil and his angels. Since he was a wealthy man and is not referred to as a criminal - except for his criminal lack of compassion toward Lazarus - his body would not have been thrown into the garbage dump. No doubt he had prepared for his funeral with a rather elaborate sepulchre and there, as Luke 16:22 says, he was buried: in hell. Several modern English versions of the bible specifically identify the rich man's grave as hades."

This is where these teachers are shown to be either bald faced liars, or are merely parroting what they have heard from other false teachers, and as a result perpetuate the lie that is being taught.

Here in this paragraph, this particular teacher equates the "sepulcher" with Hades. And it is here where the false teachers must be confronted with the Truth. Just as we have seen that there are a couple of words in the Old Testament that deal specifically with the grave, the same is true in the New Testament as well. The truth of the matter is that the Greek word for sepulcher, or grave is NOT Hades, Gehenna, or Tarturos, but in actuality it is the word "Mnemeion".

G3419

μνημειον mnemeion

mnay-mi'-on

From G3420; a remembrance, that is, cenotaph (place of interment): - grave, sepulchre, tomb.

This word is used 42 times in the New Testament, and 7 times a derivative of that word is used, and in each instance, it is obvious that the grave is being referred to. One such example is in John 5:28:

Joh 5:28 Marvel not at this: for the hour is coming, in the which all that are in the graves shall hear his voice,

29 And shall come forth; they that have done good, unto the resurrection of life; and they that have done evil, unto the resurrection of damnation.

In referring to Hell, Jesus taught about a place called Gehenna (Matt 5:29-30, Matt 10:28, Matt 18:9, etc.) and elsewhere He referred to Hades as in the case of the rich man.

Yet here in John 5:28, He mentions another place (Mnemeion) from which the dead will rise at the time of Judgment. Now, if there is no distinction between where the rich man was (Hades) and the grave, surely Jesus would have used the proper term for "grave" (Mnemeion) in Luke 16. Or, he could have used the word "taphos", which is used seven times in the New Testament.

The following verse is one instance where "taphos" is used and translated as "sepulchers".

**Mat 23:27 Woe unto you, scribes and Pharisees, hypocrites! for ye are like unto whited sepulchers (taphos), which indeed appear beautiful outward, but are within full of dead men's bones, and of all uncleanness.
28 Even so ye also outwardly appear righteous unto men, but within ye are full of hypocrisy and iniquity.**

Again at this point I would like to quote part of the statement made by a false teacher that I had referred to before so his error doesn't get overlooked:

"No doubt he had prepared for his funeral with a rather elaborate sepulchre and there, as Luke 16:22 says, he was buried: in hell. Several modern English versions of the bible specifically identify the rich man's grave as hades."

At the risk of seeming redundant, I want to make sure that the Truth isn't lost to the reader…If the rich man's abode that Jesus was referring to would

G5028

τάφος taphos taf'-os

Masculine from G2290; a grave (the place of interment): - sepulchre, tomb.

Notes

have simply been his sepulcher, Jesus would have used the word "Taphos" or the word "Mnemeion". At this point it should be very obvious that Hades and the grave are definitely two different places.

Those who adhere to the school of theology of the cults do not rightly divide the word of Truth...they twist it to conform to their own preconceived ideas, and back up their arguments with an appeal to the hearer's emotions.

Here is another statement from the same false teacher I have quoted that typifies the thinking of the cults:

"It's amazing that those who claim to teach the gospel - the good news - include in their message the unbelievably bad news of eternal torment in an ever-burning hell fire. The bible has good news, and good news."

Again, he resorts to judging God in the light of how he thinks God should be. Jesus taught the gospel, the good news, and included several times in His Teaching the warning that there was a place of eternal torment waiting for all those who rejected the Truth that He taught.

The Good news is that Jesus died, and resurrected, so that everyone might have eternal life, and that NONE would have to experience torment for eternity because of their sins.

The other good news is that Jesus never twisted scripture so that he would sound good to His hearers. I thank God that He ALWAYS spoke the TRUTH.

It should be obvious now to the honest reader that there is a difference both in the Old Testament and the New Testament between the Grave and Sheol or Hades. What Jesus Taught was the TRUTH. We don't have to wrestle with the Truth that He spoke. The Devil would love you to believe that there is no Hell, and there is no place of eternal torment awaiting the unrepentant sinner.

So we come to the end of our study of the Principles of the Doctrine of Christ. I pray this study was a blessing to you the reader, and that you will go on to perfection as you step into your Calling as a minister of the Most High God to further the Kingdom of God in your sphere of influence. There is only one other place where this particular variant of the Greek word (Strong's G5047) translated as "perfection" is used in the New Testament:

Col 3:14 And above all these things *put on* charity, which is the bond of perfectness.

Variants of the Greek Word translated as "Perfect"

G5046

τέλειος *teleios*

Thayer Definition:

1) brought to its end, finished

2) wanting nothing necessary to completeness

3) perfect

4) that which is perfect

4a) consummate human integrity and virtue

4b) of men

4b1) full grown, adult, of full age, mature

Part of Speech: adjective

A Related Word by Thayer's/Strong's Number: from G5056

Citing in TDNT: 8:67, 1161

G5047

τελειότης *teleiotēs*

Thayer Definition:

1) perfection

1a) the state of the more intelligent

1b) moral and spiritual perfection

Part of Speech: noun feminine

A Related Word by Thayer's/Strong's Number: from G5046

Citing in TDNT: 8:78, 1161

G5048

τελειόω *teleioō*

Thayer Definition:

1) to make perfect, complete

1a) to carry through completely, to accomplish, finish, bring to an end

2) to complete (perfect)

2a) add what is yet wanting in order to render a thing full

2b) to be found perfect

3) to bring to the end (goal) proposed

4) to accomplish

4a) bring to a close or fulfilment by event

4a1) of the prophecies of the scriptures

Part of Speech: verb A Related Word by Thayer's/Strong's Number: from G5046

Citing in TDNT: 8:79, 1161

Above all these things, put on Love...Perfect Love casts out fear (1 Jn 4:18). Perfect Love toward the Father allows one to walk confidently in His assurance that ***all things work together for good to them that love God, to them who are the called according to his purpose (Romans 8:28).***

Perfect Love toward one's neighbor covers a multitude of sins (1 Peter 4:8).

Perfect Love toward others will be the reflection of the Love of God for this world:

Joh 3:16 For God so loved the world, that he gave his only begotten Son, that whosoever believeth in him should not perish, but have everlasting life.

2Pe 3:9 The Lord is not slack concerning his promise, as some men count slackness; but is longsuffering to us-ward, not willing that any should perish, but that all should come to repentance.

You are now able and qualified to obey Jesus' command to "make disciples". Perfect Love for the Father will compel the child of God to Go and preach the Gospel of the Kingdom of God to those who are bound by sin. Teach them the Principles of the Doctrine of Christ, and commission them to go onto perfection, and make disciples of their own. That is the Way of the Gospel.

If you have been blessed by this study of the Principles of the Doctrine of Christ, and if you are interested in the end times, I would encourage you to consider purchasing my book, "**Three Questions; A Study of the Last Days Based on Matthew 24**".

This is a synopsis of the book:

There are so many voices in the world concerning end-time or last days prophecy. Who is right?

Will Christians be taken up in the rapture before the Great Tribulation, or will they have to go through it?

Who is the Beast of Revelation?

Who is the harlot who rides the Beast?

Who is the Anti Christ? Is he already here?

What happens after a Christian dies?

The Shemitah, the Blood Moons, the year of Jubilee - What do they mean for me as a Christian?

What is the Mark of the Beast?

The disciples asked Jesus Three Questions concerning the Last Days, and Jesus answered them plainly. This book is an exploration of the answers that Jesus gave pertaining to their questions.

It is a wake up call to those who profess to be Christians, and by the time the reader will have finished it, there will be a whole trail of sacred cows left dead in its' wake.

A lot of what you read will challenge doctrine that you have accepted as Truth for years.

Sometimes the foundation which we start with concerning a particular doctrine was a wrong foundation, but if we have just blindly accepted it as a fact, we will build our ideas and our doctrinal stance on that flawed foundation, not even realizing that is what we are doing.

The Christian who goes to the altar at a particular church will more than likely adopt it's eschatological doctrine without question. If he is a Baptist or a Church of God convert, he will be a dispensationalist pretribber. If he is a Lutheran, he will tend more to an amillennialist or a post millennialist position. On the other hand, a Presbyterian may tend more to a preterist position. And a host of non-denominational fellowships differ from one another in their position concerning end-times doctrine.

Christ and His teachings should be the foundation upon which we build.

Look for it online.

You can order it by clicking on the link found at crosscountry4jesus.com

www.ingramcontent.com/pod-product-compliance
Lightning Source LLC
Chambersburg PA
CBHW081510040426
42447CB00013B/3175